Cuttin' the Body Loose

TEMPLE UNIVERSITY PRESS ▐T▌ Philadelphia

WILLIAM JOSEPH GAVIN

Cuttin' the Body Loose

Historical, Biological, and Personal
Approaches to Death and Dying

Temple University Press, Philadelphia 19122
Copyright © 1995 by Temple University. All rights reserved
Published 1995
Printed in the United States of America

☾ The paper used in this book meets the requirements
of the American National Standard for Information Sciences—
Permanence of Paper for Printed Library Materials,
ANSI Z39.48-1984

Text design by Arlene Putterman.

Library of Congress Cataloging-in-Publication Data
Gavin, William Joseph, 1943–
Cuttin' the body loose : historical, biological, and personal
approaches to death and dying / William Joseph Gavin.
p.   cm.
Includes bibliographical references and index.
ISBN 1-56639-297-7 — ISBN 1-56639-298-5(pbk.)
1. Death.   I. Title.   II. Title: Cuttin' the body loose.
BD444.G344   1995
128'.5—dc20   94-29914

For Bonnie

It is high time for the basis of discussion
in these questions to be broadened
and thickened up.

—William James, *A Pluralistic Universe*

⟦ CONTENTS ⟧

[P R E F A C E]

THE CHAPTERS that follow stem from an insightful comment by Paul Ramsey, who noted that the more the uniquely individual and the bodily are emphasized, the more a "denial" or "rebellious"[1] attitude toward death is cultivated; and conversely, the more they are deemphasized, the more an "acceptance" model is put forth as normal or desirable. While there are always exceptions to such statements (e.g., Heidegger), for the most part this one rings true. Ramsey's statement also suggests that the term *death* does not have "meaning invariance" for us. "Meaning invariance" is the hypothesis that a word or sentence retains its content or significance regardless of the context or situation in which it is employed. As the term is used here, it also refers to the lack of recognition of the difference between what a person "means" to accomplish by employing a certain term, that is, her intent; what the term itself means, semantically; and what effect the term in question has on its audience, or its pragmatic upshot.[2]

Sometimes the claim is put forth that the *biological* definition of death is the real one, all other candidates being deemed illusory. The problem with the latter position is that there are various biological definitions of death—or at least differing biological operations we can perform in order to determine that death has occurred. Which biological definition to employ is not a biological question, but rather a normative or a cultural one.

The above issue holds true not only for the concept of death, but also for the process of dying, which many have argued is what we should be concentrating upon in the first place. After all, you are "still around" while you're dying.

Ramsey's observation, however, needs to be extended in two ways. First, while it is true that interpretations stressing individuality tend to uphold a model of rebellion ("Do not go gentle into that good night"), it must also be noted that *individuality* itself is not a concept with meaning invariance. It too is "socially constructed," that is, what one means by the term *individual* or *person* varies at least partly from culture to culture, and from one language to another.[3] Some cultures, for example, might favor a notion of individuality that is quite *inclusive* of other selves (such as family members), as in Japan. Given that social construction does take place to some degree, a simple identification of individuality and rebellion cannot be maintained. Rather, the most that one can argue for is a "relative uniqueness" of the self. Secondly, foregrounding the individual qua individual raises the question of style. That is, true emphasis upon the individual requires going from third-person to first-person language, and raises the question "To what degree can one first-person speaker view matters from the point of view of the 'other'?" In addition, emphasis upon first-person individuality raises the question as to the ability of language to capture the particular—without remolding it into essentialist categories, and thus replacing the original experience.

The text is divided into three parts. Part 1 argues for the proposition that death should be viewed historically and culturally, and that, when this is done, it becomes evident that death does not have meaning invariance. Both Western and non-Western examples are used to make this point. While death does not have one unique meaning here, there is some overlap among the various concepts. In addition, death is not viewed as an individual occurrence, but rather as a social construct; this also places limits upon a subjectivist position.

Part 2 deals with the opposite position, that is, the thesis that death is a biological phenomenon, historical accounts being of relatively minor use. Various biological definitions are discussed, as well as the issue of what kind of public policy should be adopted. The proposition that requests for a new definition are in reality pleas for allowing euthanasia is also taken up, as well as related issues concerning anencephalic newborns, letting some newborns die, and killing versus letting die. The conclusion of Part 2 argues that death does not have meaning invariance even when biologically defined, and that the distinction between the factual definition of death and the normative question of euthanasia cannot be neutrally drawn.

Part 3 commences with a criticism that discussion thus far in the text has focused, incorrectly, upon death, whereas the really important topic is that of dying. It begins with an overview of the person as an ongoing process of interactions, for whom the bodily and the affective are consequently important situating dimensions. Focusing upon the individual highlights the moral priority of "stories" of dying over the more general "stages" of dying. Three portraits are examined: Socrates, Ivan Ilych, and Zarathustra. In each case a subtext is revealed, the net result of which is to show, indirectly, that the binary opposition between acceptance and denial can, at least to some degree, be overcome—since each of us exhibits aspects of both attitudes. This conclusion is reinforced by turning to a fourth example from literature, Samuel Beckett's *Waiting for Godot*. Finally, the turn toward individual narratives raises the question of style in dealing with death and dying, requiring an investigation of the multiple functions of language. We conclude that language should be viewed primarily as *directive* rather than *descriptive*.

[[ACKNOWLEDGMENTS]]

FOR THE past fifteen years I have regularly taught Philosophy 291, "Death and Dying," at the University of Southern Maine. During that period I have benefited from numerous helpful and insightful comments from the many students who enrolled in my class, for which I am most grateful. One of them, Deborah French, provided significant proofreading support for this volume.

In May and June of 1992 Rissho University in Shinagawa (Tokyo), Japan, provided both funding and research opportunities to investigate Japanese attitudes toward death.

Jane Cullen, formerly at Temple University Press, and Doris Braendel, current senior acquisitions editor there, have been a pleasure to work with, providing continual support for the manuscript. An anonymous reviewer for the press offered extremely helpful comments on an earlier draft of the text. The reviewer's constructive criticism has served to make the present volume a much stronger one. Jennifer French, production editor, provided constant assistance throughout the entire process. My wife, Cathy, has, once again, provided continual support and encouragement, especially with the final proofs.

I am grateful to the following publishers for granting permission to reprint all or part of the following articles, with revisions:

"Language and Technology as 'Probes' into Death and Dying," *The Maine Scholar* 2 (Autumn 1989).

"*En Attendant la Mort:* Plato's Socrates, Tolstoy's Ivan Ilych, and Beckett's *Waiting for Godot,*" *Soundings* 64 (Summer 1981).

"The Gardiner Case in Maine: Summary and Reflections," *Newsletter on Philosophy and Medicine* 88 (November 1988).

"Metaphors Reveal but Also Conceal: Images of Japan," *Asian Thought and Society* 17 (January–April 1992).

Finally, the title, *Cuttin' the Body Loose,* is taken from Kalamu ya Salaam, *Banana Republic: Black Street Life and Culture in New Orleans,* quoted in "Rituals: Six Ways Americans Deal with Death," *Utne Reader* 47 (September–October 1991), p. 78.

I
Historical Contexts

[ONE]

Case Studies Conceal
as Well as Reveal

In the year 1789 Benjamin Franklin wrote, in a letter to Jean Baptiste Leroy, "in this world nothing is certain but death and taxes."[1] In a significant sense of the term, the first half of this statement is no longer true. (No doubt we would like the second half also to be false, but that is the subject of another book.) Two things caused the current ambiguity about death and dying. First, we gained the ability to prolong breathing artificially through respirators; second, we gained, and have bettered, the ability to perform organ transplants. These two technological achievements do not always march in moral tandem, as we shall see below.[2] We commence by looking at a few case studies, selected more or less at random, to see how the ambiguity arises. Or perhaps it would be better to say how the ambiguity *should* arise. For there is an important sense in which case studies as a genre, with their emphasis upon technology and upon court decisions, can serve to mask or underplay this ambiguity.

HIS BRAIN IS GONE: BUT IS HE DEAD?

The first case[3] concerns a man in his thirties who late one evening was dropped at the emergency entrance of a hospital by three anonymous friends. No sign of life was apparent. Laboratory analysis revealed heroine overdose, and lack of oxygen to the brain had left the patient in a deep coma. However the heart

3

was functioning in a normal fashion, and breathing was being maintained by a respirator. But the neurologist confirmed that the patient showed no signs of brain activity, and met the criteria for whole-brain death set up by the Harvard Ad Hoc Committee (discussed in detail in Chapter 5). He also wanted the patient's kidneys for an important organ transplant case involving a young girl.

An investigation of the hospital staff disclosed three positions concerning the patient. The first group, about 40 percent, thought that the patient was dead. The second group, again about 40 percent, believed that the patient was alive, but that "quality of life" prognosis was so bad that the patient should be allowed to die. The third group, smaller in size, believed that medical treatment should be continued.

Reflection upon these three positions reveals the following: The first group believes that brain activity of some sort is a necessary condition for being considered a live human being. We should note that it is quite possible to be considered "alive" in some sense of the term without being considered "human." Also, organisms may be kept "alive" through freezing, or other means. This first group also seems to believe that any type of brain activity is a sufficient indication of human presence. One could envision a fourth group for whom a more stipulative type of brain activity would be required.[4]

For the second group, brain activity of any type is not a necessary condition for a human being to be present; heartbeat, together with respiration, is seen as sufficient to indicate human presence; but this position seems to lead them immediately to consider the desirability of euthanasia. A series of questions arises here. First, is there a neat distinction between the seemingly factual definition of death, and the moral issue of euthanasia? Or are these more interdependent than is usually thought? Is there an inverse ratio between the "radicalness" of one's "definition" of death and one's need to deal with issues of euthanasia? Do we tend to avoid moral issues by pretending to come up with supposedly neutral epistemic definitions? Second, if one agrees with the "quality of life" decision made, is there a difference between allowing to die and terminating, and if so, is this difference one such that the moral side is always clearly identifiable? Third, the issue of quality of life is based on a concept of death with dignity. But this simply begs the question "Is death ever really dignified?"

The position of the third group is based upon the notion that it is the role of medicine to preserve life, in other words, always to do what one can. But many would disagree with this, arguing that the role of medicine is, say, to "do no harm," a position that does not necessarily entail continuing the life of a patient, since one could argue that continuance of his existence is not in his best interests.

At first glance, the issues in the case may seem clear-cut and straightforward. That is, which definition of death is "correct"? Whose rights have priority, the individual's or society's, etc. But as we have tried to show in the above set of questions, the intimation of a factually correct definition may itself be an inadequate formulation of the problematic.[5] Further, it will become a matter of extreme importance to indicate whether one is talking of the death of an organ, an organism, a person, or even a "social self." These issues will be dealt with at length in the chapters that follow.

A HYPOTHETICAL CASE

Consider a second case study, one in which you the reader play the role of attending physician.[6] A ten-year-old boy has been in an auto accident and is rushed to the hospital. He is put on a respirator, and it is noted that his pupils are dilated and he has no spontaneous movement; that is, his condition conforms to the Harvard Ad Hoc definition of death. You discuss the patient's condition with the family, and they agree to turn the respirator off, viewing this as the unplugging of a machine from an already-dead person and not as a form of euthanasia. The hospital transplant team, at this juncture, indicates that it would like to harvest the kidneys for renal transplant. This requires a thirty-six-hour wait, in order to do tissue typing. The parents consent.

Thirty-six hours later, however, the father has changed his mind, or at least developed serious reservations. He is now wondering whether the proposed action is not a form of murder, and so is inclined to refuse.

This case is less detached than the first, in the sense that it is articulated partly in the second person, that is, to you as physician, and your immediate reaction will probably be quite emotional, perhaps a feeling that "they [the parents] can't do this to me." But as Howard Brody has noted, people "may make a decision and stick to it foreverafter in the pages of ethics textbooks, but that is seldom the case in real life."[7] Assuming that you manage to put your emotions in perspective, that is, neither eliminate them nor let them dominate, there are questions to be considered in this case which are similar to those in the first. Additional questions center on whether you as doctor should offer advice to your patients, or simply let them decide on their own, or perhaps "empower" them to make a competent decision, and then demand it. Is the boy here still a person? Is it possible again that he is "alive" but is no longer a person? If the latter is the case, does the entity have any rights, or can one consider only the benefits to society? Clearly the potential for organ transplant plays an influential role in this case. But at least here there is no conflict of interest, as there was in the first case, where the patient's doctor was also the doctor involved in the transplant case. Once again, if the patient is dead, unplugging the respirator means simply removing a piece of machinery. If the patient is still "present" as a person, unplugging the respirator could be seen as a form of euthanasia. The interesting figure in the case is the father, who is unclear on the matter, who in a Socratic sense is beginning, just beginning, to "realize that he doesn't know what he once thought he knew," or at least took for granted, about death. This case is designed to present not too clear a picture, that is, one dealing with real-life situations.

THE TUCKER CASE

A third case took place in 1968, just when organ transplants were beginning to come into their own.[8] On May 25 of that year Bruce Tucker was taken to the hospital of the Medical College of Virginia at 6:05 P.M. He had fallen and suffered massive brain injury. At 2:05 A.M. an operation was completed, a craniotomy. At 11:30 A.M., however, he was placed on a respirator, with the treating physician stating at 11:45 A.M. that death was "imminent." A flat electroencephalogram (EEG) was obtained at 1:00 P.M. At 2:45 P.M. Tucker was taken to the operating room, where at 3:30 P.M. the respirator was turned off, and at 3:35 P.M. the patient was declared dead. At 4:25 P.M. and 4:33 P.M. incisions were made to remove the patient's heart and kidneys for transplant purposes. Another patient had been prepared at 3:33 P.M.

This case became famous for the number of things wrong with it. First, no attempt was made to get in touch with the patient's next of kin, even though it was established that his brother was within fifteen blocks of the hospital all day on May 25, and his business card was in the patient's wallet. Second, the tests, including the one for the flat EEG, were not repeated after twenty-four hours, as recommended by Harvard Ad Hoc. Third, it is debatable as to whether medicine has the right to decide such issues as a person's death and/or dying. The case was brought to court by Tucker's brother, with the court deciding in favor of the physicians, and newspapers stating that this case had "brought the law up to date with medicine." But the law in Virginia at the time defined death as cessation of respiratory and circulatory functions, and not as "whole brain" death as recommended by Harvard Ad Hoc. However the judge in the case sometimes seemed to direct the jury to use the new concept, something that should be decided as a matter of public policy by the state legislature. Finally, it seems extremely curious to unplug the respirator (3:30 P.M.) and then declare the patient dead (3:35 P.M.). If the patient is dead, as the surgeons seem to have thought, based on the flat EEG at 1:00 P.M. why turn off the respirator at all?[9] One could keep it plugged in at least until the heart had been removed, so as to keep the organs in the best condition, and perhaps even longer. On the other hand, if the patient is not dead, the case is not one of adopting a new definition of death. It is rather one of euthanasia, where one is dealing with a patient who is irreversibly terminal. But, once again, should this be an exclusively medical decision? Or even, for that matter, an exclusively legal one?

THE GARDINER CASE

On December 3, 1987, the Maine Supreme Court, in a four-to-three decision, upheld the decision of the Superior Court to discontinue life-sustaining treatment for Joseph Gardiner.[10] On May 11, 1985, Gardiner, who was then nearly twenty-three years of age, had suffered "severe, permanent, and totally disabling" injuries to his head when he fell from the back of a moving pickup truck. Heroic medical efforts had been undertaken; however, Gardiner had never regained consciousness, and indeed had been "in a chronic and persistent vegetative state without hope of regaining any cognitive or voluntary bodily functions by any known or anticipated medical procedures." The patient could not feed himself, nor ingest any food or drink by normal means. His nutrition and hydration were provided via the use of a Dobbhoff nasogastric (NG) tube, which was inserted through his nose into his stomach and intestines.

The majority ruling by the court was based upon public statements which Gardiner had made before the accident ever took place, concerning his desire not to be kept alive by artificial means. For example, in 1983 Gardiner had told his girlfriend, Deborah Mason, when she was working in a nursing home, that he "would want to die" rather than be kept alive by life-sustaining procedures, if such efforts resulted in the loss of human dignity. He had made similar statements to family and to friends. While a "substituted judgment" was, in a sense, made by his mother, the court based its decision primarily on Gardiner's own personal decision. In other words, the court argued that a substitute decision was not really being inserted for Gardiner's own position.

The court viewed its decision as stemming from the longstanding tradition of personal autonomy, and the right to self-determination. It argued that the right to refuse life-sustaining treatment was based on the common law doctrine of informed consent. Going further, it saw affinities between this case and others, such as *In Re Storer* (the Brother Fox case in New York; here an individual had expressly stated in public that had he been in the condition of Karen Quinlan, he would not want his life sustained by any extraordinary means).[11]

There are a few particulars about the informed-consent issue that deserve attention. First of all, Maine's Living Will Act, effective September 19, 1985, specifically excluded nutrition and hydration as procedures that can be discontinued by the author of the will. The court's majority went out of its way to indicate that it was basing its decision on Maine's common law doctrine of informed consent, stating that therefore the Living Will Act was not relevant to the question at issue, since Gardiner had not had one made up. Second, the court took notice of the fact that Gardiner was unmarried and without children, and that all testifying family members urged respect for his preaccident decision. In other words, the rights and interests of other specific individuals were not at stake. Third, the court refused to recognize an ordinary-extraordinary means of support distinction, with nutrition and hydration constituting the former of these. Against this, it argued that artificially providing food and water by utilizing an NG tube required skilled personnel, exacting standards, and specialized techniques. Going further, it agreed with the 1987 report of the Hastings Center that "all medical techniques for supplying nutrition and hydration that involve bodily invasion should be a matter of choice by the patient or surrogate." Fourth, the court rejected the thesis that providing nutrition and hydration to a patient has a symbolic importance. Rather it argued that this symbolism, deriving whatever significance it has from such contexts as the dependency between parent and infant, was inappropriate in this instance, and indeed would constitute a form of imposition. Next, the court argued that there were no state interests sufficiently strong to outweigh Gardiner's specific personal decision, made publicly and prior to his accident. The court did not see itself as making a quality-of-life decision but rather as recognizing Gardiner's decision about the quality of his own life. It did not view his decision as constituting a form of suicide, since, it argued, Gardiner had not decided to kill himself, and had not intentionally placed himself in such a position "that his continued biological existence would depend upon the provision of life-sustaining procedures." The cause of death, in other words, was seen not as his refusal to accept care, but rather as the accident itself and Gardiner's resulting medical condition.

The dissenting minority of the court argued that Gardiner's refusal to accept treatment was not really an informed one, because it was not based on any specific circumstances under which he would have wished treatment to be discontinued. Rather the minority charged that the court had paid undue attention to Gardiner's active lifestyle, a basis that it viewed as inadequate. Using a version of the slippery-slope argument, it suggested that individual rights are not absolute, and that state interest in preserving life, and in preventing suicide, was "essential to our survival as a civilization." The minority position viewed the use of NG tubes as only minimally invasive, and as causing no pain or risk to the patient. In opposition to the majority's interpretation of its own activity, the minority specifically charged the majority judges with implicitly making a quality-of-life decision about Gardiner. Finally, the minority opinion argued that identifying the accident as the cause of death was inappropriate; rather it should be noted that Gardiner was not terminally ill, and that, if the NG tube were "withdrawn, he will starve to death."

In general, this case has several aspects that align it to the cases mentioned above, as well as to several others. There seem to be two types of philosophical issues—although the difference is one of degree. First of all, there are the traditional philosophical issues over which the majority and the minority disagree: Was the informed consent really "informed"? Can the limits of personal autonomy be determined, vis-à-vis the rights of the state? And is the discontinuation of treatment really a form of euthanasia? There is also the issue of killing versus letting die, mentioned above. Here, however, the issue was somewhat sidetracked; the majority maintained that, should Gardiner's wishes be respected, his death would occur without any conscious pain or discomfort, and would "come within three to fourteen days." Less traditional but important issues concerned such matters as the ordinary-extraordinary means of support distinction, and where in this categorization NG tube feeding belongs. Here the court took a strong position, first suggesting that the distinction was contextual, and then going on to suggest that the whole distinction might be a false one. Second, in this particular case the court took a strong stand on personal autonomy, and this in the face of a Living Will Act that many wanted narrowly construed.

Finally, in this case as in so many others, the issue of "quality of life" came to the fore. In spite of recent attempts to legislate the term out of existence, and in spite of the lament by the minority that the decision was, incorrectly, based upon the quality of life, the issue seems impossible to repress. A quality-of-life decision was, one is tempted to say, inevitably, made in this instance. The only question is "Who made it?"

Other cases, some of them now famous, could be offered to flesh out the context. There is of course the case of Karen Anne Quinlan, referred to above, who had stopped breathing twice for at least fifteen minutes each time, and whose brain was therefore damaged to the extent that she was in a "persistent vegetative state." Here the New Jersey Supreme Court overruled Judge Muir of the Superior court, allowing her to be disconnected from a ventilator. It based its decision upon Karen's "right to privacy," and agreed that a "substituted judgment" could be rendered for her by her father, as someone who knew her "character" and therefore how she would (not should) choose in this situation.[12] In a sense, this case is more amorphous than the Gardiner case, in that the patient has given no direct expression of her views. On the other hand the issue of "substituted judgment" has its own flaws. It was employed in the case of Joseph Saikewicz,[13] a sixty-seven-year-old ward of the state of Massachusetts with acute leukemia, the preferred treatment for which is aggressive chemotherapy—which has considerable side effects. The court announced that it constituted the proper forum to determine the need for a guardian ad litem and the proper place to determine Saikewicz's best interests. The patient however was severely retarded, having an I.Q. of 13 or less. The use of "substituted judgment" here is therefore extremely questionable, since he had never been capable of forming specific preferences.[14] On the other hand, this may not in itself justify an exclusively paternalistic approach either.

More recently (June 25, 1990), there is the case of Nancy Cruzan,[15] who like Karen Quinlan was in a persistent vegetative state since being in an automobile accident in 1983, and whose parents petitioned to have her disconnected from a gastrostomy feeding tube. (Ms. Quinlan had required both a ventilator and a feeding tube.) The U.S. Supreme Court, in a five-to-four decision, held that the state of Missouri's "clear and convincing" evidentiary standard concerning desires to have hydration and nutrition withdrawn did not violate federal constitutional rights. In this case then, substituted judgment was not allowed, because a specific state had ruled that objective proof of Ms. Cruzan's wishes was required. On the other hand, in the process of arriving at its decision the court did explicitly recognize a competent individual's right to refuse life-sustaining treatment. It also viewed such treatment as including rather than excluding tube feeding, thus touching on one matter brought up in the Gardiner case. But the overall outlook was nonetheless rather chilling, though relegated to Missouri. Ms. Cruzan's parents were not recognized over the state, and certainty was given priority in a situation where it is rarely, if ever found.[16] Commenting upon this case, Ronald Cranford notes that "the long term effect of decisions of the Missouri Supreme Court and the U.S. Supreme Court may well be the very opposite of what was intended . . . and what was most feared . . . namely, to drive people more toward active euthanasia as the public fully recognizes how much they have lost control of their own lives and the lives of their loved ones."[17] Given the recent popularity of Derek Humphry's text *Final Exit: The Practicalities of Self-Deliverance and Assisted Suicide for the Dying*, Mr. Cranford's words seem prescient.[18]

There is a final footnote to this case study; Ms. Cruzan "died" on December 26, 1990, twelve days after her feeding tube had been removed. Her parents had requested a new hearing in November, where they produced three former coworkers of Nancy's, who recalled that they had heard her say that she would never want to live "like a vegetable." Given this testimony, a state judge ruled that "clear and convincing" evidence existed. Nonetheless, anti-euthanasia activists went to court seven times in an attempt to force resumption of feeding, but were unsuccessful each time, due to lack of legal standing. This phenomenon has come to be known as the "busybody factor," the attempted intervention by someone outside the family who seeks to force the prolongation of "life" regardless of the wishes of those more immediately involved. Ms. Cruzan's death was not only forced to be public rather than private; it was also forced to conform to a very large degree to other peoples' idea of objectivity.

CONCLUSION

Case studies like those above can be extremely illuminating. They deal with concrete situations as opposed to abstract formulas. They do not simply pit, for example, "consequentialism" and "deontological ethics" against each other in the rarefied atmosphere of a noncontextual situation. Like the recent revolt in ethics spearheaded by philosophers such as Alasdair MacIntyre, they emphasize that decision making concerning moral issues cannot be made solely upon intellectually "foundationalist" grounds, but rather involves a kind of Aristotelian "prudence" or "practical wisdom."[19] "Character" is as important a factor here as sheer rational ability. Second, case studies describe situations where a decision must be made, that is, where we do not have "world enough and time" to look at matters from every possible side. Closure of some sort does take place, though the cases can serve as models through postmortems. By looking at several of these, one can get a sense of the issues involved without necessarily succumbing to the temptation of creating overly neat classifications or eternal verities. Case studies are, in short, useful models. But like all models, one must be careful not to take them as literal descriptions of the phenomena they purport to depict. Models, to use the wording of Don Ihde, are "amplification-reduction" structures.[20] That is, they are not merely instruments, but serve rather to highlight particular aspects of the situation at hand, while marginalizing others.

The above case studies are both old (1968) and recent (1990). More important, some of them are "made up" for purposes of discussion, and some, like the Gardiner case, refer to situations that actually occurred. One point that needs to be made with regard to both of these issues (recent versus remote past and real versus rhetorical) is that in an important sense these are not the most important distinctions that demand consideration. As we shall see in Chapter 8, fictional portraits of dying have often served as our most useful studies. True, looking at the most recent legal case study often indicates the direction in which the courts are moving. This is extremely important in terms of tracking national trends and collective awareness. In addition, looking at recent cases generally reveals the latest in technological developments, such as the newest test for brain activity, or the use of nasogastric tubes. But overfocalization here can provide its own dangers. That is, it can result in a tendency to confine discussion within case studies to "meaningful" areas, in order not to get too "personal" or "emotional." This generally means suggesting that we ought not to get caught up in issues that don't have at least the possibility of a definite answer. One asks how a given case was resolved in court, or one concentrates rather narrowly upon the "facts" of the situation, especially and sometimes exclusively the "technological facts"—these being viewed as the most "objective" in an otherwise murky context. But how an issue has been resolved legally is not necessarily an indication of how it should have been resolved, as, for example, the third case described above indicates.

Going further, concentration upon the technology involved can also be counterproductive, for, like a model, a piece of technological equipment is not neutral, but from a phenomeno-

logical perspective, is rather like a probe, emphasizing some experiences and downplaying others. We can bring out what technological devices "mask" by using a simple example, slightly
"painful" but hopefully revealing. Think of what it is like to
investigate one's teeth by using a dentist's probe. Don Ihde offers
the following account:

> I can, of course, feel the tooth with my finger. In this case I do get
> the sense of the tooth's hardness, its texture and more besides.
> But compared to the sense of the tooth through the probe, I now
> note that something is missing as well. The probe not only ex-
> tended my embodiment, it *amplified* certain characteristics of the
> tooth. Through the probe I actually get a better sense of the
> hardness and softness of the tooth surfaces, a finer discrimination.
> The probe gives me what, compared to the fleshy finger, are *micro-
> features* of the tooth's surface. . . . This aspect of the use of an
> instrument is *dramatic,* it stands out. . . . But at the same time that
> the probe extends and amplifies, it *reduces* another dimension of
> the tooth experience. With my finger I sensed the warmth of the
> tooth, its wetness, etc. . . . The probe, precisely in giving me a finer
> descrimination related to the micro-features, "forgot" or reduced
> the full range of the other features sensed in my finger's touch.
>
> But this reduction of experience [if taken by itself] is not
> dramatic, it is recessive. Were I not to critically re-check what is
> possible with the tooth with my finger, I could easily not notice or
> forget the rich range of tooth features available in the flesh.[21]

The dentist's probe is a small piece of technology, usually taken
for granted. It is, supposedly, an instrument that does not affect
the end, a window through which we neutrally gaze at what is
"out there." But as the above quote makes clear, the probe is not
neutral; how we experience the tooth is textured by the probe,
or by the finger, for that matter; there simply is no "tooth in
itself." Or if there is, we don't know anything about it. The issue
remains the same if we change to a more complicated, more
expensive piece of machinery, such as an EEG, offered as an

indicator of death. That is, to the extent that it is seen as a neutral device, its use is reductive rather than dramatic. To the extent that use of an EEG is seen as not presupposing a normative decision concerning what ought to count as an indictor, its use is reductive in nature.

In sum, case studies can be looked at in both a "thin" fashion and a "thick" fashion.[22] Thinly viewed, they tend to be evaluated in terms of legal outcome and technological instrumentation. This narrowing of the problematic results in discussion focusing upon gradations of change within a very confined conceptual space. It is another version of what Whitehead has called "the fallacy of misplaced concreteness."[23] Thickly viewed, case studies strive to preserve incompatible, perhaps even incommensurate, dimensions. Idiosyncrasies are not eliminated; final closure, to the extent that it arrives, does not take place in exclusively algorithmic terms. There is no ideal "textbook case," or if there is, it is ideal because of its richness and its ambiguity. As Dena Davis has put it,

> We need thick description to allow cases to remain open to different interpretations over time, and also to enable cases to ground an ethics of care. The thicker the case, the more contextual the response. . . . People relate to narrative, and thick description allows for true psychological empathy, more powerful than the more abstract claims of shared humanity. Finally, *life* isn't as simple as thinly described cases would have us believe.[24]

The cases looked at above can be viewed either narrowly or thickly. Looking at them thickly requires not simply additional information, but a realization that the information provided may not add up, or even be commensurate. Thus the last case discussed above is "thicker" than the first three in terms of the amount of detail provided, but it remains "thin" in the sense that most of the detail provided before the analysis at the end is of a particular nature, that is, legalistic. In this sense we must remind ourselves not to be trapped within the confines of any particular discipline regarding death. The topic is interdisciplinary, and turning toward case studies should not allow this to be masked by an overly technological or legalistic approach. The temptation to seek shortcuts, to look for certainty regarding death, is a particularly strong one, given that death is something that we are "concerned" about. Nonetheless it must be resisted, and the "thicker" approach needs to be reaffirmed. Case studies are, in short, "contextualized"; they are not "recipes" to be literally replicated. By "contextualized" I mean that each personal situation possesses rich individuating characteristics of a spatial and temporal nature. Some of these are explicitly contained in language; some are implied and must be searched out. In addition, each context is moulded by the selective interest of its author. The context is, literally, that which goes along *with* the text; in other words, it is more than just other texts, but refers rather to the actual experience the person in question undergoes.[25] In short, the "model" for dying must not be allowed to replace the activity of dying.

Not only do descriptions need to be thick; they need to be *more* than just descriptions. We need to reject the old "description versus prescription" dichotomy, and to recognize that the context itself (i.e., the situated patient) is not neutral in nature, nor is our relationship to her. We do not approach impartially, but rather with our own socially constructed role of expectations. This is especially true if we happen to be in some position of power relative to the dying person. In the chapters that follow it will be argued that the implicit is as important as the explicit in language, that people often mean more, or less, than they say, that it is difficult, yet necessary, to try to see things from the point of view of the other, even when that point of view may not be clear to the other herself. Differently stated, if death is to be affirmed as a truly interdisciplinary topic, one cannot dictate in advance just what "objective" disciplines will be allowed to participate in the discussion. This entails a blurring of the distinction between science and art, or a reaffirmation of the need to view medicine as essentially requiring both features. As Robert Coles notes in *The Call of Stories:* "Our patients all too often come to us with preconceived notions of what matters, what doesn't matter, what should be stressed, what should be overlooked, just as we come with our own lines of inquiry. . . . Patients shape their accounts accordingly, even as we shape what we have heard into our own version of someone's troubles . . . an 'abstract.' "[26] For Coles, however, the physician's choice of which material to emphasize, the details considered important, and so forth constitute a different "story" in itself—one revealing the need of the physician for certainty and control. In opposition, he warns of the necessity to "worry about messages omitted, yarns gone untold, details brushed aside altogether, in the rush to come to a conclusion."[27] He takes as one of his primary role models William Carlos Williams, "the busy, street-smart doctor and the hard-working writer merged into the friendly but tough teacher who wanted his younger listener to treasure not only the explicit but the implicit, all the subtleties and nuances of language as it is used, of language as it is heard."[28] While this is not meant to say that no distinction between appearance and reality is possible, it does hold that such a distinction is always an interpretative one, and that "narrative" is a procedure to be found in both fact and fiction. Indeed, as we shall see below, some of the best models of narrative we have come from fiction.

Case studies represent a step forward from abstract theories, but stories represent an additional necessary step. Case studies begin to emphasize the importance of the individual person, but they do so in a third-person fashion. Stories begin to see matters from the point of view of the person involved. On the other hand, the point of view of the person involved is to a considerable degree a socially constructed one. Finally, even granted this, as we shall see, the emphasis upon the *relative uniqueness* of each individual self is directly correlated to whether one accepts death as a part of life, or denies it and rebels against it.

[TWO]

Historical Contexts in the West

"Philosophy," as Wittgenstein has noted, "is a battle against the bewitchment of our intelligence by means of language."[1] In our case the particular form of the bewitchment involves assuming that the terms *death,* and *dying,* have meaning invariance. Such an approach would hold that there exists, or at least *should* exist, a transcendental or acontextual definition of death, without which only conceptual chaos can reign. In opposition, in this and in the following chapters we argue that people undergo their deaths in different ways at different times. These ways are not necessarily individualistic as opposed to social, nor are they always incommensurate. But they are not always the same. "Continuity of language," as one philosopher has noted, "is no guarantee of a continuity of experience."[2] In the present chapter this position is defended by showing that death has a history, or, rather, several histories. The four authors described below differ in important ways, but they all assert that death as a topic has been viewed in too narrow a manner, that is, as acontextual, or immediately self-evident.

GEOFFREY GORER

Credit for the initial realization that death has undergone a significant change of meaning in the twentieth century is often given to the British sociologist Geoffrey Gorer. His 1965 text *Death, Grief and Mourning* contains the famous article entitled

"The Pornography of Death," and is considered a turning point. Pornography for Gorer refers to the description of taboo activities in order to produce hallucination or delusion. His major thesis is that copulation, once unmentionable in Victorian society, has now become more and more mentionable, whereas death, once quite mentionable, has now become quite unmentionable as a natural process. "The natural processes of corruption and decay have become disgusting, as disgusting as the natural processes of birth and copulation were a century ago; preoccupation about such matters is (or was) morbid and unhealthy, to be discouraged in all and punished in the young."[3] As a result, embalming, for example, has as its goal the production of a beautiful, that is, *lifelike* corpse, one that masks the reality of death. Achievements in medicine have ironically resulted in fewer and fewer young people having to deal with death in the family. Any type of extensive mourning is discouraged or forbidden; the "widow" must act as if nothing happened if she wants to be accepted. While natural death is marginalized in this fashion, death itself is not repressed; it appears rather as violent death, in such media as horror comics, war stories, thrillers, and science fiction. Gorer's opinion of the present situation is clear. He tells the reader: "If we dislike the modern pornography of death, then we must give back to death—natural death—its parade and publicity, readmit grief and mourning. If we make death unmentionable in polite society—'not before the children'—we almost ensure the continuation of the 'horror comic.' No censorship has ever been really effective."[4]

For Gorer then we have gone from an acceptance model to a denial model, from a view of death as natural to one of death as violent. His narrative fleshes out the context of this change, although he is better at describing *how* than at explaining *why* this process occurred. Perhaps this is the best that one can hope for in this area. In any event two caveats require emphasis. First, if death was a taboo subject when Gorer wrote this piece, it is not so in the same way today. As Peter Steinfels has put it, "That statement [death is a taboo subject] cannot be made today without betraying a distressing insensitivity to the climate of our society."[5] But even if death is discussed much more, this does not necessarily mean that death has become "natural" again, or indeed that there is (or was) such a thing as "natural" death that is not the result of some set of social constructs. Gorer's presentation, while illuminating, itself masks a crucial issue that we shall encounter again and again in the following chapters: namely, is any form of death "natural"? Or is this only a relative distinction?

PHILIPPE ARIÈS

In *Western Attitudes Toward Death, The Hour of Our Death,* and "Death Inside Out,"[6] French sociologist Philippe Ariès argues for the importance of context in approaching the subject of death, of our need to detach our attitudes about death "from their modernity and situate them within a broader historical perspective." He avoids at least some of the pitfalls of a sequential-stages approach (e.g., literalism, classification through habit, and lack of critical analysis) by asserting that there are both "synchronic" and "diachronic" dimensions to the process. Changes have occurred in the past, and more rapidly in recent times, but not to the extent that there is no continuity. Ariès's narrative about death contains four aspects, which he terms "tame death," "my death," "thy death," and "forbidden death," respectively. The first of these is essentially synchronic, and covers the first millennium A.D. Here most people were forewarned of their death; diseases were, in general, fatal, and if persons did not recognize their impending lot, others had the obligation to inform them. Thus Sir Gawain, for example, says, "Know ye well that I shall not live two days."[7] In addition, since the dying person knew that death was imminent, he had to prepare for it. This was done by lying down, folding one's arms across the chest, facing the wall, and other such gestures. One also, at this stage, asked for forgiveness, forgave in turn one's enemies, and in general organized and presided over the ritual of one's dying, which was a public ceremony, taking place, for example, in the dying person's bedchamber, complete with audience. In short, death was very much a part of life, and there was an appropriate way to die, an *ars moriendi*. One wanted to be buried *ad sanctos,* that is, with the saints in the cemetery. There was an "innocence or salvation by virtue of association" principle operative here. Gradually the spatial distinction between church and cemetery, operative in earlier times for health reasons (the cemetery being located outside the city) began to collapse, and cemeteries began to include of necessity charnel houses, or galleries running along the churchyards, above which were ossuaries, where the skulls of turned-over graves were placed. Death was so familiar that merchants began to sell their wares there; dancing, gambling, and socializing took place there. Indeed, an overall "macabre" aspect began to develop.

For Ariès, changes, not in the form of radical revolutions but rather in the way of "subtle alterations," began to take place in the eleventh and twelfth centuries. These changes focused upon "individualization" and consisted of four dimensions. First, the portrayal of the Last Judgment, originally depicted simply as the Second Coming when Christ would arrive to save all together, is now changed to that of individual salvation. Second, the moment of judgment is now not the last day, but rather the precise day of one's death. As such, the moment of death is itself important; it serves as the occasion for self-awareness or self-realization, because it is the last temptation to despair. As such, death begins to take on the aspect of an enemy, of something to be overcome. Third, the more concrete "transi" or worm-ridden corpse replaces the more abstract recumbent knight in portrayals of death. This too has a rather macabre, or unacceptable, dimension to it. Finally, tombs become more and more personalized, again in an attempt to indicate individual achievements, and in this sense, to "live on."

In all of this, death becomes less and less acceptable, and begins to be viewed more as a transgression, as a rupture that tears the living away from life. "In the new iconography of the sixteenth century, Death raped the living."[8] As an extraordinary event death might be admired or romanticized, but it was no longer simply acceptable. By the eighteenth century a third change has occurred in Ariès's scenario; it is the death of another person that becomes unacceptable to the survivors (thy death). People now want to go to an exact spot in the cemetery, rather than a general area; and tombs served as an indication of the presence after death of those who have departed. The relation between the dying person and his family is now reversed; the family is no longer passive. It is aided in its development by medicine, which tends to substitute a particular "sickness" for "death" in evaluating the situation. A new style of death thus emerges, a new "art of dying," in which "discretion is the modern form of dignity."[9] Thus, even if the dying person knows about his illness—which the survivors would strive to prevent— he must not be too emotional about it. On the other hand, the dying person cannot be indifferent to the efforts of those around him.

In the twentieth century we witness a new, much more intensified change in this process. Death is denied, not merely for the sake of the dying person (to keep him from harm) but for society's sake. Death, as effaced, disappears as shameful or "forbidden"; it is displaced from the home to the hospital. Death in the hospital is no longer the occasion of a ritual ceremony over which the dying person presides amidst his or her assembled relatives and friends. Death as a technical phenomenon "has been dissected, cut to bits by a series of little steps, which finally makes it impossible to know which step was the real death, the one in which consciousness was lost, or the one in which breathing stopped. All these little silent deaths have replaced and erased the great dramatic act of death, and no one any longer has the strength or patience to wait over a period of weeks for a moment which has lost a part of its meaning."[10]

For Ariès then, it is the shared, public dramatic ritual of death that is important, and not its biological description. From a critical perspective, however, he would be better off saying that an older ritual has been replaced by a newer, "scientific" one, the latter *masquerading* as nonsymbolic or objective in character. Differently stated, there are no neutral positions on death, including the latest clinical definition.

Going further, Ariès specifically ties the current, or "forbidden," view of death with the important issue of language. He argues that "death has become *unnamable*";[11] and again, that "death, that familiar companion of yore, has disappeared from our language. His naming is anathema. . . . In normal existence it no longer has any positive meaning at all. It is merely the negative side of what we really see, what we really know, and what we really feel."[12] In sum, for Ariès we have gone from acceptance to denial in terms of our approach to death; this process can be described, at least in terms of "how" if not in terms of "why." But the ironic, perhaps unintended, result of his investigations is that, at the end, death appears as *absent*, that is, as unnamable. The situation is actually more qualified in the United States, where the dead person's body occupies a more intermediate position through embalming as opposed to cremation. "Americans are very willing to transform death, to put make-up on it, to sublimate it, but they do not want to make it disappear."[13] The interdiction against death has in this sense some limitations, and one result is that death "is once again becoming something one can talk about."[14] In this context, Ariès recognizes that "there is no doubt that death is a consumer product,"[15] but, somewhat in opposition to Illich's position, developed below, he argues that "the money earned by funeral merchants [via embalming] would not be tolerated if they did not meet a profound need."[16] The causal factors, in other words, may not be exclusively or even predominantly politicoeconomic in nature. Finally, Ariès specifically associates the theme of acceptance versus denial with that of becoming a human person, or a self. "The clear correspondence between the triumph over death and the triumph of individuality during the late Middle Ages invites us to ask whether a similar but inverse relationship might not exist today between the 'crisis of death' and the crisis of individuality."[17] The position here seems to be that self-realization comes with acceptance; but as we shall see in Chapter 9, several thinkers will argue the opposite, that is, that self-realization comes with rebellion.

IVAN ILLICH

Ivan Illich also wants to focus upon the ritual nature of death. In "The Political Uses of Natural Death," he argues that each culture is dominated by a particular view of death, which in turn determines its image of health. Our industrial culture is dominated by a view of death as "natural." But what we call natural death is not really natural—it is clinical. Furthermore, this whole process is masked. "The ritual nature of modern health procedures hides from doctors and patients the contradiction between the ideal of a natural death of which they want to die and the reality of a clinical death in which most contemporary [wo]men actually end."[18] As a result of this masking, we offer "true" answers to "false" problems. That is, we try to avoid collusion among doctors, hospitals, and pharmaceutical companies; we strive for equality in health care delivery systems; and we aim for professionalism. But for Illich, improving the health care system "could render it—to use the phrase literally—more sickening."[19] The crisis in medicine then cannot be solved merely by attending to questions of reorientation. Rather one must consider the fact that these questions presuppose a ritual practice of medicine that defines a natural death as ideal, yet delivers mainly clinical death. This can be shown by looking at the cultural ideal of death as it developed over the past five hundred years in four phases.

Up until 1404 not death but rather hell was the important factor. But in that year the Duke de Berry had the first "Dance of Death" painted on the wall of the Cemetery of the Innocents in Paris. These individualized portraits changed everything. Death is no longer simply the struggle between angel and devil for one's soul; each person dances with his or her own individualized self. The dancing partner is no abstraction but a "skeleton self," inevitable, a natural force that one deals with in terms of the art of dying. By the eighteenth century however, death becomes "timely," but only for an elite group; that is, those who can financially afford to die in *active* old age, and we witness "the rise of the aging lecher." Jobs are more sedentary, and having the economic resources that would enable one to remain active up until the very end is seen as a sign of status. A few generations later the process intensifies, and we witness "the opening of the clinical eye." Having a famous doctor is seen as respectable; attention shifts from the sick person to the person's disease. "Man who must heal or die is substituted by the image of man the consumer. . . . The stage is set for the idea of unnatural death as a result of under-consumption."[20] At the end of the nineteenth century, demand for this type of "natural" (i.e., clinical) death is unionized. Workers are redefined as health consumers, and the "ideal of ending life on the job [is] turned into the right to start life after retirement from it."[21] This universalized ideal, masquerading as natural, becomes an ultimate justification for social control.

As a result, Illich charges, we have a new "Art of Dying." Death is now egalitarian once again, but as a normative rather than a factual necessity. "Man, faced by death, was . . . [in the Middle Ages] asked to be aware that he was finally, frighteningly, totally alone; society now obligates him to seek medicine's protection and let the doctor fight. . . . While the dancing partner of the Middle Ages was symbolic of something which really waits for each man, natural extinction from old-age exhaustion is a lottery ticket for only a few."[22]

In sum, we have gone from what we might term "natural/natural" death to "natural/clinical" death, in other words, to a very unnatural way of dying that pretends to be natural. Further, the evolution of this process can be explained, not only in terms of "how" but also in terms of "why." The major causal factors are economic or politicoeconomic in nature, expressible in general in Marxist categories. Finally, any attempt to impose this type of industrialized natural death upon developing, or Third World, countries constitutes "a form of imperialist intervention."[23] As with the first two authors in this section, we have gone from acceptance to denial, and this is not good.

While Illich is no doubt correct in showing that neither "health" nor "death" is a value-free term, his own narrative leaves one with a few unanswered questions. First, if a particular model of death and health dominates a specific context and does so in a masked fashion, how does one ever "break the circle"? Perhaps more important, how many people can break the circle? These are the same problems Marx had in conjuring up the "proletariat" and its "vanguard." They were not easily solved then, if at all, and the issue is no less serious here. Nonetheless, Illich's overall point rings true: One needs a rich context, communal and ritualistic in nature, within which to gain a perspective on death—whether or not one agrees with his assertion that we have gone from acceptance to denial in some sense of these terms, and that this is not a good thing.

ERIC J. CASSELL

In his article "Dying in a Technological Society" Eric Cassell also argues that "what matters is the mythology of . . . [a] society,"[24] and that what is now basic to the mythology of American society is that fate, or death, can be defeated. In his narrative we have moved from a moral to a technological context. As a result, individuals do not expect to die, since death has been redefined as a technical problem to be solved. The context of dying has changed in a similar fashion: It has moved from the home to the hospital, where "the patient's values, spoken by others, compete with the values of the institution."[25] There is a final ironic sense, in which the patient, lost among these conflicting values, dies alone. Cassell argues phenomenologically for the need to recover a multidimensional and holistic context, one that is now lost as a person enters the hospital. "It is not his blood or urine that goes to the laboratory, it is the patient. But it is not the person who holds the interest for the specialized laboratory; instead the interest centers on the person's lungs, or heart, or whatever."[26] From this perspective the hospital appears as a series of compartments, and medicine appears more and more as an analytical science.[27] The charge of depersonalization is most often leveled against young physicians, who have, we must remember, been trained on cadavers. "To the inexperienced doctor almost everything about the dying person is unfamiliar or poorly understood thus requiring the abstraction that leads to depersonalization."[28]

In opposition to this form of reductionism, Cassell argues that "there are two distinct things happening in the terminally ill, the death of the body and the passing of the person."[29] While the death of the body can be measured and defined, the passing of a person cannot. In an epoch dominated by technology, what cannot be defined is seen as unimportant, or worse, as nonexistent. Thus like Ariès, Cassell laments the fact that what is truly significant about death is ceasing to be a legitimate subject for public discourse. "Men obscure the moral content of the passing of the person by using the facts and artifacts of the death of the body as the vehicle for their interchanges—much as talk about

the weather or sports draws the sting on other occasions."[30]
There is then a twofold problem, much as exists in Illich's narrative. That is, language or discourse does exist, and it is important.
But language is being used as a diversion—as a "true" description of the wrong issue. Organisms are reduced to organs, and
those processes that cannot be controlled by existing technology,
such as cancer, acquire an ontological status of their own, independent of the person who contains them. Finally, nursing
homes for the most part serve to marginalize the failures, the
"tattered edges" of medicine viewed exclusively or predominantly as a science. It should also be noted that the view of
medicine as a science and of patients as organs is not one that
can be laid exclusively at the doctor's door. "The whole society
has shifted its public focus from moral to technical in many areas
of life; doctors are no exception to the trend. The problem cannot solely lie among physicians, or the society would not let
them get away with it."[31]

The solution, for Cassell, is not a return to a pretechnological
context. First, this is not possible, even if it were desirable;
second, people were not "inherently more moral in the past
when the moral order predominated over the technical."[32] He
argues instead for a restoration of a balance between the technical and the moral, one wherein knowledge and wonder are not
necessarily viewed as exclusive of each other.

Cassell's phenomenological description of the hospital cor-
ridor is impressive, and he shares with the other authors in this
chapter an awareness that context is important, and that one
predominant way of describing that change of context concerns
technology. But his own description of the problematic reveals
the same type of difficulty alluded to by Illich. For Cassell also,
we have gone from a form of acceptance to one of denial in going
from the moral to the technological, in reducing persons to
organs. But here too the issue is masked by a view of discourse as
neutral and descriptive, and not as directive, that is, as pointing

beyond itself.[33] As such, the problem is not apparent, and the difficulty of making it so is perhaps understated. Second, while medicine may indeed reflect the technical values of society, it also serves to intensify them and to instantiate them in a manner capable of being duplicated by few other professional areas, if any.

CONCLUSION

The four narratives described above have much in common. First and foremost, each of the authors has presented a historical account of death, as opposed to a biological one. They seem to claim that overconcentration upon the biological or the technological constitutes a reification of the problematic. Each of the four argues for the preservation of a "thick" context, and against any type of "thin" description, and each sees history, including sociology and anthropology, as *the* way or at least as *a* way to accomplish this.

Second, all of the accounts rendered above emphasize in some way the importance of ritual, of myth. In a similar fashion, Joseph Campbell has emphasized the positive dimension of myth in general, maintaining that if "a *differentiating* feature is to be named, separating human from animal psychology, it is surely . . . [that] of the subordination in the human sphere of even economics to mythology."[34] Myths for Campbell provide an understanding of the universe roughly in accord with science, but they also preserve in an individual a sense of awe about the mystery of the universe. Stemming from the recognition of our own mortality, myths guide us through life's stages, that is, childhood, old age, and so on. They also tend to support the stability of the social order through the use of rites and rituals. But while these positive aspects need to be applauded, we must also realize that myths can have negative ramifications, particularly when they are taken exclusively as literal truths and uncritically accepted. As Paul Tillich has noted on this matter, some myths need to be "broken."[35]

Third, the overriding conclusion of the four narratives is one that "relativizes" death in some sense of the term. The word *death* does not have meaning invariance; it has meant different things to different cultures at different times. More strongly put, there is no such thing as death "in itself," or, if there is, we don't know anything about it. In Kantian terminology, death appears as phenomenal rather than noumenal. Two caveats are immediately in order here. First, while the authors do not argue for a univocal definition of death, they also do not accept an exclusively individualistic approach to death. Death is not in the eye of the beholder, with each dying person telling his or her own story. Death, and the concept of self in general, is very much a social construct in these approaches. (Somewhat in opposition, Part 3 of this text will focus much more upon the individual.) The second caveat concerns the notion of change, and of explanation in general. Though each of the above accounts argues that the meaning of the term *death* has changed, none of the authors asserts that these changes cannot be explained, or at least "understood" in the broad sense of that term. We touch here upon the thorny issue of what constitutes an adequate explanation, and whether the "logical" explanations sometimes offered up by science can or should be superimposed upon historical accounts. The "explanations" offered above do not argue for such a cataclysmic degree of change that the results are "incommensurable." They can at least indicate "how," if not "why," specific changes took place. Going further, Chapter 4 will call into question the seeming exclusivity of these two types of explanation, historical and scientific.

Fourth, all the accounts given above seem to argue that we have gone from acceptance to denial, and that this is not a good thing. The historical scope utilized by each of the four authors to make his specific point differs somewhat. In Ariès we have a somewhat cursory statement about death up until the twelfth century; then a detailed account from the twelfth to the twentieth century. Illich's account takes us from the fourteenth to the twentieth century. Cassell and Gorer have narrower horizons, not exceeding the last one or two hundred years. Nonetheless, their shared point remains clear; a historical account can, or should, disclose a movement from acceptance to denial. In Part 3 we will question the exclusivity of these alternatives.

Finally, the difference between "can" and "should" alluded to in the sentence above reveals an important issue, that is, just how obvious is the problem at hand. Here Illich and Cassell seem to be more aware that the whole issue may be "masked," thereby requiring a twofold step in any attempted solution—the first of which would involve "inventing the problematic" and indicating which issues were really false ones. Going further, at the metatheoretical level, we need to ask the question "Are these accounts *themselves* neutral in nature?" Are they impartial descriptions? The answer to this question has to be no, that these descriptions are interpretations of other peoples' interpretations of experience. As such, the accounts are both partial and incomplete, as are all interpretations of our pasts. None of the authors brings this out in sufficient detail, but Illich does a better job than the rest. All the accounts given above emphasize the need to view death "from the point of view of the other," that is, at different historical moments. However, they also take for granted the availability of the "other" for inspection. This issue becomes more problematic, and more complicated, when the "other" encountered is different from one's own taken-for-granted Western culture, as in, for example, a non-Western yet modern country like Japan.

⟦ THREE ⟧

A Non-Western Example: Japan

JAPAN AS "OTHER"

No discussion about the importance of "the other" as related to Japan can fail to acknowledge the initial contribution made by Ruth Benedict in *The Chrysanthemum and the Sword: Patterns of Japanese Culture*. To her credit, Benedict commences this text by warning the reader against superimposing his or her own views or categories upon the other, or engaging in exclusive, either/or binaries. She says:

> When [an observer] writes a book on a nation with a popular cult of aestheticism which gives high honor to actors and artists and lavishes art upon the cultivation of chrysanthemums, that book does not ordinarily have to be supplemented by another which is devoted to the cult of the sword and the top prestige of the warrior.
>
> All these contradictions, however, are the warp and woof of books on Japan. They are true. Both the sword and the chrysanthemum are a part of the picture. The Japanese are, to the highest degree, both aggressive and unaggressive, both militaristic and aesthetic, both insolent and polite, rigid and adaptable, submissive and resentful of being pushed around, loyal and treacherous, brave and timid, conservative and hospitable to new ways.[1]

Benedict, in the beginning of this text, resists the temptation to label Japan once and for all, so to speak. She does, however, resort to a cataloging of the different labels available, implying

34

that it is sufficient to simply "supplement" one metaphor with another. More seriously, by the end of this text Benedict has become more logically exclusive, characterizing Japan as having a "shame" culture as opposed to European/American "guilt" cultures. She tells the reader, "True shame cultures rely on external sanctions for good behavior, not, as true guilt cultures do, on an internalized conviction of sin. Shame is a reaction to other people's criticism. A man is shamed by being openly ridiculed and rejected or by fantasizing to himself that he has been made ridiculous."[2]

Keiichi Sakuta has argued against this portrayal, suggesting that Benedict's conceptual topology is inadequate because "people first realize what guilt is through punishment from outside, and 'those who know shame' control themselves on their own."[3] And Esyun Hamaguchi argues that

> in her comparison of Oriental and Occidental cultures, Benedict began with the Euro-American notion that an individual is an independent being (an autonomous unit of action). In such a framework, consciousness of guilt (conscience) is assumed to form the core of the autonomous individual's ego structure. In contrast, shame was a suitable concept to express a non-autonomous attitude. . . . Benedict's analytical paradigm belongs to the category of methodological individualism because the point of reference for this analysis is the assumption that the individual is a free and independent being.[4]

The first of the above criticisms argues against exclusivity. That is, one should beware of utilizing one category at the expense of another, for all categories are forms of privileging. However, this criticism leaves intact the whole issue of "self" or "person." It debates how to characterize the self but does not address the possibility that the self encountered may be dramatically different from the one wanted or expected. In this sense the second criticism is more radical, suggesting that not only does Benedict superimpose adjectival qualities of one sort or another, but that she employs a notion of individuality as "normal," while it is in actuality a social construct. The notion of person or self needs to be carefully evaluated, so as not to assume the ontological existence of an acontextual entity.

As Rihito Kimura has noted: "The notion of a person is different in various cultures. Although we tend to use similar terms interchangeably, sometimes we are unable to avoid basic misconceptions due to our failure to appreciate the language and concepts of other cultures."[5] Kimura goes on to note that *ningen*, the Japanese term for "person," means "human between-ness," and states that the "individualistic Western notion of self does not reflect the uniqueness of Japanese human identity that exists in between-ness," and that, thus, "even though it may be an effective tool for analysis, the simple dichotomy of individual and group does not adequately explain the particular cultural phenomenon of human personhood."[6] Issues then, such as what we should be concerned with, whether the death of an organ, an organism, or a person, to be developed in this chapter, will themselves need to further articulate what is meant by *person*—or at least not to assume that the term has meaning invariance. Kimura perceptively connects the topic of self with that of language, and its incorrect or correct usage.[7] We would go further and suggest that language viewed as exclusively *descriptive*, that is, as an impartial account of matters from the other's point of view, will often turn out to be language as *distractive*, that is, as idle chatter, a misplaced nonaccount of the "other." To be more adequate, language must be viewed as a *directive*, as pointing beyond itself toward the other and the other's point of view, but not purporting to capture it.[8] In this sense a bigger problem emerges from Benedict's paradigm; her text can be seen as adopting what Tetsuo Najita has termed "the methodology of reducing cultural configurations to a basic stylized structure upon which to build a comprehensive interpretation of culture."[9] An approach similar to Benedict's is offered by Takeo Doi in the text *Amae no kozo (The Anatomy of Dependence),* which assumes, Najita charges, that there are "basic sociopsychological structures and patterns that could be objectively identified."[10] For Doi, however, the direct availability of the other is to *insiders* (i.e., Japanese) rather than foreigners. Nonetheless, both texts share the common foundationalist assumption, that is, the immediate availability of the other for some group or person.

A better approach is to be found in the work of Clifford Geertz, an anthropologist working off the early configurationist school dominated by Ruth Benedict and Margaret Mead. Geertz's work, ethnographical and self-consciously interpretive, "aims to replace general theoretical explanations of human behavior by particularistic, context-sensitive indigenous thought patterns. . . . Differences are always foregrounded, similarities between cultures are always backgrounded or taken for granted."[11] Geertz's self-reflective perspective is more sophisticated than Benedict's, and it is aware, as Kimura was in the above quote, that "self" or "person" is not a univocal concept. Geertz notes that "the Western conception of the person as a bounded, unique, more or less integrated motivational and cognitive universe, a dynamic center of awareness, emotion, judgment, and action organized into a distinctive whole and set contrastively both against other such wholes and against a social and natural background, is, however incorrigible it may seem to us, a rather peculiar idea within the context of the world's cultures."[12] Given this awareness on Geertz's part, the question arises as to how to proceed in coming to any awareness of the other, incomplete as that awareness may be. The twin dangers in Geertz's anthropological approach would seem to consist in, on the one hand, the projection or imposition of categories entrenched in our own society onto the other one being studied, and on the other hand, the attempts to "go native," so to speak, that is, to assume one can put oneself in the stance of the other.

To his credit, Geertz tries to show that this dichotomy of inside versus outside, first person versus third person, or phenomenological versus positivistic, is inadequate. He tells the reader: "The trick is not to achieve some inner correspondence of spirit with your informants; preferring, like the rest of us, to call their souls their own, they are not going to be altogether keen about such an effort anyhow. The trick is to figure out what the devil they think they are up to."[13]

To do this Geertz introduces the distinction between "experience near" and "experience distant" concepts. Although there is, for example, a concept of "person" (an experience distant concept) in Java, Bali, and Morocco, these are very different from our concept of "person"—not only different, but incommensurable, at least in the sense that we cannot make a point-by-point comparison. In "Notes on the Balinese Cockfight," Geertz takes one small item in the popular culture in Bali and shows how it functions on several different symbolic levels of cultural meaning. For Geertz, "societies like lives, contain their own interpretations. One has only to learn how to gain access to them."[14] Or similarly, he tells the reader that the "culture of a people is an ensemble of texts, themselves ensembles, which the anthropologist strains to read over the shoulders of those to whom they properly belong."[15] The cockfight, with its attendant betting and the accompanying rules for placing bets, is an art form—one that ultimately deals with the themes of masculinity, rage, pride, loss, beneficence, change, and ultimately, death. Finally, Geertz notes, in an obvious reference to Benedict, that the cockfight is not the master key to Balinese life. There is none, because, as we have seen, the "same people who arrange chrysanthemums cast swords."[16]

While the point of view advocated by Geertz is highly anti-reductionistic, it does, as one commentator has noted, sometimes betray "a tendency to treat the 'native point of view' as a privileged level of analysis."[17] That is, Geertz sometimes assumes that the point of view of the other, or others, is completely available to them, and, by extension, to the anthropologist looking in the right places. But, by "treating external models of culture as if they constitute culture itself, Geertz deftly bypasses the question of the relation between the system and any particular knower or actor within it."[18] In other words, advocating pluralism among cultural contexts, while laudable, may not be sufficient. It may ignore the possibility that the symbolic systems put in place by a given culture, or set of cultures, are such that they are only partly apparent to their originators, whose attitudes toward them may change over time. In sum, Benedict is less circumspect than Geertz on privileging or centering an "experience distant" notion of self or person in her text. Geertz tries not to center the self by noting that what "self" means changes from culture to culture. One can make some comparisons, but the translation, so to speak, is always incomplete. Still, in some less obvious sense, Geertz can be viewed as presuming on the "availability" of the self or selves for "interpretative" discovery.

THE CONCEPT OF "HEALTH" IN JAPAN

A more sophisticated approach to these issues is offered by the anthropologist Emiko Ohnuki-Tierney, who argues that a homogeneous sense of "self" or "other" is *not* immediately available either from without or even from within a specific culture. We do not simply reconstruct history—either our own or that of others—by using objective facts; rather, historical representations are to be seen as "incomplete, partial, and over-determined by forces such as the inequalities of power."[19] "Going native," then, would seem to be at least a partly interpretative procedure. Specifically turning to Japan, she argues that there has never been a totally homogeneous culture there, or anywhere else for that matter, and, furthermore, that there are various ways of "representing" that culture. In other words, there are multiple structures of meaning, or cultures, within Japan, and these themselves change their meaning through time and through history, becoming more or less available as items of "observation" for the participants themselves.

A specific area of concern for Ohnuki-Tierney is the concept of health and illness. She views these as "to a large extent culturally patterned, even when they are couched in biomedical terms."[20] Such a position is clearly contextual in nature, and forces her to challenge the view that modernity or modernization "produces a 'rational' individual whose behavior loses symbolic dimensions."[21] Like Illich, Cassell, and others, Ohnuki-Tierney wants to highlight the ritual and symbolic dimension of health, and of death. For her, Japan is clearly a non-Western country that has already become "modern" in terms of industrial and scientific success without succumbing to the received paradigm of identifying "Western," "rational," "utilitarian," and "nonsymbolic" as synonymous terms.

> The Japanese case . . . challenges the assumption that modernization undermines the symbolic realm of the people. . . . My own interpretation is that the notion of the "primitive" vis-à-vis the "modern" in anthropology is based on a comparison between nonmodern Third World cultures and the cultures of western intellectuals. . . . Modernization, as viewed by social scientists, is to a large extent "westernization."[22]

In opposition, Ohnuki-Tierney argues that there are "Japanese germs," and, further, that, even "in the backyards of Western cultures cultural germs lurk abundantly, although they may have different forms of expression."[23] Stated differently, illness cannot, or rather should not, be defined in exclusively biological terms. Far from being neutral in nature, such a position would, in actuality, reflect its own cultural bias—that of privileging the mechanical-biological view of disease as *the* illness. In opposition, she argues that "illness" as a sociologically defined departure from health, is different from "disease," that is, the malfunctioning of some of the chemical and physiological systems of the body.[24]

A complete analysis of Ohnuki-Tierney's outlook is beyond the scope of this chapter, but a few illustrations can provide substantiation for her interpretation. First, the Japanese concept of "hygiene" is not just based upon germ theory, but rather upon the spatial division of "inside" and "outside." "Outside" is associated with dirt—with streets, structure, crowds, impurity, and others. This area is still part of society; beyond it another area exists, mainly, "nature." One can see the difference between inside and outside appear in myriad ways—in taking one's shoes off before entering a house, so as to leave germs outside; in inside dogs (not allowed out) and outside dogs (not allowed in the house); in the use of face masks to protect the self (inside) from others (outside); in the assumption that the inside but not the outside of a homeowner's wall surrounding the property is *part* of that property, in the view of the bathroom as the dirtiest part of the house, therefore requiring a separate pair of slippers to enter. "In the Japanese logic of purity and impurity . . . the contemporary Western arrangement of having the toilet in the *bathroom* is the utmost contradiction—the juxtaposition of the most defiled place with the place for purification."[25] Purity and impurity are also generally correlated with life and death—and those activities and people dealing with death become death surrogates. Thus, the *burakumin,* a minority group currently consisting of about three million people, have been termed Japan's "invisible race"—its homeless. Traditionally their occupations were of two types: The first consisted of artists, artisans, and entertainers with specific roles in an agrarian society; the second, more germane to our topic, consisted of those whose activities involved them with death and dirt, such as "butchers, tanners, makers of leather goods, undertakers, and caretakers of tombs."[26] Actually the two groups tended to merge at the end of the sixteenth century, with the rise of feudal society. As specialists in impurity, the *burakumin* were often identified with impurity itself. This identification also had a spatial construction. "The *burakumin* resided at marginal parts of the community, just as cultural germs are seen to be located, not out in nature, but at marginal areas of society."[27] While the members of the first "artisan" type might be viewed as having both positive and negative powers, depending on correct use, the second type, living at the edge of society, is "betwixt and between"—and as such is closest to the Japanese notion of a recently dead person. "At the time of death, the dead are neither living nor dead, in that the 'freshly dead' have not become 'really dead' or ancestors. At the most abstract level of analysis, the recently dead stand between nature and culture; they no longer represent human life, which sustains culture, but they have not yet returned to soil—that is, nature."[28] In this sense the fresh corpse is most like germs or dirt—not alive and not yet compost. Death here is seen as impure and therefore as morally evil; and, for Ohnuki-Tierney the introduction of biomedical knowledge has not succeeded in undermining the tenacity of this view, just as the introduction of legal democracy has not eradicated discrimination against the *burakumin*.

Japanese attitudes toward illness and death are complex. While it is quite fashionable and legitimate to have one's very own illness, in the sense of being "down" and taking sick leave, that is, being in a dependent state, the "Japanese dread serious illness and do not discuss them openly."[29] *The* feared disease used to be tuberculosis; now it is cancer, seen as identical with a death sentence. Patients with cancer are often not told of this condition by their physician. On the other hand, suicide, or at least certain forms of it, receives cultural sanction and is even elevated to the level of an aesthetic experience. Ohnuki-Tierney resolves this apparent paradox by indicating that the explanation for the "conflicting attitudes toward illness and death lies in the basic orientation of the Japanese toward the present life, rather than the life after death."[30] That is, while they work constantly to deal with minor illnesses and weaknesses within the confines of the "pure/impure" spatial classification mentioned above, "the Japanese are pragmatically fatalistic in turning away from serious illnesses which are beyond their control. These illnesses are eliminated from their universe, which admits only ordinary illnesses."[31] Suicide is culturally sanctioned because it is seen as an act through which the individual maintains control of his or her own life. "These individuals write their own life stories to the very end." In contrast to this, a death from cancer is seen as denying the individual any active role; here patients cannot tell their own life stories. "Most Japanese would prefer to live in an illusion rather than face such a death."[32] Ohnuki-Tierney sees in cancer a condensed version of the Japanese fear of all forms of natural death, and especially the "freshly dead." Her paradigm here is actually one of a denial model, wherein, once "the dead become truly dead, Japanese culture reintroduces them into the cultural universe. Although giving little thought to how they 'live' after death, the Japanese collectively transform the dead, infants and patriarchs alike, into ancestors and then reintroduce them through an elaborate process."[33]

In sum, there are two "outsides" in Ohnuki-Tierney's paradigm, and both exert an influence upon the Japanese view of death. First, there is "nature," seen as ambivalent, both beneficent and threatening. Second, there is "the outer margin," seen as dirty or impure, but necessary.

> "Real" death and serious illnesses, both of which are beyond the control of the Japanese, are placed "outside" the Japanese cultural realm; they represent the negative power of the deities, Westerners, and others. The Japanese attempt to keep the inside clean at all times, and yet by so doing they admit the dual nature of the inside. That is, the self, like the other, is characterized by the dual quality. The difference between the dual nature of inside and

that of outside is that the former is tamed, or culturally transformed, whereas the latter is wild, uncontrollable."[34]

Ohnuki-Tierney argues for a rich contextualism as opposed to a biological reductionism in medicine—and in approaching the topic of death in Japan. Furthermore, she specifically sees "differences in cultural attitudes toward illness between Japan and the United States . . . [as] ultimately related to the concept of self in each culture,"[35] thus reiterating the importance of the theme mentioned by Kimura.[36] For her, the "Japanese family or an equivalent often act as 'patient surrogates,' who read the patient's wishes or speak for him or her, at times without explicitly consulting the patient. They are more than mediators; they are surrogates who almost become one with the patient."[37] In an important sense, as the 1979 Japanese law governing cornea and kidney transplants indicates, "the family has ultimate control over such important matters as treatment of the body after death."[38] However, definition in terms of kinship should not necessarily be taken to indicate total lack of an independent personality. Such a dichotomy needs to be rejected as too exclusive in nature.

THE DEBATE OVER THE DEFINITION OF DEATH IN JAPAN

In the previous section it was pointed out that it is a mistake to view modernity or modernization as synonymous with reason or rationality, or with Westernization. One specific example of this can be seen in the debate over the determination of death that takes place in Japan vis-à-vis the one occurring in the United States. For it is not the case that the debate in America is rational, while that in Japan is clouded with emotional or cultural issues. Rather, it is the case that in each country both rational and irrational factors are involved. That is, in each case there is an appeal to empirical data and to logic, but in addition, there is present an element of tradition, or habit on a social scale; on a personal level there is an element of preference, a "sentimental" dimension, to use William James's phraseology.[39]

In Japan the debate over brain death has been long and very public for a country so seemingly interested in indirect approaches to situations. It has also been surprisingly inconclusive. The focus of the debate concerns whole-brain death versus respiratory and circulatory failure. Each side has its advocates. Proponents of the respiratory/circulatory failure model are, to a degree, influenced by Shinto and Buddhist traditions, but there is more than a purely religious factor involved here. Many who do not consider themselves particularly religious would tend to identify their position on death as consisting of loss of breathing and blood circulation. Animism is taken seriously, coupled with a series of death rituals that go on for some time after the body is supposedly dead according to brain-dead criteria.

It must be noted that in actuality discussion of adopting a new definition of death is inextricably connected with that of organ transplants.[40] In 1968 the first and only heart transplant surgery was performed in Japan by Dr. Juro Wada. However, there is some question about whether the donor fulfilled the criteria of being brain-dead, and no record of this exists. Public outrage and suspicion of the medical profession ran high. The same doctor who was determining the patient's death was also involved with the transplant operation. The district attorney considered prosecuting, but in the end decided against it. Dr. Wada never apologized for his actions. Rihito Kimura noted in 1989, over twenty years later, that "the Japanese are still experiencing the aftereffects of the Wada Case; this is one of the reasons why Japan has not yet established any official brain-death criteria."[41] Going further, in 1979 the Act Concerning the Transplantation of Cornea and Kidney was passed, stating that these were the only two organs that might legally be transplanted from dead patients.

When this was violated in 1984 by a physician who transplanted a pancreas, another public outcry and a demand for some form of "patients' rights" ensued.[42]

On January 12, 1988, the Bioethics Committee of the Japanese Medical Association (JMA) issued a report advocating acceptance of brain death as the "new" definition of death, with some restrictions. The most important of these called for the physician to respect patients' and family members' wishes. As Kimura notes, "It is significant that these recommendations require informed consent; the patient or family can refuse to accept the use of brain criteria in the determination of death. This is a compromise aimed at introducing its use in a way that will not offend those Japanese who continue to oppose it."[43] But as Kimura himself has acknowledged, the goal of the committee was not achieved. "A negative opinion on the conclusion of the report was issued by the Japanese Federation of Bar Association on July 15, 1988."[44] The facts of the situation are not at issue here, nor the arguments offered by both sides, but rather the role of tradition, the importance of the familiar, and the place of the affective. As noted above, the Japanese are deeply influenced by an animism and a Buddhist tradition that views the body as in some sense sacrosanct. Some Japanese have found this animistic tradition frustrating to deal with, terming it "primitive" and stating that it has nothing to do with true Buddhism.[45] They charge that adaptation of such a simplistic animism results in a failure to address the key issue of *when* the sanctity of human life actually ends. Thus Omine Akira, while acknowledging that human death is "more than a medical matter," nonetheless holds that "the basis for all legal and conventional concepts of death is biological death, and it has always been the exclusive task of the physician to determine this."[46] Acceptance of the whole-brain-death definition for Akira would restore dignity to life and death by recognizing that there is "more to life than quantifiable, reducible matter." Furthermore, the refusal to accept whole-brain death "obstructs transplants, [and] shows a disrespect for the living, since it denies effective treatment to those who need it."[47] Finally, keeping the dead "alive" by continuing artificial treatment actually constitutes a violation of the dignity of their death. Japan, Akira argues, is now at odds with almost every country in the world on the issue of brain death.

Rihito Kimura also argues for acceptance of brain death, but is conscious of the difficulty of getting it accepted while the medical profession is viewed as suspect (after the Wada case). As a way of helping this process along, he advocates development of patients' rights in Japan, utilizing the traditional Buddhist teaching of "En," or relatedness, the idea that "all fellow beings are related to one another as well as to nature."[48] He believes this principle can be used to ground a strong sense of human empathy, and hence of recognition of patient rights. Kimura proceeds in this fashion because he realizes that "the concept of 'right' is originally an alien notion for the Japanese," and that "the notion of autonomy, one of the fundamental principles of Western-oriented bioethics, does not apply suitably to the Japanese socio-cultural tradition, particularly within the paternalistic medical tradition."[49] But by stressing the concept of empathy, which is indigenous to Japanese culture, he hopes to nurture more autonomy and stronger patient rights—as opposed to placing all decision-making power with doctors or with the family. However, Kimura remains realistic, saying, "I expect the Japanese public to gradually accept use of brain criteria and organ transplantation, although with serious reservation."[50]

In opposition, thinkers like Emiko Namihira hold that, "traditionally, Japanese have seen death as not only a physiological state but also a social and cultural phenomenon. It is a gradual process, not an abrupt departure from life."[51] Hence, doctors should not be given the exclusive right to determine death, and the JMA group "exceeded its professional mandate by attempting to define death as brain death, which only society as a whole has the right to decide."[52] Others argue against the new definition from what they assert is a clear Buddhist standpoint, viewing the adaptation of the brain-death criterion as the culmination of the Cartesian dualistic tradition, which it would be a mistake to import from the West. Thus, in what must be viewed as an overgeneralization of some magnitude, Umehara Takeshi argues that "since Descartes, all of Western thought has taken the individual ego as its ultimate principle," and in opposition asserts, in the spirit of the bodhisattva, that "each human life is part of an eternal cycle. . . . Death and rebirth are the inescapable fate of all life."[53] Takeshi believes that "the concept of brain death was devised to circumvent . . . doubts" about the morality of organ transplants, and argues, in opposition, that the "state of brain death is, in fact, life; as long as the heart is beating, there is life."[54] In a rather questionable attempt to condemn by association, he asserts that the majority of the Japanese people feel that organ transplants are "against the natural order of things," along with homosexuality, foot binding, and castration, and he would allow others to donate their organs only if they could be both given and received "with boundless gratitude," that is, not for selfish reasons.[55] Otherwise, the whole procedure is poisoned, so to speak.

Tomoaki Tsuchida also argues that Cartesian dualism and individualism, both unacceptable concepts in Japan, are behind the new definition of brain death.

> Among the broadly recognizable cultural traits of the United States, individualism plays a conspicuous role that is all but absent among the Japanese. The idea that one ought to be the self-dependent master of oneself seems to have been raised almost to the level of an ideal of solipsism in the United States. This idea has found philosophical and religious moorings in the Modern World (principally in Protestant tradition in particular), but so far only stands poised as a threat as far as the rest of the world is concerned. For the American, it is not only a right to exercise

control over one's own destiny, but also one's duty; death and life are one's own personal concern. The Japanese, in contrast, have lived for centuries in a highly integrated and contextualized society where even life and death have to be seen as a family affair—if not the affair of the community as a whole—as much as the affair of the particular individual. Without the consent of the family, a doctor is not expected to inform a patient of a fatal illness or even to undertake serious surgery, much less organ transplants.[56]

While there is some truth in the above quote, it relies too heavily on the either/or dichotomy between person and community. Such a stance presupposes a single definition for such terms as "person" or "self." But as we have seen earlier, such terms vary from culture to culture, and perhaps from time to time. Kimura also admits that "it might be true to say that the Japanese are group-oriented, and thus tend to suppress their individuality."[57] But he shrewdly notes that "even though it may be an effective tool for analysis, the simple dichotomy of individual and group does not adequately explain the particular cultural phenomenon of human personhood."[58] The issue, in short, needs to be addressed in ways that transcend this dichotomy; the price to be paid for such an approach however, is the espousal of pluralism in some form. As Kochi Bai, Yasuko Shirai, and Michiko Ishii note, "We ought not to assume too readily a uniformity in Japanese culture; nor, needless to say, can we ignore Japanese peculiarity. The key is to observe the situation as it exists."[59]

What is important in the overall discussion above is the appeal both sides make to social/cultural values.[60] Even those attempts to couch the problematic in exclusively biological terms seem to realize, if not to support, the important role played by tradition, that is, by the "inherited conglomerate."[61] But, once again, the issue of consensus or togetherness has functioned, in the eyes of some thinkers, to block a "pluralistic" approach. By "pluralistic" here I mean an approach that is nonreductive in nature, and which holds that there are good (i.e., warranted) reasons for maintaining more than one interpretation of the topic. Going further, such a stance may be more than merely temporal in nature. Ichiro Kato, for example, holds that there is no need for everyone to accept brain death in Japan, but charges that "the concept of social consensus . . . [prevalent there] is rooted not in rationality but in an emotionalistic penchant for acting together with the approval of all. It is a matter of mood, not logic."[62] For Ichiro, social consensus has nothing to do with the concept of "social contract" found in the West. The latter runs according to the logic of "majority rule," and the expression of individual opinion is the norm. By way of contrast, in social consensus, Japanese people "say that they cannot support something because not everyone agrees."[63] As a result of this, all serious discussion of the issue of brain death and organ transplants is deflected. No one really knows what social consensus is, or how to achieve it. In opposition to thinkers like Tsuchida quoted above, Ichiro argues that "Japanese society, with its emphasis on togetherness and conformity, is weak on tolerance of individual freedom. But unless we start emphasizing individuals rather than the group, Japan could well be left behind as the rest of the world moves forward."[64] Consensus, in short, needs to have limits.

There are, then, both similarities and differences in the debate over a "new" definition of death in Japan and in the United States. The current debate in Japan concerns whole-brain death versus respiratory/circulatory failure. In America the issue is whole-brain death versus failure of higher brain functions. In both cases an appeal has been made to tradition, to not creating too great a break with the past. And in both cultures there is debate over who really is or is not doing this.[65] Some attempts at pluralism have been advocated in each country, though these have yet to prove themselves completely successful. Most important, in *neither* case is the issue of defining death to be decided exclusively upon empirical and logical grounds. Death is, once again, to be viewed as a value-laden concept, that is, not simply something to be "discovered." An element of choice is involved in arriving at the definition, and that element cannot be eliminated by constant appeals to biology, for the question at issue is not whether to employ biology, but rather which biological definition to employ, and *that* is not in and of itself a biological question.

Finally, for many Japanese thinkers and for at least some American thinkers, the issue of a new definition of death is really the issue of organ transplants masquerading in another form.[66] This realization, when uncovered, merely serves to strengthen the thesis that the concept of death is a value-laden one. In addition, at least one Japanese thinker has gone further, charging that even the debate over organ transplants is a mask. "In Japan, there is lively debate over organ transplants, brain death, hospices, and whether a patient should be informed he or she has cancer. But we avoid the reality at the core of these controversies: the inevitability of death. And the formalistic final rites [lavish floral arrangements and funerals handled at temples by professional directors] obscure our mortality."[67] In a manner reminiscent of Ohnuki-Tierney, Yagisawa also notes that the Japanese tend to avoid face-to-face confrontation with the corpse, because "the dead have traditionally been regarded as unclean."[68] If accepted as valid, this charge would seem to indicate that the predominant attitude of the Japanese toward death is one of denial rather than acceptance. As Masami Hirayama has put it, "In the traditional religious view, death is a 'dark' or 'frightening' thing. Japanese try not to think about it. Expressions about the departed like 'He's crying in his grave' and 'She'll come back for the mid-summer memorial service' deny the finality of death."[69]

In sum, looking at the non-Western example of Japan creates problems of its own in terms of dealing with "the other." But these can be only partially overcome, thus providing further support for the thesis that the term *death* does not have meaning invariance.

CONCLUSION TO PART ONE: SOCIAL OVER BIOLOGICAL

The preceding three chapters, taken together, constitute a strong argument for viewing death historically, and hence contextually. To sum up the position, we draw upon the work of Marx Wartofsky, for whom "human death, unlike animal death, is a socially constituted fact requiring a judgment."[70] Such an approach requires that one view any biological definition of death, whole-brain or otherwise, as at most necessary, and certainly not sufficient. Defining death, now viewed as socially constructed, "is itself a matter of how we define ourselves, constitute ourselves as human, create or transform our humanity."[71] While it is admittedly the case that we are biological creatures, "the *kind* of biological creatures we are *is* socio-cultural or moral."[72] It follows that a complete separation of the biological and the cultural, and of their respective views of death, is neither possible nor desirable. Biology, in short, is "infected" with culture.

Not only biology, but also medicine itself as an entity, and the accompanying doctor-patient relationship, should be viewed as socially constructed. It would follow that medicine's view of death—since it is to medicine that we traditionally turn for the definition of death—medicine's view of death should be viewed as a social construct, *even though* its (medicine's) view is that death is to be biologically determined. Going further, even the proposal offered by the President's Commission for the Study of Ethical Problems in Medicine and Biomedical and Behavioral Research, that is, that whole-brain death be employed as a sufficient criterion, should not be allowed to pass as merely a neutral biological definition based upon "scientific" data.[73]

Human beings, being perhaps the only species that is aware of its mortality, define themselves socially and historically as a life activity, and therefore we tend to declare death as the cessation of some of these activities. "The simple fact is that what is at issue is not death as such, but the conditions under which a human being is to be declared dead."[74] It is important to realize, however, that there exist different ontological paradigms that might be employed to indicate this, for example, science, medicine, philosophy, sanctity of life, or cost-allocation, and "the way the question is posed, and who poses it, already determines in large part what will count as an answer."[75] Assuming this to be the case, the idea that there is a definition of death separate from the determination that it has occurred must also be rejected, and technological instruments, as extensions of human sensation, must themselves be viewed as socially constructed. There is both a pluralism involved here and a rich contextualism. Any attempt to see the biological as sufficient should be viewed as reductionist in nature. "Human reality, as a social reality, or human ontology as a social ontology, can't . . . be reduced to animal biology,"[76] although it must be emphasized that human reality is a social one, and not that of the abstract individual offered by Descartes. Self-consciousness evolves over time and through cultural context.

The argument for the social construction of death is bolstered if we turn briefly to Wartofsky's presentation of "disease" as a social construct. Indeed, it parallels to a significant extent Ohnuki-Tierney's portrayal of "Japanese germs." "It is not the *organ,* nor yet the organism which is the appropriate basic entity in . . . [the] domain [of medical practice], but rather the *disease;* and . . . [the] appropriate characterization of the disease is precisely the one which takes it as a socio-historical and cultural phenomenon."[77] There are two strong indicators of the veracity of this position. First, even a cursory analysis of a patient's medical history will disclose that it is essentially social and historical in character, containing such things as age, membership in a particular class, and family history. Ironically here, the very attempt to individuate a patient takes place in and through social categories rather than in spite of them. "The medical facts are *themselves* socio-historical facts."[78] Secondly, the doctor-patient relationship does not take place in a vacuum, but rather in a specific social context or institutional setting such as a private office, emergency room, or a big-city hospital. The "patient" is a product of these historical developments, taken together with his or her genetic inheritance. The social, however, must not be reduced to the biological, or "nurture" reduced to "nature," for even the nature that now exists is the result of human social practices that evolved as we adapted to an environment.

The patient cannot be reduced to a number of organs, nor should the organism be taken as the final unit. Such a view of the individual as merely atomic constitutes a new form of abstractionism. Disease ought not to be viewed as a pathology of an organ, or even of an organism; disease is rather "the property or characteristic of a population, i.e., of a system of individuals in a given socio-historical context."[79] This can be seen most easily by focusing upon mass diseases, such as epidemics or plagues; diseases ethnically defined; or specific pediatric or gerontological diseases. These last also vary from culture to culture, since the concepts of "infancy" and "old age" are also socially constructed. Even isolable somatic diseases should be viewed as socially constructed, given that "a given form of medical practice—including here its methodology, its institutional forms, etc.,—picks out certain syndromes as typical or characteristic ones in its repertoire."[80]

It should be pointed out that Wartofsky does not want to *replace* biology with culture, only to add to it and to criticize the viewpoint that takes biology as sufficient. His statement that he is "not out to deconstruct death"[81] and that he is arguing more as a Hegelian or Marxist than as a Derridean is a further indication that he is leery of being accused of holding a "death is in the eye of the beholder" position. Whether he wanted to or not, he is credited with at least some deconstructionist achievements by Charles Scott, who notes that Wartofsky "did succeed nonetheless in suggesting that practices and knowledges centered in a unified definition of whole-brain death must be deconstructed by a way of thinking that respects the essential diversity of human lives and deaths."[82] Scott articulates the conclusion to be drawn from the historicist approach in perhaps its most forceful form:

> This social-historical understanding of human being means not only that the "fact" of human death is constituted by social judgments. It means further that no one way of dying is definitive of human beings. Not only is biological or "animal" death only one dimension of human passing away. In the essentially human dimension of dying, many different definitions of death are legitimately possible. Different social-historical patterns—different traditions and subtraditions—mean that a pluralization of the time and definition of death is necessary if we are to treat human death appropriately.[83]

In short, the historical/cultural approach has made an extremely strong argument for the thesis that the term *death* does not have meaning invariance. But it has tried to restrict the pluralism that it wants to espouse to the level of social categories rather than individual ones. Death is not in the eye of the beholder but rather varies from culture to culture—somewhat. But as Wartofsky himself noted, asking the physician to stop treating an organ or an organism and start treating the population as a whole gives her or him a "notoriously abstract entit[y] . . . to treat."[84] That is, even if this can be accomplished, it may be at too high a price, namely, not letting the dying person tell his or her own "personal" story because it does not fit well into *available* social and cultural categories.

Indeed, some advocates of the social/historicist model of death have already traveled considerably far down the road toward "personal" choice of a definition. Thus John Lachs, for example, also starts out from the premise that "there can be no objective solution [to the debate over the definition of death] because there is no empirical disagreement; neither side offers an alternative biology."[85] For Lachs too, the standard used in defining death "is not written into the nature of things and, accordingly, cannot be read off from the facts of biology."[86] Death is rather to be viewed as a biologically based social choice, a choice regarding activities no longer performable, and costs. Such choices, of course, have value-laden presuppositions, and as such are perspectival in character. The choice, by physicians, to use the biological paradigm as *sufficient* needs to be rejected as an impoverishment, and one way this can be disclosed is through cultural comparisons, for example, of our culture with that of the Eskimo. "The absence of this cross-cultural or anthropological perspective renders much contemporary discussion of the criteria of death one-dimensional and the deliberations of the President's Commission sterile and unsatisfying."[87]

Thus far, Lachs's position is clearly the historical/cultural one. But he goes further than this, advocating an individual-centered, multiple-criteria view. Pointing with approval to the spread of living wills, Lachs suggests that "we have failed to recognize the remarkable fact that such laws empower each individual to adopt his or her own criterion."[88] Basing his stance on the importance of liberty, autonomy, and freedom in our culture, Lachs views the determination of death as essentially a private matter, best left to individual determination. Although there must be limits to self-determination, "the decision is best left to the person involved: only she can judge what is of paramount importance in her life and when her existence is no longer worth its cost."[89] The major caveat necessary here is that the term "individual" is itself at least partially socially constructed, as was seen in the case of Japan, and as was at least obliquely noted in the reference to other cultures by Lachs himself. That is, the values associated with individualism in our culture, and the disassociation of individual and society that at least seems prevalent here, may well not be so clearly espoused by other cultures. So while one might indeed want to uphold the importance of self-determination, and support the need for each dying person to tell his or her own story, we must come back at least a small ways toward the historical/cultural position. That is, we must realize either that we are promoting one view of what it means to be an individual at the expense of others, or we must allow for the possibility that activity on the part of individuals in other cultures that we view as nonautonomous, such as allowing the family to make the decision concerning one's state of being, may be considered by the principle "person" involved as perfectly appropriate. An individual develops in time and through cultural contexts, and may indeed take on characteristics different from those contexts, or adopt characteristics from competing contexts, thereby forcing choice among them.

This issue of individual choice is pursued in Chapter 5, where the legal ramifications of a relativized or pluralistic definition of death are discussed, and again in Part 3, where the main theme is personal *dying* rather than death. But first, let us develop the argument for the priority of the biological over the historical.

II
Biological Contexts

[FOUR]

Science and Medicine

The three previous chapters have focused upon the richness and diversity of approaches to death. They argue that different cultures view death differently; that the same culture views death differently at different times; that case studies are not uniform in nature, but rather diverse and idosyncratic. In response, it might be argued that these descriptions are indeed accounts of what death has meant to different people or communities, but that this is entirely different from the definition of death itself, which is capable of being formulated with scientific rigor, and demonstrated via a specific operational procedure. Failure to do so, it might be further argued, would render one's legal system chaotic, and leave "death" itself as a mere "theoretical entity." Historical and anthropological approaches, while containing information that is interesting, and perhaps even useful at times, cannot measure up to the more rigorous standards of objectivity found in the natural sciences. If one wants to attain objectivity in the area of death then, one has to turn to science, or at least to an analysis of what science is, that is, to the philosophy of science.

There is a parallel between attempts in the philosophy of science to reduce all theoretical terms (what we might call the "superstructure") to their observational base through operational definitions of basic terms; and attempts to view medicine as first a science rather than an art—a science whose province includes the topic of death. From this perspective death appears as a problem, a "theoretical entity" or final "disease" that can be precisely defined via operational procedures, and perhaps, as a disease, even ultimately overcome.

Grounds for the assumption that medicine either is a science, or is well on the way to becoming one, are readily available. Though he ultimately rejects the argument, Ronald Munson admits that "the new understanding of disease processes and pharmacological mechanisms contributed by biochemistry and molecular biology, the establishment of therapies on the basis of experimental research, and the development of new modes of acquiring and utilizing precise laboratory data are just a few of the factors that contribute to the sense of medicine's being rapidly transformed into science."[1] Daniel Callahan argues that although in some respects it may be viewed as conservative, "medicine gradually became by the end of the nineteenth century one of the most enthusiastic acolytes of the Enlightenment ideal of progress. Through basic biological knowledge and its clinical application, medicine can constantly advance the frontier of human health: the possibilities of progress are unlimited."[2] From this position, Callahan argues, death is viewed as a correctable biological deficiency that medicine has a *moral* obligation to defeat. As medicine achieves more and more success in overcoming specific diseases, death is transformed into the one disease yet remaining to be solved. In a sense then, we have, Callahan charges, a new form of "tame death," one wherein the issue is defined as a problem—and hence as having at least a possible solution that we are getting closer and closer to. "The . . . belief is of a . . . subtle kind: that medicine can, in its conquest of disease, remove the unpleasant, distressing *causes* of death, thus transmuting it from a condition to be feared to one that can be managed and tolerated."[3]

Some time ago the American philosopher John Dewey argued that "it is a familiar and significant saying that a problem well put is half-solved."[4] But Dewey also argued that "if we assume, prematurely, that the problem involved is definite and clear, subsequent inquiry proceeds on the wrong track."[5] While granting the insight of this position, we would go further and suggest that some issues are not problems, and that this condition is not a transitory one—that, as Peter Steinfels has argued, "death must be viewed as a mystery, not a problem."[6] Characterization of death as a problem then will result, as was the case in Ivan Illich's analysis, in our offering "true" solutions to false issues.

There are then, three "problems" or issues here: first, there is a "problem" with the problem itself, that is, the viewing of death as a problem; second, there is a problem with the assumption that the problem, as a problem, has a solution, that is, with the view of death as a theoretical entity capable of being operationally defined; and third, there is a problem because the problem is not seen, or viewed *as a problem,* in other words, it is taken for granted as "normal," "self-evident," or even desirable. Differently stated, the roots of the received view are deep and well entrenched. Callahan argues that the notion of death, and its causes, as something that can be managed, has its roots in Francis Bacon, "who first called for medicine to seek the cure of disease."[7] Bacon's approach was one of induction, though of an impure type; that is, it relies on a quasi-essentialist theory of the "nature" and "forms" of objects. A second variety of induction can be found in the twentieth century, with the rise of the positivist tradition in science. This tradition had its roots in Hume, with its emphasis on sense impressions, and it ultimately argued that all theoretical terms should be reduced to an observational base. Ironically enough, this type of induction also proved to be an impure one—ultimately revealing that the line between observation and theory was an interpretative and value-laden one. Let us briefly see how this came about.

WHAT MAKES A THEORY "SCIENCE"?

Attempts to answer the question as to what makes a given theory "scientific" initially involved a specific description of the relationships among facts, laws, and theories. That is, one distinguished between scientific and nonscientific (e.g., philosophical or religious) explanations by declaring that the former had to have its theories, and the theoretical entities contained therein, "tethered" to the empirical "soil" of observation through a set of correspondence rules and operational definitions. Theoretical terms were viewed as necessarily reducible in this manner if science was not to be seen as synonymous with metaphysics. The most famous version of this view was termed "operationalism," as articulated by P. W. Bridgman in 1927. It held that all basic terms had to be definable exclusively in terms of a specific set of possible operations.[8] Thus, terms like "length" and "hard" had as their entire meaning a specific operation involved. A given object was hard, if and only if, if one dragged the object across a piece of glass, it scratched the piece of glass, or $Xh \equiv (Xg \rightarrow Xs)$. Problems arose, however, when it was realized that there were logical problems with operational definitions. These were articulated in detail by Rudolf Carnap in his famous article "Testability and Meaning" in 1936–37.[9] Carnap showed that, given the way "material implication" is defined, the operational definition turns out to be true even when the operation is *not* performed. The only time the relationship is false is when the antecedent is true and the consequent is false. All other possibilities render the relationship true. This would seem to damage severely the whole goal of operational definitions. We might term these undesirable alternatives "false negatives," a term that will be used below. Carnap remedied this problem via his so-called reduction sentences, which can be rendered as follows: $Xg \rightarrow (Xh \equiv Xs)$. This formulation says, *if* you place an object upon a piece of glass, then the object is hard if and only if it scratches the piece of glass. This remedies the problems involved with the first formulation, but at a price: It gives only a *partial* specification of the meaning of the term in question. In terms of the logic involved, we could then have "false positives." Furthermore, this is not a temporary problem, but one stemming from the very nature of the logic. Once again, the entire purpose of operational definitions seemed to be in jeopardy.

Important for our purposes here is the realization, even from some proponents of a formal approach stressing objectivity and rational reconstruction of what the scientist did, that operational definitions seemed to be either incomplete, or more than really operational in nature. As we shall see in Chapter 5, a similar conclusion is drawn by Robert Veatch concerning operational criteria for death, that is, the measurements used by physicians to determine that death has occurred.

The realization that at least some terms in a scientific theory could only be partly specified led to the conclusion that the "fact/theory" distinction was not a neutral one, that facts were "theory laden," and that the whole distinction between facts and theories was one made from inside an already assumed "paradigm." It would follow from this even more clearly that facts do not have meaning invariance, but rather gradually take on a specific meaning within the confines of a specific system. The foremost proponent of this position was Thomas Kuhn, first in *The Copernican Revolution*,[10] a text that constituted a "thick" case study of one event in science; and second in *The Structure of Scientific Revolutions*,[11] where Kuhn offered his overall outlook on progress in science—or the lack thereof.

There are two major theses in *The Copernican Revolution*, an interdisciplinary thesis and an epistemological thesis. The following quotes are representative of the first of these:

> Though the Revolution's name is singular, the event was plural. Its core was a transformation of mathematical astronomy, but it embraced conceptual changes in cosmology, physics, philosophy, and religion as well.[12]

> To describe the innovation initiated by Copernicus as the simple interchange of the position of the earth and sun is to make a

molehill out of a promontory in the development of human thought. If Copernicus' proposal had had no consequences outside astronomy, it would have been neither so long delayed nor so strenuously resisted.[13]

No fundamental astronomical discovery, no new sort of astronomical observation, persuaded Copernicus of ancient astronomy's inadequacy or of the necessity for change. Until half a century after Copernicus' death no potentially revolutionary changes occurred in the data available to astronomers. Any potential understanding of the Revolution's timing and of the factors that called it forth must, therefore, be sought principally outside of astronomy, within the larger intellectual milieu inhabited by astronomy's practitioners.[14]

The second thesis, the epistemological, has as its specific goal the rejection of the division of experience into objective and subjective components, or, more precisely, the rejection of the logical empiricist division of language into verifiable and logical terms on the one hand, and psychological terms on the other. It is contained, for example, in the following texts:

Conceptual schemes have psychological as well as logical functions, and these do depend upon the scientist's belief or incredulity.[15]

Historically the process of revolution is never, and could not possibly be, so simple as the logical outline indicates. . . . Though scientists undoubtedly do abandon a conceptual scheme when it seems in irreconcilable conflict with observation, the emphasis on logical incompatibility disguises an essential problem. What is it that transforms an apparently temporary discrepancy into an inescapable conflict? How can a conceptual scheme that one generation admiringly describes as subtle, flexible, and complex become for a later generation merely obscure, ambiguous, and cumbersome? Why do scientists hold to theories despite discrepancies, and, having held to them, why do they give them up?[16]

The net result of these two theses is the assertion that the change from one scientific framework to another in this particular instance is not completely rational. This conclusion, which constitutes in nascent form the major thesis of *The Structure of Scientific Revolutions* (at least up to the "Postscript") is argued for ostensively in *The Copernican Revolution*. Commencing with Aristotle's view of the heavens as his example, Kuhn argues that this view is intimately connected with: (a) Aristotle's overall metaphysics; (b) Aristotle's theory of motion; (c) astrology; (d) Christianity; (e) politics; and (f) a commonsense feeling of "being-at-home-in-the-universe." In brief the "received view," that is, the Ptolemaic universe, seemed to have established a strong and widely entrenched position, leading to the question "Why did the revolution occur *at all*? In answering, Kuhn lists the following as contributing factors: (a) the discovery of new Aristotle texts, leading to questions of consistency; (b) the optical relativity argument; (c) a new theory of motion—the impetus theory; (d) the revival of Neoplatonism; (e) the Renaissance; (f) the Protestant Reformation; (g) the discovery of America; and (h) the demand for calendar reform. However, while all these factors may have helped, at least in the sense of there being so much going on, taken collectively they do not explain *why* the revolution took place. Furthermore, this is not a temporary situation that can be alleviated merely by the accumulation of more information.

In *The Structure of Scientific Revolutions* Kuhn generalizes his case study into a theory about change in the history of science. The latter is not, as a whole, incremental; indeed, science does not exist as a whole. Rather is it to be divided into two types of science—normal science and revolutionary science. Normal science is science based on an assumed "paradigm," a term employed frequently and not univocally by Kuhn.[17] As used in this context, a paradigm is a model or standard illustration, or scientific achievement, which includes law, theory, application, and instrumentation together and is more basic than any of these.[18] "Normal science" is cumulative because progress is defined in terms of an already assumed paradigm. "Revolutionary science" describes what occurs as we move from one paradigm to another. Such movement is cataclysmic. In some sense, a conversion experience is involved. There is no meaning invariance (in terms of a common observation language) that endures through the transition from one paradigm to another. Objectivity is not to be found in this process, since normal science is ideological and revolutionary science is not completely rational. Taken as a whole, science is not a cumulative activity. Paradigms seem to be incompatible and incommensurate with each other.

In a "Postscript" written seven years later, Kuhn admits that he has used the term *paradigm* in a rather vague fashion, and he attempts to defend his outlook against the charge of irrationality. He does so by making several qualifications to his position and by distinguishing between a scientific community previously identified sociologically, and its "disciplinary matrix." A disciplinary matrix consists of a formal structure, beliefs in particular models, shared values, and use of an "exemplar."[19] This last term is Kuhn's revised equivalent to *paradigm,* and refers to the "concrete problem-solutions that students encounter from the start of their scientific education, whether in laboratories, on examinations, or at the ends of chapters in science texts."[20]

Kuhn's reply to the charges of irrationality need concern us here only to the extent that he seems to have replaced one form of certainty (science, e.g., physics) with yet another (sociology); and also to note that his "new" position is far less radical than the old one, prompting one commentator to say: "I find the new, more real Kuhn who emerges in it [i.e., the Postscript] but a pale reflection of the old, revolutionary Kuhn. Perhaps this revolutionary Kuhn never really existed—but then it . . . [would be] necessary to invent him."[21]

Nonetheless, Kuhn's analysis remains important for our current issue of whether or not medicine is a science, for his presentation as outlined above serves as an important reminder that the question "What makes something a science?" cannot simply presume that the term *science* itself has meaning invariance. By the time Kuhn has finished his analysis, the term *science* means something significantly different than it did in the positivist tradition (even though Kuhn himself has a positivist side). It is here that the historicist rejoinder to the biologist would no doubt take place, that is, that there really is no nonhistorical alternative, since science too is subject to the sands of time. Failure to see this results in dealing merely with logical abstractions.

In sum, two different "paradigms" vied for domination over the issue of how to describe the activity of science in our century—what we might oversimplistically term the "logical" paradigm and the "historical" paradigm. One of these placed significant emphasis upon the purity of operational definitions; the second, noting that any paradigm included law, theory, application, and instrumentation *together,* argued that any instrument utilized or operation performed carried theoretical presuppositions. The second view has emerged as the more adequate position.

IS MEDICINE A SCIENCE?

The conclusion reached so far should give us pause when we consider whether or not medicine is a "science," since this term has now been shown to have more than one possible meaning. But there are still additional difficulties to confront. The question of whether or not medicine is a science is often couched within the larger question of what else (in addition to science) medicine might be construed to be. Cassell's statement in Chapter 2 that we have moved from the moral to the technological order may serve as an entry to the issue, but as was the case in that chapter, it is one that must continue to give us pause. Herrman Blumgart has noted that "without scientific knowledge, a compassionate wish to serve mankind's health is meaningless."[22] But Blumgart himself would be the first to assert that this attribute, while necessary, is by no means sufficient. "The science of medicine consists of the entire stockpile of knowledge accumulated about man as a biologic entity. The art of medicine consists in the skillful application of scientific knowledge to a particular person for the maintenance of health or the amelioration of disease. For the individual physician, the meeting place of the science of medicine and the art of medicine is the patient."[23] For Blumgart then empathy is crucial, but "*appreciation* of another's feelings and his problems is quite different from *joining* in them."[24] A physician needs to be concerned with the needs of one's patient, but such a compassion should remain detached in character, a sort of "neutral empathy," as opposed to sympathy. Entering into the feelings of another and becoming affected by them entail a loss of objectivity and perspective that is not desirable.

This approach, while commendable in its own right for preserving a rich context in medicine, that is, seeing the latter as both an art and a science, does not go far enough. It suggests that there is some kind of objective science that needs to be married to something else. As such, it "masks" an important epistemological issue concerning the supposed base or neutral ground of medicine and health care in general. As Richard M. Magraw has pointed out, such an "objective" approach is built into the very framework of medical education.

> Perhaps all of us should pay more attention than we do to the fact that a physician's training consists not only in progressively acquiring an enlarged data base and set of skills, but also in encountering a graded series of "patient models." . . .
>
> The first "patient" the student is introduced to is the cadaver. The cadaver is obviously a highly complex model for the beginning student, yet understanding the cadaver is often easier than trying to understand the living, responding, feeling persons

whom the student will ultimately meet and work with when he becomes a practitioner.[25]

Magraw points out that subsequently the student will be exposed to other models, such as "heart-lung preparations" and specimens of blood and urine. The results of this, while useful, are quite dangerous. "The first human patients the student examines in his physical diagnosis course and later talks to are in a sense functioning as manikins for him. His interaction with them is quite perfunctory." It is to be hoped and expected that the student will grow out of such a reductionistic position, and will come to view patients as fully blown human beings, part of "a complex fabric or network of family, marital, social, and occupational contexts."[26] Magraw's phenomenological approach is more subtle than Blumgart's, because it discloses how the myth of objectivity is built into the system from the beginning. It is, then, a more complicated matter than simply "adding on" a subjective factor (art, ethics) to an objective one (science), even if the latter exists, which after Kuhn's analysis is quite doubtful. Arthur Kleinman has made this point in an insightful way, noting that

> practitioners [in medicine] . . . are not trained to be self-reflective interpreters of distinctive systems of meaning. They are turned out of medical schools as naive realists, like Dashiell Hammett's Sam Spade, who are led to believe that symptoms are clues to disease, evidence of a "natural" process, a physical entity to be discovered or uncovered. They are rarely taught that biological processes are known only through socially constructed categories that constrain experience as much as does disordered physiology. . . . The upshot is that practitioners, trained to think of "real" disease entities, with natural histories and precise outcomes, find chronic illness messy and threatening.[27]

In this chapter we have argued that operational definitions, uncritically accepted, constitute one form of naive realism, either in science or in medicine, when dealing with death. Going further, if the real issue or "problem" requiring analysis and understanding is not death but *dying*, the latter may well appear, as we shall see in Chapter 7, as more akin to chronic illness, in other words, "messy and threatening."

The approach of H. Tristram Engelhardt's is also insightful, in that it refuses to acknowledge that there is some neutral Platonic concept termed "health," "disease," or "medicine." For Engelhardt, medicine is a "uniquely value-laden" phenomenon, one wherein "there are no simple, pure facts . . . , but . . . [rather] all facts appear in and are influenced by contexts of expectation and value."[28] It follows from this position that "disease" is no thing in itself, but rather a relational concept, "a structure inferred in order to apprehend coherently a particular state of the organism (disease state) in connection with other factors—the cause, the history of the organism, etc."[29] The disease pattern is "read into" the appearances. While there are different levels of explanation apparent in identification of "syndrome" versus "disease proper," in neither case is the explanation merely a neutral account. Syndrome identification is often followed by causal identification; such a move in abstraction, if taken as sufficient, results in the "fallacy of reification." That is, multifactorial or pattern-relation analyses of disease variables are ignored.

> The patterns of nature, the signs and symptoms clustering and cohering in a syndrome, can be recognized, explained, and predicted through relations apprehended in thought, analyses of multiple factors involved in the observed syndrome. An excellent example is coronary artery disease, which can be correlated with genetic, pathophysiological, psychological, and social variables, and, therefore, could possibly be construed as a genetic, anatomical, metabolic, psychological, or social disease. By allowing the emphasis to fall upon relations rather than upon thing-causes, one is free to conceive of the disease in different fashions for different purposes."[30]

The above presentations all react negatively to the question "Is medicine a science?" either by stating that medicine is *also* something else, for example, an art or a moral practice, and that this latter factor cannot be ignored, or by refusing to deal with the subjective/objective binary as presented, and arguing instead that the terms *medicine* and *health* are normative. Each approach attempts to build a thicker context for medicine than the physiological or scientific model would allow for. If one assumes that at least some of the arguments given above are persuasive, is there any remaining reason to consider the proposition that medicine is, or should be viewed exclusively as, a science, in the old positivistic sense of the term? The answer seems to be that there is, to the extent that we fail to realize that there are different operational definitions possible, that these have different theoretical presuppositions, and that the decision as to which biological definition to employ is itself *not* a biological one, but rather cultural and normative in nature—in short, when we forget about the "thickness" of the context. Going further, we are most prone to doing this at times, like the present, when we feel vulnerable because of the ambiguity and uncertainty caused by technological advances in medicine.

OPERATIONALISM IN DEATH AND DYING

Martin Pernick has noted that death "has never been completely definable in objective technical terms."[31] But he has also astutely realized that "some historical periods demonstrated far more discomfort over these uncertainties than did others. One era of particularly intense concern began about 1740 and lasted through the middle of the next century or longer."[32] The reason for this concern was a series of important technological discoveries such as artificial respiration, resuscitation, suspended animation, and use of anesthesia. As a result of these discoveries there was increased difficulty in determining when a person was in fact actually dead, coupled with an intense fear of premature burial. Indeed, the mortuary was created to prevent premature burial by simply delaying interment. Corpses could be watched there for an extended period of time for the slightest movement. Further, burial often took place in a technologically elaborate casket. Here is one narrative account of this procedure:

> The Victorians contrived an elaborate series of warning and signaling devices to enable a dead person to make known his resuscitation. A wealthy individual might be buried with a length of iron pipe connecting his casket to the ground above, and a trusted family servant would be required to remain at the cemetery, day and night, for a month or more, on the chance that the deceased would suddenly awake and begin to call for help. Persons buried above-ground, in family vaults, were often placed in patented, spring-loaded caskets, with a complex maze of wires attached to arms and legs, so that the slightest movement of the body would throw open the coffin lid.[33]

What is important to see in the above description, besides its confirmation of Ivan Illich's observation that death comes differently to the rich and the poor,[34] is that it conforms precisely to an operational definition—and to all the problems attendant thereon. That is, a person is dead if and only if, if placed in a spring-loaded casket the lid remains closed: $Xd \equiv (Xs \rightarrow Xc)$. Or, if there is a bell connected by a string through the pipe to the subject's hand, the person is dead if and only if the bell remains silent: $Xb \rightarrow (Xd \equiv Xs)$. The problem with such constructions is that they are subject to the "false negatives" and to "false positives" mentioned above. For example, the casket could spring open because of external vibration, or deficient spring mechanism, or an animal running across the casket. Discoveries such as that of the stethoscope in 1819 alleviated but did not completely do away with uncertainty, and the fear that accompanied it. Finally, the irony of this situation is that it has reappeared once again in our own century.

As we noted in Chapter 1, two things occurred in the 1950s to reintroduce a heightened sense of uncertainty regarding the determination of death. Once again they were technological innovations: the development of respirators on an extensive level and the ability to engage in organ transplants. We shall take up the results of these in detail in the next chapter. For the present we concentrate on one aspect of the development, namely, the possibility that death could be redefined as, for example, neocortical failure *and* that the latter could be operationally defined as the failure to register on an electroencephalogram. Such a position, if accepted, would surely clear up any ambiguity about death. However, it too is subject to the same types of problems encountered above in terms of false negatives and false positives. For example, a decision must be made as to whether the new definition is replacing earlier operational definitions, or merely clearing them up. Both alternatives are fraught with difficulty. If the first alternative is adopted, it immediately follows that the term *death* not only has no meaning invariance, but indeed changes its meaning from one technological discovery to the next. If the second alternative is accepted, it follows that there is some other, "deeper" meaning to the term *death* than the operational definition can encompass. Similar difficulties would develop for any attempted operational definition of the intermediate position, that is, whole-brain death.

In sum, death viewed as a theoretical entity or as a problem to be solved by the science of medicine is an inadequate paradigm. Autonomous operational definitions of death, even if desirable, seem unattainable, or at least not attainable without enormous difficulties. In the next chapter it will be argued that, even if attainable, such definitions are unacceptable. Merely the realization that there are competing operational definitions available, and no decision-making process agreed upon, renders the issue a contextual one—rather than one allowing for certainty. Medicine may indeed have a necessary scientific dimension or component to it, but we should reject any attempt to view medicine, and its view of death, in an exclusively operational fashion. Overconcentration on operational definitions as sufficient is misleading because the entity in question is at least very often not synonymous with the operation to be performed. This was found to be the case in the philosophy of science in the "transition" from logical positivism to Kuhn. It will also be seen to be true in medicine's concern with the topic of death. Finally, the temptation to employ operational definitions uncritically, in addition to ignoring cultural differences, masks a more complex philosophical controversy, namely, what is it exactly that is at issue here, the death of a body, a brain, or a person.[35] The following chapter takes up this topic.

[FIVE]

Harvard Ad Hoc and Its Critics

As noted at the end of the last chapter, the development of the respirator and the ability to engage in organ transplants posed a problem for the traditional definition of death, as found for example in *Black's Law Dictionary* (4th edition, 1951). It defined death as follows: the "cessation of life; the ceasing to exist; defined by physicians as a total stoppage of the circulation of the blood, and a cessation of the animal and vital functions consequent there upon, such as respiration, pulsation, etc."[1] Since respiration could now be prolonged for an extensive period of time, an attempt to update the old decision was undertaken by the Ad Hoc Committee of the Harvard Medical School in 1968. The committee stated that its primary purpose was "to define irreversible coma as a new criterion for death," and argued that improvements in resuscitation now placed great burdens on patients who had suffered loss of intellect, as well as on their families, hospitals, and society in general. In addition, obsolete criteria were blocking attempts to obtain organs for transplantation purposes.[2] The committee argued that irreversible coma takes place when a patient shows the following characteristics: (1) unreceptivity and unresponsivity to external stimuli; (2) no spontaneous muscular movements for at least one hour, and no attempt to breathe, if a respirator is turned off for a period of three minutes; (3) no reflexes—pupils of the eyes are fixed and dilated, no attempts to swallow, yawn, and such; and (4) a flat electroencephalogram (EEG)—the latter being viewed not as necessary, but as of great confirmatory value. These procedures were to be repeated at least twenty-four hours later, and the conditions of hypothermia and central-nervous-system depressants (e.g., barbiturates) would be excluded.

The committee's report, however, contained serious flaws. The definition of irreversible coma might be viewed as a descriptive question, that is, one of technological precision (though even here, as we shall see, there is room for argument). However, the decision to use irreversible coma as a sufficient indication that a *person* is no longer present is a normative or ethical question. It must be argued for, and ultimately decided upon—not simply alluded to as factually obvious. To go even further, the decision for one position and against another may well involve a preferential or nonrational dimension. Yet the committee failed to carry out even the logical argument necessary, in spite of the fact that it clearly recognized that "more than medical problems are present."[3] It seems to have assumed that a patient suffering from irreversible coma is also brain-dead, and that (only) when the entire brain is gone is a person no longer present. Indeed, it remains unclear in the report exactly what entity—body, brain, or person—or all of these—is being declared dead. To recapitulate, there are at least three issues here: First, what, exactly, is irreversible coma; second, is it an adequate definition of death; and third, the death of what—a body, a brain, or a person.

Going further, the committee listed as justification for updating the definition of death the new burdens these technological advances have placed upon patients, families, hospitals, and society. But it left unresolved the possibility that the interests of these various entities may often come into conflict, and it did not prioritize among them. This can have serious moral consequences, especially since the second justification given by the committee for updating is to facilitate the ability to obtain organs for transplant purposes.

Third, the committee was concerned in its report "only with those comatose individuals who have no discernible central nervous system activity."[4] This seems to be an attempt to distinguish clearly between those patients who are to be termed "dead," and those who might be allowed to die, for example, where euthanasia might be warranted. Such a line can of course be drawn, but the drawing itself is by no means a neutral act, as we shall see. Furthermore, it immediately renders the definition of "comatose" offered as only partial. Peter Black defends the stance of the committee here, saying that if "they . . . leave a large number of patients with irreversible severe brain damage 'alive' by their guidelines, that is acceptable. In declaring death there seems a strong advantage to being conservative."[5] But Black himself admits that this position cannot be completely justified on logical or empirical grounds, and that "tradition, rather than clear clinical or pathological data, will have determined our use of the term 'brain dead' "[6] in the future. Once again, cultural values, based upon habit and custom, seem to play a more vital role than is initially realized.

Finally, the report stated that "death is to be declared and *then* the respirator turned off."[7] While the intent of this stipulation is clear, namely, avoidance of homicide charges, stipulation of this sequencing runs afoul of other problems, namely, those concerning the new ontological status of the corpse.[8]

Each of these issues is given a more extensive presentation in the following critiques of the Ad Hoc Committee's attempt to update the definition of death.

THE CRITIQUE OF ROBERT VEATCH

Perhaps the most sustained critique of Harvard Ad Hoc's position has been offered by Robert Veatch in texts such as *Death, Dying, and the Biological Revolution.*[9] Here Veatch develops two arguments, one general and the other more particular. Both are important to our analysis. The general argument is a critique of *any* attempt to set up a single operational definition of death as sufficient by itself. As such it is analogous to our critique of operationalism offered in the preceding chapter. For Veatch, "the very meaning of the word *definition* is ambiguous. Some of the issues are indeed matters of neurobiological fact. . . . But judgments about facts made by scientists with expertise in a particular and relevant field can be called *definitions* only in an operational sense. The debate over the definition of death also takes place at philosophical, religious, and ethical levels."[10] In opposition, Veatch argues that we need to distinguish four separate levels in defining death: a level of formal analysis, a level dealing with the concept of death, one dealing with the *locus* of death, and one dealing with the criteria to be employed in determining death. Any attempt to leap immediately to the last of these, that is, to operationally define death, tacitly presupposes a philosophical concept of death. One literally would not know where to look, or what tasks to perform, without such a presupposition. A purely formal definition, on the other hand, is also insufficient. Death, defined as the loss of essential characteristics, provides a framework for further analysis, but by itself is merely an empty shell, since we are not told just what those characteristics are that are essential to a human being, as opposed to, say, a plant.

This last question concerning what characteristics are essential to being human is a philosophical one, and, ultimately an ethical one involving choice on our part. Veatch offers a fourfold topology of competing concepts of death: (1) irreversible loss of the flow of vital fluids, (2) irreversible loss of the soul from the body, (3) irreversible loss of the capacity for bodily integration, and (4) irreversible loss of the capacity for social interaction. The first of these is associated with the traditional way of defining death; it seemed to function well until the invention of respirators—though even here study of the fear of premature burial in the eighteenth and nineteenth centuries reveals that this image may be an illusory one created through a revisionist historical approach.[11] The second concept also has a long-standing tradition, based upon vitalism. However, it is not useful in the hospital setting where so many people today find themselves facing these issues. The third is the concept generally associated with the stance of the Harvard Ad Hoc Committee. The fourth concept of death stresses loss of the capacity for social interaction, as opposed to mere bodily integration, as constituting what makes us human.

Only after a concept of death has been selected can one turn to the *locus,* that is, the place to look to determine whether a person has died. Thus, having selected irreversible stopping of vital fluids, one can then turn to the heart and lungs as the appropriate place to take measurements; having selected irreversible loss of capacity for bodily integration one can then turn to the brain; having selected irreversible loss of the capacity for social interaction one can turn, probably, to the neocortex. Even here, however, there is room for debate. For example, one could agree with the last concept of death mentioned without necessarily agreeing with the locus suggested, or for that matter, with the operations or measurements being suggested—such as an EEG in this case. The latter could conceivably provide false positives. Focusing his attention upon the stance of Harvard Ad Hoc, Veatch accuses them of unjustifiably assuming that irreversible coma is synonymous with brain death, and that the latter is identical with the passing of a person, and, even further, of assuming that irreversible coma means loss of *all* brain activity and not simply loss of consciousness. In opposition, he holds that it is the loss of the ability to engage in social interaction, that is, the "higher functions," which constitutes the passing of a person; irreversible coma should be viewed as loss of consciousness, and this can most probably be measured by a flat EEG.

In sum, Veatch has provided a scathing critique of any seeming neutrality in selecting a definition of death on the biological level. He has done this by showing that any seeming operation (at least of those currently available) presupposes a decision, based on warranted assertability to be sure, but nonetheless a decision, as to which concept of a person is correct. Second, he has himself selected, from the four possibilities provided in his phenomenological topology, the last of these, the loss of the capacity for social interaction, as most truly indicative of the passing of a person.[12]

THE CRITIQUE OF ROBERT SCHWAGER

The foremost critique usually brought against Veatch's position is that it constitutes too radical a break with tradition. Whether or not this critique is accepted, it immediately points up the role being played by habit or custom in this issue, as an additional ingredient to empirical data and logical analysis. One version of this "radical break" critique is provided by Robert L. Schwager in his article "Life, Death, and the Irreversibly Comatose." In actuality Schwager accuses Veatch's view of being both too conservative and too radical. To make his case Schwager focuses on the term *irreversible coma,* and reminds us that there are two kinds of comatose patients. Those patients whose capacity for cerebral activity has been *totally* destroyed are termed "decerebrate." Those whose capacity is irreversible without being decerebrate are termed "irreversibly comatose simpliciter (ICS)." As noted above, Harvard Ad Hoc dealt only with the first of these. It specifically did this in an attempt to keep separate the issues of determination of death vis-à-vis allowing to die. Schwager agrees that a truly decerebrate individual is dead, and, going further, that an ICS patient (with neocortical failure) should be allowed to die. In his opinion, Harvard Ad Hoc did not offer a new definition of death, but rather reemphasized the traditional understanding that a person has died. Decerebrate individuals do not respirate spontaneously, whether or not there is a mechanical aid involved. "Thus the underlying concept of death remains unchanged. What changes are the criteria for deciding that death has taken place. Rather than turning off the respirator and waiting for the heart to stop beating, death can be pronounced while heartbeat continues, since, given the total and irreversible loss of cerebral function, *that* heartbeat is no sign of life."[13]

ICS patients, on the contrary, might indeed maintain spontaneous respiration and circulation. Veatch then is too radical in "permitting the burial of individuals who respirate and circulate themselves." On the other hand, Veatch is too conservative in "asserting that *only* the death of patients justifies discontinuing certain medical treatments."[14] In opposition, Schwager argues that ICS patients ought to be allowed to die. "The loss of what gives life its value is not identical with the loss of life. It may, however, be identical with the loss of any good reason for striving to preserve that life."[15] Finally, any and all treatments may be removed from ICS patients, since any attempt to determine what can and cannot be discontinued based upon the so-called ordinary-extraordinary distinction in actuality begs the question, or assumes a consensus in customary practice that simply does not exist.

Schwager alludes to, but stops short of discussing, the supposed distinction between "killing versus letting die," that is, discontinuing treatment as opposed to actively intervening to bring about death. Like the Harvard Ad Hoc Committee, he wants a clear distinction between facts and values, though Harvard was quick to admit that "more than medical problems" were present. As we shall see below, the killing versus letting die dichotomy has recently become more problematic, and it may well be that so too has the distinction between a definition of death and a decision to let die, especially if the former is necessarily linked to a particular philosophical or religious worldview.

Thus far, then, we have the following positions concerning death and letting die, or "facts," versus "values." First, a "new" definition of death was offered by Harvard Ad Hoc, or if not a new definition, at least a new criterion for determining that death has occurred. There is a substantial issue here as to whether the concept of death remains a constant over time and only the criteria for determining its occurrence change, or whether the only notion of death we have changes from operation to operation. While we have, in an earlier chapter, rejected the adequacy of operational definitions, we have already noted in Chapters 2 and 3 that the concept of death does indeed change from culture to culture. The Harvard Ad Hoc Committee took no position on euthanasia. A second definition of death was offered by Robert Veatch, with no accompanying position on euthanasia, but also with the clear realization that all definitions of death are value-laden. A third definition of death was offered by Robert Schwager, who clarified Harvard's position and tied it to a position on passive euthanasia. Schwager also attempted to uphold some distinction between facts and values, that is, between the definition of death concerning decerebrates and the decision to let ICS patients die (with the additional acknowledgment that more analysis needs to take place concerning two competing values, passive versus active euthanasia). If the assertion put forth by Veatch is accepted, that is, if no definition of death is value-free, the fact/value distinction drawn by the other two positions is undermined. Further evidence that a definition can only *pretend* to be neutral is provided when we recall that the second reason offered by Harvard Ad Hoc to update the definition was to facilitate obtaining organs for transplantation purposes. Indeed there are some who believe that this is the primary, or perhaps the only, reason that the proposal for a new definition exists.

THE CRITIQUE OF HANS JONAS

In "Against the Stream: Comments on the Definition and Re-definition of Death," Hans Jonas argues that what the Harvard Committee really defined was "not death, the ultimate state, itself, but a criterion for permitting it to take place unopposed—e.g., by turning off the respirator."[16] Their report, however, purports to have defined death, that is, to be merely definitional or theoretical in character. However, Jonas views the desire to save other lives through organ transplants as an "intrusion into the *theoretical* attempt to define death which makes the attempt impure."[17] Practical concerns have overwhelmed theoretical attempts to define death, and what we have as a result is a value-based position *masked* as a definition. One is reminded here of Ivan Illich's critique of "natural death," as presented in Chapter 2. The main difference is that his is more cultural in tone, whereas Jonas stresses the personal or existential dimension of the situation. In Jonas's opinion, an attempt has been made to turn an essentially vague situation into a nonvague or clear one through linguistic legerdemain. In opposition, Jonas argues for the importance of the vague. In a manner somewhat similar to that of William James, he says: "Mine is an argument—a precise argument, I believe—*about* vagueness, viz., the vagueness of a condition. Giving intrinsic vagueness its due is not being vague."[18] And again: "We do not know with certainty the borderline between life and death, and a definition cannot substitute for knowledge."[19] If Jonas is correct, the whole attempt to update the *definition* of death is essentially flawed, and it is by no means neutral or merely epistemic, *regardless* of which definition is selected. "The decision to be made [about a person in irreversible coma, regardless of the 'spontaneity issue'] is an axiological one and not already made by clinical fact. It begins when the diagnosis of the condition has spoken: it is not diagnostic itself. Thus . . . no redefinition of death is needed; only, perhaps, a redefinition of the physician's presumed duty to prolong life under all circumstances."[20] The attempt at pretended neutrality has, for Jonas, disastrous consequences concerning the ontological status of the newly defined "dead corpse." If the patient is no longer present, why turn the respirator off at all? Why not protract the in-between state for which a new name will have to be found—"simulated life," perhaps.

Willard Gaylin made a similar point in his article "Harvesting the Dead," alluded to in Chapter 1.[21] If the patient is dead he or she no longer possesses any rights since there is no longer a person present. Somewhat with tongue in cheek Gaylin suggests that the term *neomort* be employed to identify their new ontological status. Neomorts could well serve in several capacities, for example, as an improved replacement for cadavers in medical school, as an organ bank, and as an entity upon which to try out experimental drugs. Jonas agrees entirely with this fear, stressing that there will be strong pressure brought not to turn the respirator off. "We must remember," he says, "that what the Harvard group offered was not a definition of irreversible coma as a rationale for breaking off sustaining action, but a definition of death by the criterion of irreversible coma as a rationale for conceptually transposing the patient's body to the class of dead things, *regardless* of whether sustaining action is kept up or broken off."[22] In opposition to this, Jonas argues for a conservative position that would "lean over backward toward the side of possible life" in this context of marginal ignorance that cannot be cleaned up by linguistic definition. He predicts the ironic return of a new variant of Cartesian dualism, "brain/body," which will view the body as merely a tool or instrument, and strives to reaffirm the sacrosanctity of the latter by reminding us that mind and body are phenomenologically codetermined. "The body is as uniquely the body of this brain and no other, as the brain is uniquely the brain of this body and no other"; and again: "My identity is the identity of the whole organism, even if the higher functions of personhood are seated in the brain."[23]

In sum, the biological context may, at first glance, have seemed to offer the promise of a more "objective" way to deal with the redefinition of death than that offered by the historical context. But if the above discussion is at all indicative of the situation, and we would offer that it is, such is not at all the case. Harvard Ad Hoc and the Schwager critique did try to adopt some version of the "fact-value" distinction, that is, they suggested that a line can be discovered, not invented, that demarcates the definition of death from the decision to allow someone to die. However, the critiques offered by Veatch and Jonas have as one result a pincerlike attack upon any sort of foundationalist position.

Two specific issues emerge out of this dual attack. First, Veatch has suggested that *any* biological definition of death presupposes a philosophical worldview. It is, in this sense, not neutral. One result of Veatch's critique, if accepted, concerns public policy. Where there are competing definitions, and where several of these seem to be of equal power, can we attain closure through legislation? Should we? Or, should one legislate pluralism? Second, Jonas has charged that the new definition of death is not necessary and is certainly not neutral in character or effect. He is suggesting that the whole discussion so far has been misconstrued, and in two specific ways. First, it has downplayed the demand for organ transplants; second, it has been on death and not on *dying*.

The remainder of this chapter will first take up the issue of public policy raised by Veatch's critique. Chapter 6 will then deal with three ramifications of Hans Jonas's critique: the use of anencephalics as organ donors, letting some newborns die, and killing versus letting die. The final issue raised by Jonas, that of death versus *dying*, will be taken up in Part 3.

DEATH AND PUBLIC POLICY

Harvard Ad Hoc itself raised the issue of public policy by referring to court cases such as *Thomas v. Anderson,* which noted that
"death is not a continuous event and is an event that takes place
at a precise time,"[24] and *Smith v. Smith,* in which it said that the
Arkansas Supreme Court "considered the definition of death to
be a settled, scientific, biological fact."[25] In opposition, however,
Harvard suggested that "responsible medical opinion is ready to
adopt new criteria for pronouncing death."[26] Ironically it did not
think that any statutory change in law was necessary, viewing
the question as "one of fact to be determined by physicians."
However, in an issue as important as that of life and death, it
would seem necessary to involve the public in some way. But
how? The instigation of public dialogue on the subject might
well be deemed necessary, but is it sufficient? Also, as has been
the case in Japan, it might not reach any conclusion. For whatever reason, several (actually most) states have by now gone the
route of instigating a statutory definition of death. The first of
these was the notorious Kansas Statute, introduced in 1970,
which provided two separate criteria, that is, "alternative definitions of death." It said: "A person will be considered medically
and legally dead if, in the opinion of a physician . . . there is the
absence of spontaneous respiratory and cardiac function. . . .
[Alternatively a] person will be considered medically and legally
dead if, in the opinion of a physician . . . there is the absence of
spontaneous brain functions."[27] The problem with this definition, which was indeed enacted into law, was that it advocated
two different definitions of death without specifying any relationship between the two. It offered, as David Lamb has suggested,
"two concepts . . . and [two] sets of criteria."[28] It was, presum-
ably, left up to the physician to decide which definition to employ in a given case.[29] An attempt to clear up this ambiguity was
offered by Capron and Kass in their article "A Statutory Defini-

tion of the Standards for Determining Human Death: An Appraisal and a Proposal." Arguing that death was not just a technical matter, and that therefore the public had to be involved to some extent, they also recognized that "courts operate within a limited compass" and that they "are not inclined to depart from existing rules."[30] With this in mind, they offered the following alternative proposal for defining death:

> A person will be considered dead if in the announced opinion of a physician based on ordinary standards of medical practice, he has experienced an irreversible cessation of spontaneous respiratory and circulatory functions. In the event that artificial means of support preclude a determination that these functions have ceased, a person will be considered dead if in the announced opinion of a physician, based on ordinary standards of medical practice, he has experienced an irreversible cessation of spontaneous brain functions. Death will have occurred at the time when the relevant functions ceased.[31]

This definition is not so general as to be merely "philosophical" in nature; on the other hand, they argue, it is not so specific that it would change with each new specific test invented, or with any new operational criteria to be employed.

The authors were trying here to distinguish between the meaning of death and the criteria used to indicate that death has occurred, and to maintain the former as a constant. "In other words, the proposed law would provide two standards gauged by different functions, for measuring different manifestations of the same phenomenon."[32] The Kansas Statute clearly did not do this, proposing instead two alternative definitions. On the other hand, solving the problem by espousing reliance *solely* upon brain activity, Capron and Kass argue, would constitute too sharp and unnecessary a break with tradition.

It is clear that this proposed law was geared to read so that one definition can replace the other in the event that the first can no longer be used. It maintains, as David Lamb puts it, "one concept of death but two alternative sets of criteria."[33] However, not all states adopted the Capron and Kass version; seven states did. Four others adopted versions of the Kansas Statute; five others adopted a statute preferred by the American Bar Association. Two states adopted a Uniform Brain Death Act and seven others had "nonstandard" statutes. Several states did not have any statute at all.

To remedy all this, a President's Commission for the Study of Ethical Problems in Medicine and Biomedical and Behavioral Research was formed, and issued its report, *Defining Death*, in 1981. The commission offered a definition that it hoped would be adopted as a statutory law by all states, thus attaining uniformity. The proposed law read as follows:

> An individual who has sustained either (1) irreversible cessation of circulatory and respiratory functions, or (2) irreversible cessation of all functions of the entire brain, including the brain stem, is dead. A determination of death must be made in accordance with accepted medical standards.[34]

This proposal, which is actually quite close to the Capron-Kass suggestion, has by now been enacted into law in most states. However, it has also been criticized in the literature for *not* accomplishing precisely what it set out to do. Thus Bernat, Culver, and Gert, in "Defining Death in Theory and Practice," charge that "the model statute that the Commission recommends should not be adopted because there are significant flaws in it."[35] Specifically, the phrase "irreversible cessation of circulatory and respiratory functions" is highly ambiguous, and does not provide a genuine standard for death since it could refer either to spontaneous or to artificially supported functions, and *neither* of these is acceptable. The first (loss of spontaneity) would define a person wearing a pacemaker as dead.[36] The second, loss of artificially supported functions, may be sufficient, but it is not necessary,[37] since the commission itself holds the view that someone who is being artificially supported but whose *total* brain functions have ceased, be considered dead. The problem arose, they charge, because the commission did not distinguish carefully between a "standard" and a "test" for death. In an attempt to avoid any radical break with tradition, the commission argued that "any statute on death should . . . supplement rather than supplant the existing legal concept."[38] The old standard was based on spontaneous functions, and these are now recognized as inadequate by the commission. But by adding a second standard rather than a second test for the same concept of death, the commission has merely deepened the issue.

> Cardiopulmonary tests may be adequate in the overwhelming number of cases, and brain-based tests may be used in only a small portion of cases, but this belongs in the practical part of the statute, not in the statutory definition of death. The Commission has thus created a statutory definition of death that is seriously misleading and that contains the most serious flaw that the Commission finds in previous statues; it provides two independent standards of death, without explaining the relationship between them.[39]

Two issues emerge consistently in this discussion, and in actuality they are intertwined. The first is, can one completely distinguish between the concept of death and the criteria to indicate that death has occurred? This issue arose in Chapter 4 when an analysis of operationalism was presented. There it was shown that operationalism by itself was insufficient, in that it led to a radical fractionalization of the concept under discussion. But now the converse difficulty must also be recognized. Retaining a universal, Platonic concept of death seems to be getting more and more difficult. One point the commission tried to emphasize was that "most Americans still feel they recognize the manifest signs of death. . . . The heart and lungs move when they work; the brain does not. Thus, since any incorporation of brain-oriented standards into the law necessarily changes the *type* of measures permitted somewhat, a statute will be more acceptable the less it otherwise changes legal rules."[40] The problem with this stance, as David Lamb notes, is that the "change in the criteria for death necessitated by resuscitation technology, *does* require a radical transformation of concepts of death and human life, and that, contrary to the President's Commission such a redefinition cannot be viewed as a mere supplement to the traditional concept."[41] In opposition, Lamb advocates a "one concept and one set of criteria approach," like that proposed by the Law Reform Commission of Canada. This solution is shared by Bernat, Culver, and Gert. Their proposed statute reads:

> An individual who has sustained irreversible cessation of all functions of the entire brain, including the brainstem, is dead
>
> (a) In the absence of artificial means of cardiopulmonary support, death (the irreversible cessation of all brain functions) may be determined by the prolonged absence of spontaneous circulatory and respiratory functions.
>
> (b) In the presence of artificial means of cardiopulmonary support, death (the irreversible cessation of all brain functions) must be determined by tests of brain function.
>
> In both situations, the determination of death must be made in accordance with accepted medical standards.[42]

This is indeed one "solution" to the ambiguity of the situation, but it perhaps underestimates the role of habit and tradition in different cultures, as well as that of "the manifest image" of death as opposed to "the scientific image."[43] The new definition is logically more acceptable than earlier models proposed, but this emphasis upon logic masks a bigger issue. This can be brought out most effectively by noting what the last proposal foregrounded, namely, *whole*-brain death, as opposed to neocortical failure. This is the second remaining central issue referred to above. That is, the President's Commission, Lamb, and Bernat, Culver, and

Gert, all share an aversion to a definition of death as the cessation of "higher brain functions," like the one offered by Veatch—though each might express this aversion differently. (The President's Commission favors "whole brain failure"; Lamb favors the term "brain stem failure.") However, it must be noted that this favoring is itself based partly upon nonrational features—either preference or custom. One way to bring this out more clearly is to return to the position of Robert Veatch, and specifically to his critical response to one of the three advocates of whole-brain death mentioned above, namely, the President's Commission.

In "Whole-Brain, Neocortical, and Higher Brain Related Concepts" Veatch charges that the commission nowhere provides an adequate defense of its decision to adopt "whole-brain" as opposed to "higher brain" formulation of the problematic. Rather, it invalidly went from the premise that there exists no consensus on death to the conclusion that therefore the whole-brain definition should be chosen. This is a position that purports to be both centrist and conservative. That is, it adopts a middle-of-the-road position that supposedly causes little or no break with the past. Veatch has two criticisms of this position. First, it constitutes a form of imposition; he suggests instead pluralism and tolerance, an outlook he had also maintained in *Death, Dying, and the Biological Revolution:*

When dealing with a philosophical conflict so basic that it is literally a matter of life and death, the best solution may be individual freedom to choose between different philosophical concepts within the range of what is tolerable to all the interests involved. . . . There must . . . [however] be limits on individual freedom. At this moment in history the reasonable choices for a concept of death are those focusing on respiration and circulation, on the body's integrating capacities, and on consciousness and related social interactions. Allowing individual choice among these viable alternatives, but not beyond them, may be the only way out of this social policy impasse.[44]

Death here is not "in the eye of the beholder" so to speak, but
neither is the ambiguity of the situation, as described above by
Jonas, legislated away by legal fiat. Veatch continues to argue
that his position of "higher brain functions" is the preferable
one. But he realizes that it too is only one philosophical/religious
worldview, and as such it is no more neutral than its alternatives.
Therefore Veatch's stance on public policy is not to do away with
the alternatives but to preserve a place for them.

Regarding the issue of conservatism and breaking with the
past, Veatch argues that his position of higher brain functions is
actually *closer* to the Judeo-Christian tradition, where he claims
to stand, than the newly proposed "whole-brain" death, which
is actually a form of animalism—itself a particular religious/
philosophical worldview.

Veatch purports to have arrived at his position without any
necessary concept of "person."[45] Apparently bristling at the decision on the part of the President's Commission to "reduce"
his higher brain formulation of death to one involving personhood,[46] Veatch states that this is entirely unnecessary; rather, all
that is needed is recognition of a series of behaviors (mourning,
stopping medical interventions, reading the will, and so forth).
"Since the 1960s I [Veatch] have maintained that 'death' is
simply the name we give to the condition when these behaviors
are considered appropriate. It may be that we now have to come
to the conclusion that not all of them should occur at the same
instant. In that case death as we know it would cease to exist.
It would be replaced by a series of discrete events signaling
the appropriateness of the various social behaviors."[47] But it is
Veatch himself, in arguing for his higher brain position, who
says, "I do not want to be confused with my gagging,"[48] and who
states that, as a member of the Judeo-Christian tradition, "I
maintain two things. First, I maintain that the human is fundamentally a social animal, a member of a human community
capable of interacting with other humans. Second, I maintain

that I am in essence the conjoining of soul and body—or to use the more modern language, mind and body. If either one is irreversibly destroyed so that the two are irretrievably disjoined, then I—this integrated entity—no longer exist."[49] As Richard Zaner has pointed out, statements like this surely contain at least an implicit theory of "person."[50] Indeed, the President's Commission tried to avoid the "personhood" issue for much the same reasons that Veatch does, namely, there is no general agreement on what "person" is. As the commission put it, "Crucial to the personhood argument is acceptance of one particular concept of those things that are essential to being a person, while there is no general agreement on this very fundamental point among philosophers, much less physicians or the general public."[51] The commission exercised a sort of "damage control" here, relegating the problem to one specific definition of death, namely, Veatch's. This will not do, as Veatch has pointed out so well. Veatch for his part tried to avoid the "thicket of personhood" by stressing behavior patterns. But this will not do either, given his own powerful argument that any attempt to operationally define death already presupposes some particular religious/philosophical worldview.

In short, Veatch's position here seems more radical than he at times realizes. He sometimes tries to avoid the issue of personhood. When he does talk about the self, his public policy position seems to be libertarian, yet he claims to stand within *the* Judeo-Christian tradition. However, one should, as William James noted long ago, beware of the definite article.[52] Here, it creates too monolithic a picture of a multifarious tradition. But even more is involved, for at least some Christian traditions seem to stress community and covenanting rather than libertarianism—so much so that Richard Zaner has doubts about Veatch's Judeo-Christian roots, suggesting instead that "what Veatch in fact endorses is . . . Hobbesian individualism."[53]

Regardless of whether or not one accepts all of Zaner's critique here, one point is clear. Veatch does seem to take for granted a concept of person; however, this is masked under language of "behavior patterns" concerning death. This tends to deemphasize the fact that death is a personal issue for each of us, as well as masking the realization that the notion of person varies somewhat from culture to culture, as we have seen in the instance of Japan, and perhaps even *within* a culture such as the Judeo-Christian. The upshot of this masking, if not realized, is unfortunate. First, the radical dimension of Veatch's position loses much of its edge. Second, the masking constitutes a form of denial and as such plays into the hands of Jonas's major critique that we are not really dealing with the major issue—dying.

CONCLUSION

In closing this chapter, we should not fail to see that the ultimate irony here is that we have in a significant way returned to the beginning of our discussion on public policy. That is, the initial reaction to Harvard Ad Hoc came in the form of a particular statute that legislated choice, namely the Kansas Statute, which left it up to the physician to decide which definition of death to employ. Ensuing positions such as that of the President's Commission tried to avoid choice about the definition of death by separating this issue from the issue of euthanasia and by advocating statutory approval of the Uniform Definition of Death Act. In rebuttal, Veatch, like the Kansas Statute, wants to advocate choice, but the person choosing is now different, namely the patient rather than the physician.

Our analysis of the public policy debate reveals several attempts to confine the discussion to a biological context, and to do away with ambiguity through law. However this ambiguity seems to be an essential aspect of the situation that will not, and should not, go away. It is this ambiguity that forces choice, including the choice of who gets to choose. Ultimately it may force us to deal with the issue of "allowing" one to choose versus "enabling" one to choose.[54] It may also force us to deal with various definitions of the "persons" doing the choosing, and whether they see themselves as isolated from or intermingled with "the other."

The need to preserve the ambiguous or the "vague" here, even as it concerns the law, is captured by Patricia D. White, herself a lawyer and professor. She says:

> It seems to me mistaken . . . to *assume* that there is a specifiable point of division between life and death and that all hard cases must fall on one side or the other. . . . The Commission was operating in a context within which (1) there were (and still are) explicit and specific legal standards for determining death and (2) the clear expectation was that a proposal or proposals would issue which undertook to update and make more uniform the various formulations of those standards. It is not surprising, therefore, that the report which accompanies its proposed Uniform Determination of Death Act shows little evidence that it considered seriously the possibility that it should instead have fashioned a systematic retreat of the law from the business of defining death.[55]

The critique of the President's Commission offered above by Bernat, Culver, and Gert, suggested that ironically, after over a decade of attempted legislation, we still have not come up with an adequate definition of death, *but* that one was waiting around the corner, so to speak, in Canada. White's critique is more radical, in that it suggests that even if this is around the corner, we should avoid going there. The assumption that there is an answer to the question "What is death?" and that the answer is available, or will be soon, is one that the law should not make. In sum, her position is much like that of Roger Dworkin, who many years ago charged that "amazingly, the current definers of death not only overlook the obvious point that death only matters in terms of its consequences, but also ignore the fact that the law has long recognized that death occurs at different times for different purposes [e.g., property laws, homicide, tax law, inheritance, bigamy, etc.],"[56] and that therefore we should constantly strive to view death "in context."

The examination of the biological aspect of death and of the public policy matters presented above bear witness to the veracity of Dworkin's concern for "thick contexts."

[S I X]

Ramifications of Jonas's Critique

ANENCEPHALICS AS ORGAN DONORS

One of the most obvious instances that might substantiate Hans Jonas's fear that death was being redefined primarily for "impure" reasons concerns anencephalic newborns. Anencephalics are generally defined as not possessing skull, scalp, or forebrain at birth. They do, however, possess some brain stem activity, allowing them to perform circulatory and respiratory functions. There are "approximately 2,000 to 3,000 anencephalics . . . born each year"[1] in the United States. Estimates vary as to what percentage of these are born alive, from 25 percent to 50 percent.[2] "Approximately 40 percent of these infants who are born alive survive at least twenty-four hours. Of these survivors, one of three will be living at the end of the third day and one of twenty will live to at least seven days."[3] On the other side, there is clear evidence of need. As Richard Zaner notes, "If the approximately 2,500 anencephalics born each year in the United States could become organ donors, the estimated 40 to 70 percent of babies who die while currently on transplant waiting lists could be saved."[4] Finally, while there is not yet any track record to indicate a high degree of success in transplanting organs from anencephalics, "early indications suggest optimism."[5]

There is, in short, the recognition that anencephalics cannot live for long, the need to help others, and the ability, at least in some instances, to do so. There is also a desire by some parents to assist others by providing organs from their anencephalic newborn. On March 22, 1992, Theresa Ann Campo Pearson, "Baby Theresa," was born anencephalic. Her parents, Laura Campo and Justin Pearson, knew of her condition beforehand, but wanted the infant's organs donated in order to save others. The parents were very much pro-life, and indeed had had other children, but realized that in this case the outcome was inevitable. The courts refused their petition, stating that the infant did not meet the requirements for being defined dead, that is, whole-brain death. An appeals court refused to intervene in the lower court's decision. Baby Theresa lived for nine days before "dying"; only her corneas were then capable of being used, and this for research.

The problem here revolves around the fact that neither Baby Theresa nor any other anencephalic meets the requirements for being considered brain-dead, according to Harvard Ad Hoc. Should he or she therefore be termed "alive," and perhaps allowed to die because of the dim prognosis? Or, should the definition of death be changed again so that anencephalics would be included? Or, finally, should anencephalics be placed in a third category of their own?

One advocate of the first position is Alexander Capron, who argues that

> adding anencephalics to the category of dead persons would be a radical change, both in the social and medical understanding of what it means to be dead and in the social practices surrounding death. Anencephalic infants may be dying, but they are still alive and breathing. Calling them "dead" will not change physiologic reality or otherwise cause them to resemble those (cold and nonrespirating) bodies that are considered appropriate for post-mortem examinations and burial.[6]

For Capron, the decision by Harvard Ad Hoc to advocate whole-brain death did *not* constitute such a radical break, but rather only an updating of the means for determining the *old* definition of death. Physicians do not consider anencephalics as dead, and starting down this "slippery slope" could have disastrous consequences. If their lethal neurological condition is to be used as the determining characteristic, then other states might also fall in this category. Microcephaly, for example, is a condition covering a number of problems, including cases in which the brain hemispheres fail to form. These latter would be *"conceptually* indistinguishable" from anencephalics. Placing anencephalics into the category of "dead" persons useful for organ donation would result in an unfortunate loss of certainty over the definition—an implication that there are different kinds of death. This ambiguity, for Capron, is simply unacceptable. He asks, "Is *any* particular patient,—and not just an anencephalic baby—*really* dead? Or do the physicians mean only that the outlook for the patient's survival is poor, so why not allow the organs to be taken and bring about death in this (useful) fashion?"[7] Far better to keep the neutral univocal definition separate from the issue of when to "let die." Recognition of anencephalics as dead "would amount to the first recognition of a 'higher brain' standard" advocated by thinkers like Robert Veatch. Taking an anencephalic to be a "person," that is, "live birth of the product of a human conception,"[8] Capron argues that, particularly as the most vulnerable patients, they ought not to be used as the "opening wedge" in the attempt to revise the organ donor process. An extension of this line of thought implies that women might have their autonomy usurped, or at least that they might be pressured by society to bring anencephalic fetuses to term in instances where they might otherwise opt for abortion.

Richard Zaner is a clear advocate of the second option—as also is Robert Veatch. For Zaner, the problem is not with the use of anencephalics as organ donors, but with the whole-brain definition of death. He goes so far as to state that "anencephaly . . . constitutes one of the clearest, most convincing instances demonstrating the need for a statutory revision of the definition of death as death of the person," that is, absence of higher brain functions.[9] Borrowing a concept from H. Tristram Engelhardt, Zaner criticizes Capron for failing to make the necessary distinction between "human personal life" and "human biological life."[10] In actuality, what Capron has done is to list one specific *criterion* to determine that death has occurred (that is, irreversible cessation of whole brain activity) as a *concept* or definition of death, thereby begging the very point at issue. The point, for both Zaner and Engelhardt, is that anencephalics are *not* dying persons; they were never alive as persons in the first place.[11] Use of anencephalics for purposes of organ donorship, it follows, does not constitute a violation of "personal dignity." Going further, abortion for purposes of organ transplant in this instance, even in the third trimester, is morally justifiable. (Fetal organs are not mature enough for transplantation until the third trimester.) This becomes clearer when one realizes that *Roe v. Wade* incorrectly identified "viability" exclusively with gestational age, whereas in reality "viability [is] a matter of reasonable medical judgment."[12]

As to the slippery slope argument, fears about "organ farms" or commercialization of fetal tissue can be overcome by placing sensible checks at critical points. One does not want "absolute prohibition but the contrary, great caution and specific justification at every stage."[13] As Mahowald, Silver, and Ratcheson have put it, slippery slope arguments have no more or less validity here than they do in issues such as abortion or withdrawal of treatment. "The roadway traveled by those who make ethical decisions is unavoidably a slippery slope. To traverse it successfully requires placing wedges at the right places, in order to restrict or stop travel at those points where one is most likely to fall."[14]

Michael Harrison advocates the third position mentioned above, that is, creating a new category, considering the anencephalic not as "brain-dead" but rather as "brain-absent." The concept of whole-brain death, when it was developed, did not have anencephalics in mind, but rather was concerned to protect those patients in coma whose brain injuries might never heal. "Obviously, this precaution need not and should not apply to an anencephalic who never had and can never have the physical structure necessary for higher brain activity or cognitive function."[15] Failure of brain development then would constitute the only exception to the whole-brain statute. He thinks the anencephalic should be looked at as a "dying person" whose death is inevitable at or shortly after birth, but hopes and believes that "brain-absent" will come to have the same medical-legal implications as "brain-dead." That is, life support can be withdrawn and organs can be retrieved.[16]

The most obvious problem with this approach is that "it is an overtly utilitarian move, possibly justified in this case, but inviting additional special categories as social demand for organs increases."[17] In addition the term itself does not capture the actual condition of the anencephalic, who after all does have some brain activity. As Mahowald, Silver, and Ratcheson note in this context, " 'Nonviability' is a more accurate description; this term would apply not only to anencephalic infants, but also to fetuses or individuals whose imminent death is unavoidable."[18]

In actuality, the proposal to create a new category here for anencephalics forces one to deal with the wider issue raised by Jonas in the first place: Did we "redefine" death, or merely create a social policy to help resolve a problem?[19] At a minimum, it must be admitted that a loss of certainty has occurred here, if indeed it ever existed. That is, the fact that there are three dissenting positions regarding the ontological status of anencephalics would seem to constitute at least *prima facie* evidence for the need for some form of pluralism here, especially when one recalls the attack upon the supposedly neutral definition of death mounted by Jonas and Veatch above. Norman Fost has noted that "several scholars believe they have discovered . . .

[the] true definition of death; unfortunately, their views are not entirely compatible with each other."[20] We would agree, questioning only whether or not this is an unfortunate condition. That is, as will become more evident in Part 3, the personal dimension of dying needs to be given its due, and this entails a pluralistic and contextual approach to situations at large.

DEATH AND DYING OF NEWBORN INFANTS

In the above section on anencephalics, reference was made to a distinction made by H. Tristram Engelhardt between "human personal life" and "human biological life." It should be noted that the implications of this distinction, if granted, go far beyond the topic of anencephalics, to the issue of personhood itself. For Engelhardt, the term *human person* or *human life* does not have meaning invariance, but rather must be contextually articulated.[21] "Not all instances of human biological life are instances of human personal life. Brain-dead (but otherwise alive) human beings, human gametes, cells in human cell cultures, all count as instances of human biological life. Further, not only are some humans not persons, there is no reason to hold that all persons are humans, as the possibility of extraterrestrial self-conscious life suggests."[22] Given the ambiguity of the situation, Engelhardt initially bases his distinction on Kant. Persons are self-conscious and self-determining. They are to be treated as ends and not as means. That is, their autonomy is to be respected, since they are moral agents. In return, they have the duty or obligation to treat other persons as ends in themselves. It follows, as Michael Tooley has argued, that not only fetuses but also newborn infants, since they are not rational self-conscious beings, do not qualify as persons.[23]

Engelhardt accepts the consequences of this distinction as it applies to fetuses and anencephalics, but is uncomfortable with its application to other newborns. As a result he decides to restructure the issue by offering two concepts of "person" (more than this probably exist in his opinion). In the strict initial sense of "bearers of rights and duties," infants are not persons. But they may be treated *as if* they were persons, even though in the literal sense of the term they are not. In a mother-child relationship, for instance, "the infant is treated as if it had the wants and desires of a person—its cries are treated as a call for food, attention, care, etc., and the infant is socialized, placed within a social structure, the family, and becomes a child."[24] Important for our purposes is Engelhardt's clear realization that a shift is taking place here in developing this second concept "from merely biological to social significance. The shift is made on the basis that the infant is a human and is able to engage in a minimum of social interaction."[25] Infants, in short, become *socialized* into the role of "person"; they live "in and through their families." They have rights, but not duties—that is, they are treated as if they have rights because this benefits society in the long run. "It should be stressed that the social sense of person is primarily a utilitarian construct. A person in this sense is not a person strictly, and hence not an unqualified object of respect."[26] While children appear then in some sense of the term to be persons, and while they have great value, they are not moral agents in the strict sense. While adults might in some specific circumstances select a form of euthanasia, even active euthanasia, with moral justification based on preserving their rationality and autonomy, children are not able to make any such decision. In their stead, Engelhardt argues, "parents [i.e., not doctors and not society at large] can properly refuse life-prolonging treatment for their deformed infants if such treatment would entail a substantial investment of their economic and psychological resources."[27]

Specifically then, Engelhardt would argue that one can cease to care for anencephalics on the grounds that they are not, and will never be, persons. But one can also with moral justification cease treatment of some children born, say, with meningomyelocele, on the grounds that the cost of any cure would be very high, the quality of life very questionable, and the resulting suffering and anxiety inflicted upon parents very great. The role of the physician here is to provide all necessary information in a comprehensible form, and once again, the parents, as the primary caregivers, are the ultimate decision makers, within limits. "Society must value mother-child and family-child relationships and should intervene only in cases where (1) neglect is unreasonable and therefore would undermine respect and care for children, or (2) where societal intervention would prevent children from suffering unnecessary pain."[28] The justifications previously listed (cost/benefit, anxiety, etc.) are primarily of a utilitarian nature, but Engelhardt also believes that additional Kantian support may be provided by recognizing the "injury of continued existence." That is, "certain qualities of life have a negative value, making life an injury, not a gift."[29] Under these circumstances (such as Tay-Sachs disease, or Lesch-Nyhan disease), it could be argued, under the principle of *primum non nocere,* that medicine has a duty not to treat, that it is in the newborn's own self-interest not to have its life prolonged. Such an argument would go far toward trying to see matters from the point of view of the "other," in this case, the child.

It is important to note, before leaving Engelhardt, that for him the important distinction to draw with precision is between moral agents and nonmoral agents—and *not* the distinction between nature and nurture. "Exactly where one draws the line between persons in the social sense and merely human biological life is not crucial as long as the integrity of persons strictly is preserved."[30] But this way of focusing the issue simply bypasses the whole question as to whether any concept of "self" or "person" is not socially constructed. Engelhardt has just offered a version of one for newborns. But there is nothing in the Kantian sense of "self" as autonomous moral agent that prevents it from being viewed also as socially constructed. This becomes clearer when we remember that in some other cultures, such as Japan, the primary or only sense of self recognized is one where one lives "in and through one's family" and is not self-possessed. Ironically, while Engelhardt may have thought that Tooley's argument proved too much in that it proved infants not to be persons in any sense of the term, his own argument may suffer a similar fate, that is, disclosing more radically than he perhaps wished, how fragile the sense of "self" or "person" is, upon which we base our ethical arguments.

A much different position is advocated by David Smith in "On Letting Some Babies Die." Smith proceeds by assuming that newborns *are* persons, although admitting that not every product of the human womb should be so characterized. The case of anencephalics, for example, is described as "problematical,"[31] and is simply not dealt with by Smith. Whatever "person" means for Smith, it does not entail the sense of self-consciousness demanded by Tooley and probably by Engelhardt's concept of person in the "strict sense." Since newborns are persons, any decisions concerning possible termination of care constitute a form of euthanasia. Questions revolve around who should decide, since clearly the newborn cannot, and what criteria should be used in making the decision.

Smith commences his discussion by referring to a case that has become a symbol or icon—ultimately leading, after several changes, to the "Baby Doe" legislation in 1985. The case, dramatized in the film *Who Should Survive?*,[32] is a composite based upon several Down's syndrome babies born at Johns Hopkins Hospital in 1971. It concerns a newborn who has Down's syndrome and who also has duodenal atresia (blockage between the higher duodenum and the lower stomach which prevents passage of food and water). The parents, primarily the mother, decide not to allow the relatively minor operation necessary; the hospital honors their wishes, though the film does not bring out the fact that the mother, a nurse, had worked with Down's syndrome children before. The newborn is then "allowed to die" over a series of days.[33]

Smith agrees with Engelhardt that the primary decision maker should be the family, while admitting that medicine will inevitably retain considerable power and *technical* competence. As to what criteria should be employed by the family in making the decision, Smith adopts a version of the "just war" theory, and as a result generally rejects any claim for euthanasia based upon the threat of the newborn to others. The argument that the newborn would be a drain upon society's or a family's resources "proves too much," and would justify killing anybody who was a social liability. Furthermore, the actual people being threatened, that is, the family, have other options available, such as institutionalization. A deserted child constitutes an even lesser threat, since one cannot even identify specific individuals threatened. Regarding the argument for letting an infant die based upon the infant's own interest, Smith argues that there is no agreement on which criteria are adequate in, for example, cases of spina bifida; that the possibility of erroneous diagnosis always exists, and that no personal contextual judgment is possible for the newborn—as would be the case, for example, in advocating euthanasia for an adult who had a medical history and whom one could decide had "begun to die." Since passive euthanasia is not considered justifiable, the issue of active euthanasia is not taken up, being considered even less so.

In brief, for Smith, treatment of defective newborns should not be withheld unless one can show that some specific person is threatened in an unavoidable manner, or unless the infant cannot be cared for in any other manner. While not advocating the use of extraordinary treatments in all cases, he wants to avoid the comparison of sick newborns with limited capacities with so-called normal babies. "Such an approach leads one to think that the ideal result is either a 'perfect' baby or a dead baby."[34] In opposition, he advocates resolving whatever difficulties may be presented through better allocation of our limited resources.

Smith's position amounts to a virtual prohibition upon the termination of newborns, though, once again, it fails to deal with anencephalics. The case it began with, and others similar in nature, led the Justice Department and the Department of Health and Human Services to decide that neither parents nor doctors were the primary or exclusive decision makers, but that "imperiled newborns were . . . handicapped citizens who could suffer discrimination."[35] Denial of treatment would therefore constitute violation of their civil rights. Initially, signs were to be posted in hospitals, saying "Discriminatory Failure to Feed and Care for Handicapped Infants in This Facility Is Prohibited By Federal Law."[36] Hospitals violating the law risked loss of federal funding. A hotline was established, whereby anyone could report abuses. All of this was adamantly supported by those advocating the right to life, and opposed as at least an infringement by the American Academy of Pediatrics. The results of the final outcome, that is, the regulation put into effect in 1985, are debatable. On the one hand, from a conservative vantage point, the term "medical neglect" was broadened, originally in 1984, to explicitly include withholding medically indicated treatment from a disabled infant with a life-threatening condition.[37] On the other hand, there are three exceptions to the rule, and each of these is sufficient in itself to justify cessation of treatment, *except* for appropriate nutrition, hydration, and medication. These are:

> The infant is irreversibly comatose; or . . . the provision of such treatment would merely prolong dying or not be effective in ameliorating or correcting all the infant's life-threatening conditions . . . or . . . the provision of such treatment would be virtually futile in terms of the survival of the infant and the treatment itself under such circumstances would be inhumane."[38]

Previously included specific examples were now omitted, and "clarifying definitions" were relegated to an appendix and re-termed "interpretative guidelines." Both sides, in short, could claim victory, and did so.

But as Thomas Murray has noted, "the rule is more anti-climax than climax."[39] Indeed, in some ways the symbolic legal victories seemingly achieved only serve to mask more crucial moral issues, and one in particular, namely, killing versus letting die. Reflection upon the question of why food and water received such special attention, constituting exceptions to the non-treatment options, reveals that the image of a newborn with Down's syndrome and an accompanying problem that needs correction "shaped debate on the general issues."[40] In actual fact, the case was the Bloomington Baby Doe case, where the newborn has Down's syndrome and tracheoesophageal fistula (gastrointestinal malformation). The parents chose not to operate. This time the hospital went to court, but at each level in Indiana the court ruled for the parents. An attempt to get an emergency stay at the federal level was rendered moot by the actual death of the infant.[41] As in the Johns Hopkins case, attention here was focused upon the symbolic value of nutrition, and on the seeming necessity for medicine always to provide such nutrition. But decisions such as the one involving Baby Doe "concern not *whether* an infant should be allowed to die, but how that death will be managed."[42]

In conclusion, the apparent appeal for pluralism put forth by Smith is to be applauded; one does need a thicker context. But his own plea for pluralism seems to be undermined by the refusal to accept nothing less than certainty in making a decision regarding when infants might be allowed to die, and his plea for better allocation of resources seems to deflect attention from the interest of the newborn, and from Engelhardt's assertion that continued existence could at least sometimes be considered as wrongful.

The Reagan administration's emphasis upon "nondiscrimination" referred to above is, as John Arras has argued, "fatally flawed," in that it "overlooks the very real possibility that there may well be *morally significant* differences between . . . [normal and handicapped] children that *justify* . . . differential treatment."[43] While agreeing that the "best interests of the child" approach is the right way to go, Arras shrewdly points out several limitations of this approach. For example, even if one confines the analysis to the infant's interests, as opposed to considering the impact upon the family that Engelhardt brought up in the section above, does one take into account the economic status of the newborn? Severely impaired newborns born in poverty are likely to wind up in the back wards of ill-equipped institutions. On the other hand, the degree of wealth is not a "morally significant difference" in allocating health care to two equally deserving recipients—or at least it should not be. But we all know that it is. "At this point in the argument," Arras argues, "we have clearly entered a 'moral blind alley'—that is, a situation so structured that whatever course we take, we end up doing something morally unacceptable."[44] The child's socially caused problems should not count; unjust social conditions should be alleviated. Yet such a stance does nothing for a case *presently* at hand. Secondly, Arras recognizes how difficult it is to actually see things from the point of view of the "other," in this case the handicapped newborn, even if one is alerted ahead of time to the bias of "normalcy." "We must ask not whether a normal adult would rather die than suffer from severe mental and physical impairments, but rather whether this child, who has never known the satisfactions and aspirations of the normal world, would prefer nothing to what he or she has. . . . Adopting the child's viewpoint would be difficult in practice, but it would conform more closely to the spirit of the best-interest standard."[45]

This approach of seeing things from the point of view of the other will result, Arras admits, in a rather strict standard concerning when nontreatment is allowable. But it should *not* be allowed to function as an all-covering rule requiring treatment in all cases. Specifically, the best-interests standard has its own limitations and "tends to view the absence of pain as the only morally relevant consideration."[46] That is, if a newborn is not in unmitigatable pain, treatment should persist, regardless of the infant's other characteristics. As a supplement, Arras adopts a "relational potential standard," arguing that for "grievously afflicted children . . . [with] no distinctly human capacities, and thus no human interests, the activity of keeping them alive is pointless from the moral point of view."[47] Important for our purposes here is his clear realization that such a standard is not transcendental or foundational in nature, but rather must result from "social intersubjective inquiry," and that "ethical ambiguity pervades the issue."[48] Such ambiguity, however, is far preferable to the alternative, that is, "an illusory and counterproductive quest for moral certainty."[49] In short, as we noticed in Chapters 2 and 3, the difficulty of seeing matters from the point of view of the other needs to be recognized, while at the same time preserving a contextual approach to the situation at hand.

This point about recognizing contextual uncertainty and responding to it appropriately is reinforced by a report on "Imperiled Newborns" produced by the Hastings Center in 1987. It identifies three possible responses in treating defective newborns: a statistical approach, a wait-until-near-certainty approach, and an individualized approach.[50] In the first of these, an "across-the-board determination" is made "that infants fitting a particular statistical profile are unlikely to benefit from treatment," which is therefore withheld. In the second, all newborns are treated "until it is certain that a particular baby will either die or be so severely impaired that under any substantive standard, parents could legitimately opt for termination of treatment."[51] The last approach begins treatment on all infants, but "allows parents the option of termination before it is absolutely certain" in the sense described under the second option above. While each approach has its merits, and while on the face of things the "wait until certainty" approach might seem the most moral position, in actuality it removes all moral decision making except in cases where the baby is going to die for certain or be in a comatose state. In other words, the "extreme uncertainty" is removed by being "explained away." It tends to make doctors depend more and more on new technology and reduces parents to mere onlookers. In opposition, the authors of the report opt for the contextual approach, believing that "it is morally preferable to decide on the basis of the individual infant's prognosis."[52]

The issue of imperiled newborns, and the possibility that at least in some rare cases treatment should be withheld, raises one additional question. In these cases, should the infant be "allowed to die," or should active intervention to hasten its death be condoned? Going further, is there any moral difference between these two, between killing and letting die?

Previous chapters have argued that overemphasis on the supposedly absolute distinction between the definition of death and the moral status of euthanasia has sometimes served more as a hindrance than an advantage. Analogously, as we shall see, insistence that there is an absolute distinction between passive and active euthanasia, and that one is sometimes morally permissible but the other never so, can at least sometimes result in an inability to conceive of the problematic in humane terms, that is, from the point of view of the "other."

KILLING VERSUS LETTING DIE

The same image or symbol, that is, a newborn infant with Downs' syndrome and an accompanying congenital defect, served as the catalyst for the most widely known article against the distinction between killing and letting die, "Active and Passive Euthanasia" by James Rachels. In it Rachels argues that once the decision to terminate has been made, the decision to let die is less humane than a quick termination of suffering. While he can see that some would oppose all forms of euthanasia and others might advocate active euthanasia (himself included), he argues that, in this instance, the decision to distinguish between active and passive does not make sense, or worse, is immoral. "The doctrine that says that a baby may be allowed to dehydrate and wither, but may not be given an injection that would end its life without suffering, seems so patently cruel as to require no further refutation."[53] In addition, it leads to decisions on a life-and-death issue being made on irrelevant grounds. "It is the Down's syndrome, and not the intestines, that is the issue." Finally, the distinction between active and passive is based, wrongly, on the distinction between killing and letting die, and the assumption that the former is always worse than the latter. In the first example Rachels uses, Smith goes into the bathroom to drown his cousin so as to inherit a fortune. In the second, Jones goes into the bathroom *with the same intent,* but his cousin slips, hits his head, remaining underwater, and Jones "merely" lets him die. To assert, Rachels argues, that in the first case one does something but in the second one just stood there, "can only be regarded as a grotesque perversion of moral reasoning."[54] Analogously, if a doctor decides, for humane reasons, to let a patient die, "he is in the same moral position as if he had given the patient a lethal injection for humane reasons."[55] It is inadequate to assert that the doctor's intention in the second case was different; the intentional cessation of treatment in this case *is* the intentional termination of life.

Why then do we cling so adamantly to the distinction between killing and letting die? Indeed, our entire legal system seems to be predicated upon it. For Rachels, it is a matter of enculturation. "Most actual cases of killing are clearly terrible (think, for example, of all the murders reported in the newspapers), and one hears of such cases every day. On the other hand, one hardly ever hears of a case of letting die, except for the actions of doctors who are motivated by humanitarian reasons.

So one learns to think of killing in a much worse light than of letting die."[56] Once again, the issue needs to be viewed in terms of cultural context, and not in absolute, either/or terminology. For here too there are more than rational factors involved in the argument.[57]

One form that this enculturation has taken consists in the attempt made to draw the distinction between killing and letting die in terms of "commission" versus "omission," or the "withdrawing" of treatment versus the "withholding" of treatment. The idea is that the physician actually does nothing in withholding treatment, whereas in the withdrawal of an initiated procedure he or she is engaged in a positive act. But many have argued against this outlook, noting that, while no physician is obligated to take on a patient, once he or she does so a special relationship exists within which the distinction between omission and commission disappears.[58] However, while it may well be the case that this perception is agreed upon by a broad consensus of scholars in medical ethics, as a *Hastings Center Report* holds, neither the public at large nor local legal officials can be counted upon to view matters in the same way.[59]

Several thinkers have tried to cast doubt on Rachels's position, and to at least partly reinstate the distinction between active and passive euthanasia. Tom Beauchamp, for example, concedes that the bare difference between killing and letting die does not carry any moral weight. We cannot make the distinction on the basis of commission versus omission. "It is true that different degrees and means of involvement entail different degrees of responsibility, but it does not follow that we are *not* responsible and therefore are absolved of possible culpability in *any* case of intentionally allowing to die. We are responsible and *perhaps* culpable in either active or passive cases."[60] However, Beauchamp believes that a form of rule utilitarianism, when conjoined with a slippery slope argument that stresses gradual

erosion of moral principles, can be used against active euthanasia. Rules against killing are not isolated items, but rather form
a moral web; removal of a strand weakens the remaining whole.

> If, for example, rules permitting active killing were introduced, it
> is not implausible to suppose that destroying defective newborns
> (a form of involuntary euthanasia) would become an accepted
> and common practice, that as population increases occur the
> aged will be even more neglectable and neglected than they now
> are, that capital punishment for a wide variety of crimes would
> be increasingly tempting, that some doctors would have appre-
> ciably reduced fears of actively injecting fatal doses whenever it
> seemed to them propitious to do so, and that laws of war against
> killing would erode in efficacy even beyond their already abysmal
> level.[61]

Against such a litany or avalanche of possible consequences, we
should perhaps recall Mary Mahowald's comment earlier that
the best way to deal with the slippery slope is not to refuse to ven-
ture out on it, but rather to place wedges at the appropriate points
of danger. Certainty, in other words, is not to be had before
skiing. Indeed, Beauchamp himself, having made the distinction
between active and passive euthanasia to his own satisfaction on
moral grounds, admits he is "uncertain" as to whether or not
"we *ought* to accept . . . [it]. This problem is a substantive moral
issue—not merely a conceptual one—and would require at a
minimum a lengthy assessment of wedge arguments and related
utilitarian considerations."[62] This may be granted, but not any
intimation that studying the problem long enough will necessarily result in a solution. Rachels may have overstated his case in
saying that the distinction between active and passive euthanasia is always morally irrelevant, but Beauchamp's "conclusion"
that society is faced with a dilemma here understates or masks
the sentimental personal or cultural features involved. That is, it
might serve as a compelling argument as to why society ought
not to condone as "public policy" the active intervention of

physicians to intentionally cause the death of their patients. But it does not deal well with those who would hold that, in the case of, say, a patient who is conscious and in extreme pain, at a specific point there simply is no difference in terms of consequences between those who would advocate treating the pain aggressively with the accompanying increased risk of death, and those who would advocate active termination of the patient. A possible response to this might be made in terms of "intentions," that is, intending to cause death to alleviate the pain versus intending to treat the pain aggressively while risking the possibility of death.[63] However, we would argue that here as elsewhere, these intentions are at least partly socially constructed.

CONCLUSION

After all the numerous arguments made and positions taken on the three major topics discussed in this chapter, it must be noted once again that the outcome achieved depends to a considerable degree upon the "invention of the problematic."[64] That is, the way the issue is couched to some extent determines the outcome. As Maurice A. M. de Wachter has noted, "Definitions are not morally neutral."[65] The specific topic he has in mind here is euthanasia, and the customary classification of it into "active" versus "passive," and "voluntary" versus "involuntary." The most radical part of the ethical debate in the United States has turned upon the former of these. Indeed, involuntary euthanasia is already condoned in terms of surrogate decision makers in some circumstances deciding to forgo life-sustaining treatment. This is seen as less vulnerable to slippery slope arguments than the active-passive issue. But in the Netherlands the term *euthanasia* itself means the active termination of a patient's life at his or her own request, freely given and persistent in nature. Hence, "in the Netherlands 'voluntary euthanasia' is a tautology and 'involuntary euthanasia' a contradiction in terms."[66] We might extend this point to the more general concept of "individual self-determination" utilized by Dan Brock to advocate voluntary active euthanasia in some specific circumstances, and by Daniel Callahan as a principle that has "run amok" and that should therefore be rejected.

For Brock, self-determination, that is, "people's interest in making important decisions about their lives for themselves according to their own values" is itself a fundamental value—and one that entails pluralism.[67] It can be melded to the principle of individual well-being and a strong case then carved out for each person's controlling the timing and circumstances of his or her own dying and death, including, with safeguards in place to prevent abuse, the use of active voluntary euthanasia. Killing, in short, is not always ethically unjustified in medicine. In opposition, Callahan argues that "self-determination" has limits, that "the acceptance of [voluntary active] euthanasia would sanction a view of autonomy holding that individuals may, in the name of their own private, idiosyncratic view of the good life, call upon others, including such institutions as medicine, to help them pursue that life, even at the risk of harm to the common good."[68] In actuality, this is not a form of self-determination, "but of a mutual, social decision between two people, the one to be killed and the other to do the killing."[69] While this second position does recognize at times the social construction of "self-determination" here, it seems to argue that once this is seen we will return to the "true" notion of self-determination, that is, the one predicated upon autonomy, and simply recognize that it has limits placed upon it by society. But if the very terms of the debate are to some degree socially constructed, the issue is not that of individual versus society, but rather which role model of self is found in a particular culture.

Still a third version of "inventing the problematic" can be couched in terms of being "alone" versus being "autonomous." Those advocating the first of these will tend to structure the primary plight of the patient in terms of her being abandoned or left alone. They will see the primary needs of the patient to be the provision of comfort and support during the dying process. Hence both physician-assisted suicide and active voluntary euthanasia will be downplayed. By contrast, an emphasis upon autonomy tends to result in an attitude favoring physician-assisted suicide and active voluntary euthanasia. But, once again, the notion of autonomy being accepted here is one already carrying around the exclusionary bias of self-determination versus social control. As we have noted in Chapters 2 and 3, the cultural contextualization of "self" needs to be recognized and preserved if one is to deal with the *richness* of the problematic. As de Wachter has argued, "Definitions . . . may serve two purposes quite apart from their logical function: they may legitimize what they describe; and they may encompass other things that people perceive as being relevantly similar."[70]

Fourth and finally, the trio of topics discussed here, that is, anencephalic newborns, letting some babies die, and killing versus letting die, serves as a reminder that not only *specific* problems about death but indeed the problematic *in general* may be misconstrued. That is, the most important issue may not be which biological definition of *death* to employ as an overall public policy, or even how much pluralism to tolerate among competing definitions, but rather the more personal process of *dying*.[71] We turn to this theme in Part 3.

III
Personal Contexts

[SEVEN]

Death Versus Dying

In Chapter 5 Hans Jonas stated that perhaps the entire issue was being misconstrued, and that we should be focusing upon the issue of euthanasia rather than trying to come up with either a new definition of death or a revised version of the old one. He is only one among several thinkers who believe that we have fundamentally misconstrued the problematic—once again offering true answers to false questions, and therefore once again engaging in a form of denial. The problematic for these thinkers is not death but rather dying, and just as one would not identify a melody with the last note in a score, so too one should not focus on the last moment of dying, that is, death, at the expense of the entire process of dying. This form of denial results in a depersonalization of the dying process through displacement and self-deception.

This theme will be developed in three ways in the present chapter. First, death as a process versus death as an event will be taken up, focusing on the debate over this issue between Robert Morison and Leon Kass. Second, the possibility of viewing a person as a process rather than a substance will be discussed, using John McDermott's analysis of the doctor-patient relationship. The basis for McDermott's position is William James's view of person, which will be described in some detail.

If the above two accounts succeed in elevating the theme of dying to at least the same level of importance as that of death, then the same critical questions should be asked of it as were asked of the latter, namely, is a neutral account or description of the process possible, or desirable; and, is the process best viewed as one of acceptance or as one advocating some form of denial or rebellion? This will constitute the third theme of the present chapter, and it will focus on the work of Elisabeth Kübler-Ross, whose presentation of an acceptance model will be followed by several critical reactions, most of them charging that her acceptance model is in actuality a new form of denial. One of these accounts, the analysis of Lawrence Churchill, will receive particular attention, for it is Churchill who advocates the moral primacy of stories over stages. As such, his account returns us to the critical analysis of case studies versus "thick description" presented in Chapter 1, as well as pointing the way toward Chapter 8, which focuses on individual portraits of dying persons. Throughout the analysis the issue of acceptance versus denial or rebellion will continue to move toward center stage, as well as the question as to whether or not this binary can be transcended, and if so, how.

ROBERT MORISON: DEATH AS PROCESS

In "Death: Process or Event?" Robert Morison charges that we engage in "the fallacy of misplaced concreteness"[1] insofar as we tend to replace participles and adjectives like "living" and "dying" with abstract nouns like "life" and "death." All too often this results in the objectification of death as a thing capable of moving about on its own. "In many cases . . . Death is not only reified, it is personified, and graduates from a mere thing to a jostling woman in the marketplace of Baghdad or an old man, complete with beard, scythe, and hourglass, ready to mow down those whose time has come."[2] This leads to a discontinuity Morison sees as artificial, and a consequent denial of the more correct view of growth and decay as a continuous process. He argues that the truth of this position can be brought out by our remembering the difficulty of pointing out the precise moment of death when dealing with primitive organisms, as well as by our realizing that constant tinkering with our own machinery has made it difficult, if not impossible, to identify death as an event any longer—or even a "configuration."

Morison believes that a redefinition of death is not a sufficient solution to the problem. Rather we must realize that practical matters of great importance are at issue, such that "it appears that parts of the dying body may acquire values greater than the whole."[3] He believes it better to face up to this, and to make choices about euthanasia, than to engage in the type of self-deception that views human life as an absolute, concentrates upon redefining death, and refuses to deal with euthanasia. In opposition, Morison adopts a process metaphysics wherein the human being is constituted through a complex set of interactions with the environment, and where the value of life changes as the value of these interactions changes. This will result in our having to make decisions on when the value of life has ebbed to the extent that one will not only no longer utilize all means of support, but also engage in passive, or even active, euthanasia. "The intent appears to be the same in the two cases [active and passive] and it is the intent that would seem to be significant."[4] An individual should not be restrained by law or social attitudes from "taking an intelligent interest in his own death,"[5] that is, at least sometimes rationally contemplating suicide. We must then, for Morison, shoulder the responsibility of deciding when the trajectory of an individual's declining life intersects with society's needs.

In sum, for Morison, death viewed as an event constitutes a form of denial. Death should be accepted, but looked at correctly, that is, as process. Such a view will require more concentration upon ethical issues concerning euthanasia, as opposed to a quest for new definitions.

While there are many attractive aspects to this position, three disquieting points need to be made immediately. First, ordinary language does *not* mean by the term "death" a process, as Morison's own analysis seems to reveal. But language is not a coat that we can simply take off at will. It is more like a skin. The alternative solution is to say that Morison is introducing a new "theoretical" definition of death as "dying." This solution would be available only to "experts," so to speak, that is, process philosophers. Neither of these approaches seems desirable.

Second, Morison's article tends to foreground continuity at the expense of discontinuity. Alarmed at the tendency to create the thing "death" as discrete from dying, he tends to view living and dying as one continuous process. But as William James noted long ago, we need to pay attention to both the disjunctive and the conjunctive transitions when looking at consciousness—or at life itself.[6] This omission will have particular consequences for the concept of "person as process" in the next section.

Third, this overemphasis upon the continuous shows up most clearly in Morison's assertion that there is an "intersection" between the downward curve of an individual's life and the needs of society in general. It is necessary to at least consider the possibility that these curves may in some instances never intersect.

These points, and others, are taken up in the critique offered by Leon Kass.

LEON KASS: DEATH AS AN EVENT

In "Death as an Event" Leon Kass accuses Morison of confusing "aging" and "dying"—and actually of confusing "living," "aging," and "dying." Aging is what renders an individual more and more prone to die from some accidental cause. "As distinguished from aging, dying is the process leading from the incidence of the 'accidental' cause of death to and beyond some border, however ill-defined, after which the organism (or its body) may be said to be dead."[7] The factual definition of death is important, and it must be clearly distinguished from the issue of euthanasia. Morison, Kass charges, is concerned only with the question of prolonging or not prolonging life, and not with the question of when a person is in fact dead. For Kass there *is* an answer to the last question, and it is based upon preserving the distinction between the concept of death and the operational criteria used to indicate that death has taken place. Using an Aristotelian metaphysics, as opposed to the process approach offered by Morison, Kass offers that what dies is the organism as a whole, and that "questions about *when* and *how* cannot be adequately discussed without some substantive understanding of *what* it is that dies."[8] For Kass then, the whole is greater than the sum of its parts, and Morison's biology is reductionist in nature. Analogously, David Lamb has argued that

> most of the confusion underlying the "event" versus "process" debate is generated by a failure to distinguish between clinical death—death of the organism as a whole—and biological death—death of the whole organism. Clinical death can be defined as an event which marks the "cessation of the integrative action between all organ systems of the body." . . . Biological death, on the other hand, involves the irreversible loss of function of all the body's organs.[9]

For Kass, if the tinkering of humans with their machinery has caused confusion, this confusion should be viewed as ours, and not as nature's. Here Lamb goes even further in defending Kass's position against Morison's: "If technology has blurred the traditional distinction between a man alive and a man dead then there is an urgent and pressing reason to restore clarity";[10] and again: "It may be that medical science has encountered very serious difficulties in formulating criteria for death, but the answer lies, as it does in every other scientific problem, in more research, more analysis, and better science, not in skepticism."[11]

Turning to the moral issue of allowing to die as opposed to the fact of death, Kass charges that Morison wants to have it both ways in upholding patient needs and also those of society. "But the ethic of allowing a person to die is based solely on a consideration of the welfare of the dying patient himself, rather than on a consideration of benefits that accrue to others. . . . Medicine cannot retain trustworthiness or trust if it . . . [acts] otherwise."[12] It is misleading then to suggest that we can locate the moment of "curve intersection" that Morison suggests. Finally, there is for Kass a major difference between active and passive euthanasia. "The intent is not the same, although the outcome may be. In the one case, the intent is to desist from engaging in useless 'treatments' and to engage instead in the positive acts of giving comfort to and keeping company with the dying patient. In the other case, the intent is indeed to directly hasten the patient's death."[13]

In sum, Kass offers us an acceptance model of death as an event, though he acknowledges that "we need to recover both an attitude that is more accepting of death and a greater concern for the human needs of the dying patient."[14] Views of death as a disease and of medicine's possible victory over it will "not succeed, for death is not only inevitable, but also biologically, psychologically, and spiritually desirable."[15]

Kass's position, however, is not without serious flaws. First, the distinction that the confusion caused by our constant tinkering with our human machinery is ours and not nature's is quite questionable. In any case, the "pragmatic upshot" is the same, that is, we will still have to make decisions about when death takes place. Appeals to substance over process, to "what" versus "when," simply reveal competing metaphysical systems—not any factual definition of death. Further, as Barbara MacKinnon has wisely noted, it is not inconceivable that the tinkering actually changes the situation, perhaps even changing death from an event to a process.[16] Second, we have already seen that the distinction between the definition of death and the criteria utilized to indicate that death has taken place may not be possible to draw.[17] Third, appeals to "more science" as a solution to the current confusion betray a particular progressivist view of science not necessarily acceptable in a post-Kuhnian context. Fourth, even acceptance of the "holistic" approach offered in the article does not necessarily free one from deciding, contextually, *when* the person as a whole has died.

Both Morison and Kass offer "acceptance" models, but acceptance of different things—or one thing (death) and one process (dying). Kass maintains a view of the person as substance, with accompanying attributes, based upon an Aristotelian metaphysic. Morison's process position tends to "merge" the individuality of personhood into the environment—a series of complex interactions "working out . . . a complicated tautology"[18] after the novelty of the chromosomal pattern is formed. There is a nascent view of the person as process here, but it needs to be developed in a more Jamesian or Deweyan fashion. Finally, each author accuses the other of a form of self-deception and denial, and argues that one should rebel against the false portrayal of the situation, but accept the true one.

The answer to the question "Is death a process or an event?" may well be yes. That is, these two alternatives may not be mutually exclusive, or it may be more fruitful to locate the debate elsewhere.[19] Nonetheless, overemphasis upon death as an event does mask the importance of the process of dying. But that process should not be articulated in general terms that emphasize the conjunctive transitions only. This results in the loss of the personal dimension of dying, including the affective aspect. As Sartre has noted, it is in the ability to say no, that is, to engage in disjunctive transitions, that human freedom dwells.[20]

PERSONAL DYING: WILLIAM JAMES AND JOHN J. MCDERMOTT

In "Against the Stream" Hans Jonas has charged that the main issue was not being addressed, namely dying, and that vagueness was an essential component of the real-life situation.[21] Further, he argued against the imposition a new form of dualism, namely, brain/body. "My identity is the identity of the whole organism, even if the higher functions of personhood are seated in the brain. How else could a man love a woman and not merely her brains? How else could we lose ourselves in the aspect of a face?"[22] In a similar fashion, the American philosopher William James had consistently argued for "the reinstatement of the vague and inarticulate to its proper place in our mental life."[23] Initially concerned to paint a picture of consciousness in *The Principles of Psychology,* James later realized that the distinction between consciousness and existence could not be maintained, and he subsequently developed a metaphysics of "pure experience" wherein much of what he earlier said of consciousness was now applied to reality at large. Important for our purpose is James's rejection of the subject/object dichotomy, his clear realization that the affective is important, and that it is essentially vague. For James, those experiences that he terms "*appreciations* . . . form an ambiguous sphere of being, belonging with emotion on the one hand, and having objective 'value' on the other, yet seeming not quite inner nor quite outer."[24] An experience of a painful object is usually also a painful experience; a perception of loveliness is a lovely perception, and so on. "Sometimes the adjective wanders as if uncertain where to fix itself. Shall we speak of seductive visions or of visions of seductive things?"[25] In James's metaphysics, each present moment of experience, as it drops into the past, is classified as consciousness or as content, or both of these. However, the world of the affective or the prerational is more real, in the sense that it preserves the original given vagueness of experience. "With the affectional experiences . . . the relatively 'pure' condition lasts. In practical life no urgent need has yet arisen for deciding whether to treat them as rigorously mental or as rigorously physical facts. So they remain equivocal; and as the world goes, their equivocality is one of their great conveniences."[26]

For James, what is "present" at the most primordial level of experience is *not* immediate, but rather passing, or flowing. Reality is the fringe, the vague, the "more." Affectional experiences are more real than others to the extent that they preserve vagueness. However, experiences do become classified as subjective or objective, conscious or content, mine or yours, or both of all these. These distinctions come upon the scene. They are not primordial, but rather arise with and through language. One must therefore be continually careful not to let language *replace* the personal experiences that it purports to *represent*.

In "Feeling as Insight: The Affective Dimension in Social Diagnosis" John J. McDermott takes a Jamesian approach to medicine and the doctor/patient relationship. Arguing that unfortunately diagnosis all too often proceeds from a fixed point of view, that is, one wherein the "diagnostician assumes the contours of human behavior as known and deduces from those limits a set of symptom-question relationships," McDermott charges that this results in "vicious intellectualism" wherein questions are structured to elicit specific responses, and "alternatives, not being sought . . . never surface."[27] Asking that the uniqueness of each individual context be preserved, McDermott hopes that the "sensitive diagnostician will not fit . . . [patient] articulations into an a priori context but will strive to unearth their experienced roots so as to better follow the multiple hints and leads which yield genuine insight into the real and felt needs of the person or community."[28] However, even when this attempt to acknowledge the "other" is undertaken, the success achieved is only partial, as we have seen in Chapters 2 and 3. The issue becomes even more difficult when one fails to deal with the *inarticulate*, which James deemed so important, in this case with experiences that patients undergo but that are vague or difficult to describe. "How frequent it is that people retreat to a studied anonymity because the complex quality of their experience defies the recognized patterns of expression and explication."[29] Such insensitivity can be overcome only if we cease treating the other person as object, and view her or him rather as "relational process" wherein both the mind *and* the body play an active role. "In effect, we lead with our bodies, or better, our bodies are knowers in a primal way."[30] As James himself put it,

> Where the body is is "here"; when the body acts is "now"; what the body touches is "this"; all other things are "there" and "then" and "that." These words of emphasized position imply a systematization of things with reference to a focus of action and interest which lies in the body. . . . The body is the storm centre, the origin of co-ordinates. . . . Everything circles around it, and is felt from its point of view. The word "I," then, is primarily a noun of position, just like "this" and "here."[31]

The body here is how we "intend"; it is a probe, an extension of our being into the world. Intentionality as such is not limited to the rational but necessarily includes the affective as well. The world is such that human beings can structure a place for themselves through rejection and assimilation, definition and inference. But there is no guarantee of success in advance. The Jamesian self here is articulated in terms of both conjunctive and disjunctive transitions; slippage, even death, is always possible. Finally, each dying person has his or her own narrative to tell.

The Jamesian self is more than the comparatively impersonal one offered by Morison, but less than the more fully blown Aristotelian self offered by Kass. The human being, from this perspective, is best viewed as a creator, a sculptor in James's terms. But the environment in recent years, McDermott charges, has become less and less available for our creative endeavors, mainly through our own activity. Listlessness and anomie have been the result of our failure to accompany "breakthroughs in technology with a rerouting of bodily interests into other areas of experience. . . . We [have] witnessed a steady loss in the role of our hands in the penetration and shaping of the world."[32] We are in this sense, atrophying, "dying," and deaesthetization should be viewed as a social disease that medicine must attend to, even at the expense of ignoring more startling technological breakthroughs of limited scope.

The Jamesian self as viewed here is active, yet fragile. Constructed from a cultural web of relational interactions with the environment, it can ebb and grow, but within limits. Progress is possible, but not all is progress. As James asked in *Pragmatism,* "Doesn't the fact of 'no' stand at the very core of life? Doesn't the very 'seriousness' that we attribute to life mean that ineluctable noes and losses form a part of it, that there are genuine sacrifices somewhere, and that something permanently drastic and bitter always remains at the bottom of its cup?"[33] In short, there is an individual self in James, but it is not foundational in any Cartesian sense. Rather does it come upon the scene through evolution. Once arisen however, it has some fragile sense of individuality that cannot be explained by being explained *away,* that is, as its being just another part of nature. Going further, the self is embodied, and grows, or dies, through interaction with its contexts—cultural and otherwise. Loss of open or challenging or inviting contexts will ultimately result in loss of self, that is, death. The Jamesian self is both processive and cumulative in the way described above, both an event and a process; it is also a self that cannot be generalized about in acontextual third-person discourse. Each self is in this sense "different," and these differences need to be preserved, difficult as this is to do while using language. It is through the bodily and the affective that such a variegated or pluralistic context is maintained. Finally, this perspective is one wherein death is "accepted" as inevitable, yet rebelled against. In a way not dissimilar to Pascal, James sees the human self as finite, yet refusing to accept the inevitability of the situation. Local rather than transcendental progress can be made. Furthermore, there is an important sense in which "the nectar is in the journey." Everyone tells, or should be allowed to tell, his own story. But in order for this to occur, the Jamesian description provided here, "thick" and individualistic as it is, must be pushed one step further, to a recognition of first-person creations over third-person accounts. We shall return to this theme in Chapter 8.

ELISABETH KÜBLER-ROSS:
THE STAGES OF DYING

Without doubt, the person most responsible for turning our attention to dying, as opposed to death, has been Elisabeth Kübler-Ross. She too begins her most famous work, *On Death and Dying*, with an attack on technology. The patient

> may cry for rest, peace, and dignity, but he will get infusions, transfusions, a heart machine, or tracheostomy if necessary. He may want one single person to stop for one single minute so that he can ask one single question—but he will get a dozen people around the clock, all busily preoccupied with his heart rate, pulse, electrocardiogram or pulmonary functions, his secretions or excretions but not with him as a human being. He may wish to fight it all but it is going to be a useless fight since all this is done in the fight for his life, and if they can save his life they can consider the person afterwards. Those who consider the person first may lose precious time to save his life! At least this seems to be the rationale or justification behind all this—or is it? Is the reason for this increasingly mechanical, depersonalized approach our own defensiveness? Is this approach our own way to cope with and repress the anxieties that a terminally or critically ill patient evokes in us? Is our concentration on equipment, on blood pressure our desperate attempt to deny the impending death which is so frightening and discomforting to us that we displace all our knowledge onto machines, since they are less close to us than the suffering face of another human being which would remind us once more of our lack of omnipotence, our own limits and failures, and last but not least perhaps our own mortality?[34]

As an alternative to this form of repression Kübler-Ross offers a phenomenology of dying that, she asserts, occurs in five "stages": denial, anger, bargaining, depression, and acceptance. Denial is the stage of "No, not me!" My chart has been mixed up with someone else's; a misdiagnosis had occurred, or some such. Although Kübler-Ross sees initial denial as a "healthy way of dealing with the uncomfortable and painful situation,"[35] she views the stage as temporary, and considers maintained denial to be a rarity. Anger is the stage of rage and envy, where the patient asks, "Why me?" "Why not the person next to me or down the street?" This is a stage that is difficult for the patient's family and the hospital staff to deal with, as the anger is displaced in all directions and projected randomly. Failure of those surrounding the patient to realize that the patient's anger has little or nothing to do with the people who become the target of their anger often results in truly tragic situations. The third stage, bargaining, is one wherein the patient enters into a sort of pact or agreement with God, for example, saying something like "All right, I have cancer, but just let me live to see my son married." Or, "OK, I'm dying but let me live to see the garden I planted come up." In other words, the patients are asking for an extension of life, promising afterwards to accept their situation. However, patients do not keep their original promises, but try rather to renegotiate the bargains into which they have entered. The fourth stage, depression, actually consists of two types. The terminally ill patient initially undergoes a "reactive" depression where he or she grieves over the loss of something once enjoyed in the past, such as good looks or a full head of hair. The second type, "preparatory" depression, consists of a patient's grieving over impending losses, that is, the loss of *all* love objects in the near future. These two "types" of depression are different in nature and should be dealt with differently. Specifically, some encouragement, in terms, say, of available breast prostheses for a cancer

patient is helpful for the first type of depression. But too much
encouragement in the second instance "hinders [the patient's]
emotional preparation rather than enhances it."[36] This last type
of depression is usually silent and is a tool to facilitate the fifth
and final stage, acceptance. "If a patient has had enough time
(i.e., not a sudden, unexpected death) and has been given some
help in working through the previously described stages, he will
reach a stage during which he is neither depressed nor angry
about his 'fate.' "[37] This is the acceptance stage, which is not a
happy one, but rather one almost void of any feelings.

Several questions arise at this point. To begin with, is it inevitable that all patients arrive at this stage? And, is it desirable
that they do so? In the chapter of *On Death and Dying* entitled
"Hope," Kübler-Ross states that "the one thing that usually
persists through all these stages is hope,"[38] which she says, at
least for some patients "remains a form of temporary but needed
denial."[39] Hope seems to be connected here with a form of non-
acceptance, perhaps even with a frail sense of rebellion against
one's situation, and if "all our patients maintained a little bit of it
and were nourished by it in especially difficult times,"[40] this
raises serious questions about the desirability of the acceptance
stage. Going further, Kübler-Ross had stated at the beginning of
this text that "this book is in no way meant to be judgmental";[41]
but it does indeed sound as if arrival at the fifth stage is viewed as
optimal. This impression is only deepened when she says, in a
later text: "I think most of our patients would reach the stage of
acceptance if it were not for the members of the helping professions, especially the physicians, who cannot accept the death of
a patient. If we as physicians have the need to prolong life
unnecessarily and to postpone death, the patient often regresses
[from acceptance] into the stage of depression and anger again
and is unable to die in peace and acceptance."[42] The language of
"regression" here is clearly value-laden or normative in tone and
sounds contradictory to the claim to be neutral. However, when

challenged about this, Kübler-Ross responded by saying that "it's a matter of semantics. The ideal would be if both the dying patient and the patient's family could reach the stage of acceptance before death occurs. . . . It is not our goal, however, to push people from one stage to another."[43] Even while acknowledging that patients will tend to die as they have lived, that is, in anger/rebellion or depression, for example, she continues to speak of only one stage as an "ideal" one. "Patients who are in the stage of acceptance show a very outstanding feeling of equanimity and peace. There is something very dignified about these patients."[44] This sounds like dignity is reserved for those in acceptance; further, it raises the more ominous question, to be discussed in Chapter 9, as to whether "death with dignity" exists at all, and whether it can be conferred by one person upon another.

CRITICS OF KÜBLER-ROSS

Without doubt Kübler-Ross's stages made a significant contribution to our understanding of the dying process. In actuality the "stages theory" was so successful that for some time criticism was hard to find. However, it did slowly begin to appear. Thus in "Is Acceptance a Denial of Death? Another Look at Kübler-Ross," Roy Branson makes two central criticisms. First, he accuses Kübler-Ross of prescribing as opposed to describing, that is, of recommending completion of a sequence. Why not, he asks, term denial, anger, bargaining, depression, and acceptance "types" of dying as opposed to stages?[45] Kübler-Ross's refusal to accept such a suggestion is only rendered more questionable when we remember that she herself distinguished two different *types* of depression in stage four. Second, Branson bristles at Kübler-Ross's portrayal of dying as a *natural* process, and as such, one that we should accept. To this tradition of "classical naturalism" which goes back at least to the Stoics, Branson opposes the Christian tradition, for whom death is the result of sin, in other words, unnatural and abnormal. The point of this opposition is not to advocate a blind acceptance of religion, but rather to argue that the Christian is the true realist who refuses to idealize either death or dying as simply the biological counterpart to birth.

> Dr. Kübler-Ross is not convincing when she tries to make death more acceptable as part of some natural cycle. Indeed, the Christian may become persuaded that the author's stages of dying describe a circle of their own: from denial through anger, bargaining and despair, back to another form of denial called acceptance. In fact, it may well be that acceptance of death returns the dying to a juvenile inability to face the facts; that the infantlike dependence and passivity of Kübler-Ross's stage of acceptance is the greatest sort of denial of death's reality.[46]

Similar criticisms of Kübler-Ross are leveled by James Carpenter, who charges that her "five stages of dying are divided into negative [denial, anger, bargaining, and depression] and positive [acceptance] responses to death."[47] There is no reason, for Carpenter, to say that someone who has been a fighter all his or her life and chooses to defy death has died badly, or achieved less somehow. Carpenter is most upset about Kübler-Ross's portrayal of the role of religion, as she describes it in a later text, *To Live Until We Say Good-bye*.[48] Religion's task, she claims, is to help patients finish up "unfinished business" in this life so that we can accept death, and to provide objective evidence of life after death. Such a view of religion, for Carpenter "requires too little of us, for what we seek is already assured and at a price that asks only our assent."[49] We are underwhelmed in this portrayal of religion, as opposed to, say, the function of religion for a thinker like Søren Kierkegaard. Rather, "the role of religion in death and dying is ideally not a comfort but a reminder to commit ourselves now to what we would make of ourselves. Supporting either acceptance or denial of death amounts to withdrawing from the struggle for life and meaning between these two extremes; both positions finally are untenable."[50] Here we witness again a hint that the binary of acceptance/rebellion needs to be transcended.

The most cynical critique of Kübler-Ross is Ron Rosenbaum's article, "Turn On, Tune In, Drop Dead." Rosenbaum believes that "things have gotten out of hand"[51] with this "whole misbegotten love affair with death" promoted by Kübler-Ross. His "solution" to the incurable suffering of dying patients would be a purely pharmacological one—the "Brompton's Cocktail," a "combination of equal parts of pure heroin and pure cocaine, with a dash of chloroform in an alcohol-and-cherry-syrup base."[52] However, such a solution is unavailable in the United States, at least not legally. The substitute drugs utilizing morphine and Thorazine do not constitute a similar solution—Thorazine actually being a treatment for psychotics. This failure is overcompensated for, Rosenbaum charges, by massive injections of sentimentality; we celebrate death, and turn adults into children, compliant dying children who happily accept death as a result of this behavior control. We have actually gone through a series of metamorphoses, or "stages" as Rosenbaum calls them with tongue in cheek, going from "worshipping the dying," or having reverence for the wisdom of the terminally ill; to "longing to be dying," or devoting one's life to preparing for death; to "playing dead," in terms of the romance of the near-death experience; to "playing with the dead," in terms of communication with the "other side." "By Stage 4, the dead are not really 'dead' at all."[53] Finally, there is stage five, or "going to bed with the dead," a reference to a cult church Kübler-Ross allied herself with in 1980, and whose minister, Jay Berham, claimed to be a sexual medium to the other world.

Rosenbaum does not present a very sustained argument to support his own position. He clearly favors a biological solution to the problem at hand. In addition, he shows himself to be unsympathetic to any form of Eastern thought, viewing it as "metaphysical heroin, a Brompton's Cocktail of the mind."[54] In spite of this, his conclusion is a challenging one, for it far transcends his own article, possibly applying, for example, even to readers of the present text. He tells the reader:

> Death has claimed another victim, the mind of Kübler-Ross. Another sad but predictable triumph of death over reason, another case of an interesting mind committing suicide. It begins to seem that thinking about death is, like heroin, not something human beings are capable of doing in small doses and then going about the business of life. It tends to take over all thought, and for death 'n' dying junkies, the line between a maintenance dose and an O.D. becomes increasingly fine.[55]

One wonders, however, whether this warning applies to the author himself, whether he would prefer to describe his own piece as an "unthinking" one, or, finally, whether he alone has managed to do just the right amount of thinking about this topic.

The most sustained critique of Kübler-Ross comes from Larry Churchill. In "The Human Experience of Dying: The Moral Primacy of Stories over Stages," Churchill commences by acknowledging that Kübler-Ross's "stages" have done a great deal of good in the health care community. But too literal an interpretation of the stage metaphor has resulted in the latter being blinding as well as illuminating. Churchill's initial critique is similar to the one offered by Branson and Carpenter, that is, that there is a "progressivist bias" to Kübler-Ross's presentation, rendering it prescriptive in nature. She also espouses a view of the acceptance stage as the only one that is aesthetically pleasing. The result of this is a tendency, especially on the part of nursing students or concerned laypersons, to engineer the process of how people ought to die. Viewing the fifth stage as the only aesthetically pleasing one tends to divide the whole process into two parts. Part one is "the battle," followed by part two, "the victory," that is, stage five. While the categories may help the health care professionals who work around the dying, Churchill charges that "to put the dying into stages is to control them and to deny them the needed opportunity to tell us what dying means to them."[56] Indeed, the labels, by creating expectations, serve to control not only the dying person but the very meaning of the experience itself. In this sense the dying become victims of the stages and are not allowed to interpret their own deaths.

Where Churchill's critique of Kübler-Ross makes a significant advance over the others discussed here is in his sketching out of a positive and more personal alternative to the stages theory. This alternative consists in defending a view of the person wherein "stories" have moral primacy over "stages." A story "is an account of incidents or events in a narrative or dramatic form."[57] Only individual dying persons are able to tell their particular stories, because only they know how the storyline goes. To use stages as replacements for stories, therefore, constitutes a form of "moral hubris."

> The point at issue here is that "story" is a category of interpretation for the experience of dying which is logically prior to "stage." The stories of dying persons are the primary data: stages are formal abstractions created by professionals who attend the dying. Stories are the primary texts; categorizations into stages are best seen as commentaries on these texts. Stories employ the words of patients; stages are couched in the languages of psychiatry, clinical psychology and the behavioral sciences. Stages are second-order creations.[58]

Each person, then, for Churchill, is best viewed as a narrator or storyteller, and the story of each cannot be generalized about without significant loss of meaning. Going further, stories, as opposed to stages, may or may not be progressive in nature; they may well proceed in a zigzag fashion, and may contain contradictions. Stories also are not always fully logical or consistent. "The narration of the meaning of death does not follow a catenarian, or chain-like sequence, but follows the story-line, with inconsistencies, sudden turns, and proleptic movements."[59] Advocating "acceptance" then is insufficient precisely because it is too acontextual. One needs to ask rather, "What does *this* particular acceptance mean?" Stages, in short, are not true to how dying people have their experiences; they *replace* the latter rather than recapturing it.

Most important, the binary contained in the stages between "anger versus acceptance" or "denial versus acceptance" is rejected by Churchill. "Many persons combine acceptance of terminal illness with defiance toward both the disease and, in some instances, God. We do these persons a disservice if we try to describe their responses solely in terms of a psychological understanding of anger."[60] Many patients accept the inevitability of their impending death, and still continue to evince hope or courage. Here again it is the vagueness or the rich ambiguity of the situation that is forcing a rejection of any articulation of the problematic in too exclusive a fashion. Going further, even if the stages were an accurate description of how dying persons undergo their experiences, which they are not, they should not be forced upon dying people. "Self determination remains the cardinal ethical principle."[61]

Much as William James asked that "the basis of discussion . . . be broadened and thickened up,"[62] and as Dena Davis called for "thick description" in case studies,[63] so too Churchill here calls for a "thick sense of narrative,"[64] wherein idiosyncratic space is not only tolerated but nurtured, and where the dying assume a teaching role. "What the dying have to teach the living is not that they all uniformly cope with dying in stages, but that each is as unique and individual in dying as in living. Nobody dies by the book."[65] Finally, only as the dying are allowed and encouraged to function as storytellers do they maintain their status in a

community, as opposed to being abandoned or avoided. Ironically enough, it is through the affirmation of personal narration
that the bifurcation between the individual and the community
can be overcome—if the dying person can be viewed as a narrator in two senses of the term. First, he or she is the author or
creator of a life story, including its final moments, and, as such,
should be allowed to function as "artist" until the very end. But
second, the dying person as narrator also functions as a teacher,
in the sense of describing and explaining her life to others. "The
dying teach those who attend them what their experiences of
dying mean. . . . The narratives of the dying support the living by
providing structures of meaning to which the living can relate
and from which they can draw strength, comfort, or at least
interpretability."[66] There is, to be sure, a creative tension involved here, between what an individual intends by a specific
expression, and what that expression means to her audience.
The richest interpretation of the dying process will preserve both
the first-person and the second-person aspects of narration. This
approach will also serve as a reminder that there are limits to the
concept of "self-determination," since the latter comes to us
filtered through social construction.

Churchill's critique focuses upon the personal and the affective, in a way not unlike John McDermott's presentation of
the affective dimension in the doctor-patient relationship. Both
thinkers are suspicious of an overly rationalistic approach. Both
emphasize the body. Both worry about the power of language
and yet its inability to deal with the inarticulate or personal.
Finally, in both of these accounts, as well as elsewhere in the
discussion, there seems to be emerging a correlation between the
affirmation of the individual person qua individual and a refusal
to *completely* accept the acceptance model. That is, the more one
emphasizes the body's uniqueness, the more one upholds the
need for hope, the more one does *not* see the self as part of a long
ongoing process (Morison) or as part of the cosmos (Stoics), the

more difficult it seems to be to rest content with acceptance. This theme will be taken up in some detail in Chapter 9.

CONCLUSION

The present volume began with several case studies, which is the way issues about death and dying are most commonly discussed nowadays. While these can indeed be illuminating, as opposed to formal ethical systems that are universal and acontextual in character, it was also noted that we need to preserve "thick" descriptions, and to question the impartiality of descriptions in general. With an eye toward doing this we turned to several historical contexts, to see if death had changed its meaning from epoch to epoch or culture to culture. Several authors argued that we have gone from "acceptance" to "denial," as we "progressed" from, say, the fifteenth to the twentieth century. The implication of these pieces, for the most part, was that this was not a good thing. The issue of acceptance versus denial arose in a similar though by no means identical manner in Japan, in the Japanese view of death as "outside," and in the ongoing debate over which definition of death to employ.

This was followed by several thinkers who argued that this form of articulation was not the problem at all, that is, that the issue was biological and not historical, and that perhaps medicine could be looked at as a science. From the point of view of these thinkers, therefore, the historical/cultural approach constitutes a form of denial, and the biological one a form of acceptance. A sub-battle took place at this stage among advocates of a particular biological definition of death, whether respiratory/circulatory failure or whole-brain death or neocortical failure. This debate terminated in the charge that this also was not the problem, that a new definition of death was not what was needed, only more concern for the *dying*.

To some degree it can be argued that Morison and Kübler-Ross argue for acceptance of the process of dying on a general level, while McDermott and Churchill argue for the importance of the personal, the particular, or the affective, even if this results in some form of denial or rebellion. On the surface, the position most often credited with bringing back the primacy of acceptance is that of Kübler-Ross. However, the cumulative impact of her several critics is enough to cast serious doubt upon this assumption, and to raise the question as to whether complete acceptance is either possible or desirable.

This same question may then be asked about complete denial or rebellion, and subsequently the exclusivity of the alternatives may be challenged (as has been done to some degree already by Churchill in the article discussed above). This challenge emerges most clearly when one dwells upon the particularity of a specific dying person, and does not jump too quickly into categories. Doing so requires a willingness to preserve the vagueness, the idiosyncrasy, the ambiguity of the situation, including its affective dimension. This task is rendered doubly difficult when one realizes that language per se is ill equipped to do this, being by nature much more at home with universal formulations, abstractions, and third-person descriptions. On the other hand, language is all we have, and so one has, as William Carlos Williams said:

> To make a start,
> out of particulars
> and make them general, rolling
> up the sum, by defective means . . .[67]

In the following chapter, the "particulars" consist in individual portraits of people dying. Here too at first glance the portraits will appear to be a straightforward description of Socrates, Ivan Ilych, and Zarathustra. But here too language is, or can be, deceiving, especially when it is viewed as exclusively descriptive in nature. In opposition, we shall argue that language in these portraits functions on several different levels. Viewing language as functioning on only one level, that is, the descriptive, would, from this perspective, constitute another form of denial.

[[EIGHT]]

Three Portraits of Dying:
Socrates, Ivan Ilych, Zarathustra

In the last chapter it was noted that the work of Elisabeth Kübler-Ross has been met with wide acclaim, and that one of its central tenets was the reintroduction of dying as a very natural part of life. However, we also witnessed critics who have attacked this view as being not merely a description of how people die, but rather a covert prescription of how people ought to die, with acceptance viewed as an optimum state. On the other hand, advocates of the acceptance position point out that Kübler-Ross's analysis of death as "natural" is actually nothing new; they often turn to two specific portraits of persons who "accepted" death: Plato's Socrates and Tolstoy's Ivan Ilych.

In actuality the two portraits referred to here are more complicated than might initially appear. In addition, it will be seen that portraits as a genre are prescriptive rather than merely descriptive. As such, they deny and repress at least some aspects of their subject matter. Further, there is irony in both portraits, although the irony is *intended* in Plato's account but not in Tolstoy's. Finally, the intended irony alluded to in the case of Plato's Socrates will serve as an anticipation to the also ironic conclusion of the present volume, that is, that you cannot wait or prepare for death, and also that you cannot avoid/deny waiting or preparing. This point becomes clearer as we compare and contrast these two portraits with a third one, that of Nietzsche's Zarathustra.

PLATO'S SOCRATES

In the dialogues on the actual death of Socrates, we are given a picture not of death but of the process of dying. I want to suggest that Plato was an excellent student of the art of dying. He tells us in the *Phaedo* that "those who really apply themselves in the right way to philosophy are directly and of their own accord preparing themselves for dying and death."[1] In the *Apology, Crito,* and *Phaedo,* therefore, we might expect great attention to be paid to the details of Socrates' dying. And indeed, we are not disappointed.

First, in the *Phaedo* the poison-giver asks Socrates not to talk too much because it will overheat him. Here we are presented with a straightforward "medical" plea not to upset the applecart, to "kick off" according to schedule. Although the jailer feels sorry for Socrates, his death is something that must be carried out. One is reminded of a family attending a sick member at a hospital, and viewing the sick person's dying as a discomfort for others. Indeed, much the same point is made in the *Crito,* where Crito himself tries to dissuade Socrates from going through with dying because people will say that he (Crito) has let Socrates down, and because Socrates' actions will result in his (Crito's) losing a friend.[2] Finally, Crito accuses Socrates of taking the easy way out. Here Socrates' death is seen as inducing anger, perhaps as a defense mechanism against impending grief, but also because Socrates' death is being perceived in terms of "the family" and not "the patient." In the *Phaedo,* Crito again tries to deny the reality of Socrates' death. Even after the arguments concerning the immortality of the soul have been presented, he tries to convince Socrates that it is too early to take the hemlock, that the sun has not really set yet, and so on.[3] Here again Plato gives us a picture of someone trying to interpret Socrates' death for his own benefit. Crito seems to grieve over Socrates' imminent death, but also to feel anger at Socrates' deserting him.

At first glance then, most if not all of the psychological responses described by Elisabeth Kübler-Ross are to be found in the dialogues. The responses are not placed within one character but rather distributed among several. Some feel grief, some anger. Depression at impending loss characterizes some of Crito's arguments, and at one level at least Socrates seems to exemplify acceptance. Why the responses are spread among several characters rather than located in one is a matter of conjecture. But one possibility is that the complexity of the human individual was something that Greek philosophy was only beginning to focus upon. This interpretation is strengthened when we recall that Plato later moved from a two-part to a three-part theory of the soul in the *Republic*.[4]

The above description constitutes one perspective on Socrates' death. On the surface, he looks like someone who simply believes in the afterlife, and who is therefore resigned to this life and to dying. Philosophy is the preparation for death, and death is the departure of the soul from the body. In this sense, Socrates is a proto-Stoic and death is not really extinction or annihilation; it is, rather, a transition.

However, there is another level to Plato's Socrates, and this one revolves around the ironic, the paradoxical. We must remember that in the *Symposium* Socrates is portrayed by Alcibiades as someone who "spends his whole life playing his little game of irony, and laughing up his sleeve at all the world."[5] Also, the *Apology,* which is the reaffirmation of his life in the face of death, ends with a quip. Socrates says to the jury: "Now it is time that we were going, I to die and you to live, but which of us has the happier prospect is unknown to anyone but God."[6] The *Phaedo* ends with another ironic comment. Socrates, while dying, offers a cock to Asclepius, the god of healing.[7] In the *Crito,* Socrates, with tongue in cheek, says that since he (Crito) is not to die in the morning, he is not likely to have his judgment upset by this (Socrates') impending calamity.[8] In short, the very pervasiveness of this ironic cast of mind demands our attention.

A clue can be found in Robert Downs's novel *Going Gently,* the story of two people, an academic and a salesman, both of whom have terminal diseases. The salesman rages against his impending doom, but the stance of the teacher remains that of sarcastic irony. A revealing passage in the novel gives the reason for this difference.

> "Jesus, but I see red sometimes," Mr. Flood [the salesman] said. "You're most fortunate," Mr. Miller [the academic] answered. "All the books I've read say that getting angry is the best therapy. I'm afraid, however, that is not in my repertoire of counter-attack."[9]

Gregory Vlastos makes a similar point about Socrates' general character in an insightful article entitled "The Paradox of Socrates": "Jesus wept for Jerusalem. Socrates warns Athens, scolds it, exhorts it, condemns it. But he has no tears for it. One wonders if Plato, who raged against Athens, did not love it more in his rage and hate than ever did Socrates in his sad and good-tempered rebukes."[10] Leaving aside the question of who really loved Athens more, it does seem that anger is not in Socrates' repertoire of feelings. However, as we have seen, he often indulges in extreme irony. The "cruelest" joke of the *Phaedo* is that the arguments for the immortality of the soul don't work. And Plato's Socrates goes out of his way to show the reader that they don't work. To begin with, Simmias and Cebes voice objections to the argument from opposites and the argument from recollection. In a more ironic vein, Socrates "proves" that, since soul is defined as the principle of life, there is no such thing as a "dead soul"—which is not the same as to prove that an immortal soul exists.[11] Indeed the final argument involving the Forms comes down to something like the following: If there are eternal Forms there must be an eternal part of us to know them. Like any implication statement, this one does not necessarily establish the truth of either proposition. Finally, the *Phaedo* ends with a myth, a "likely story" about the afterlife. It is important to remember that myths become more and more important in Plato. This one has religious, scientific, and geographical dimensions. As Paul Friedlander has noted, by use of myth, Plato

> escapes the danger of a metaphysical dogmatism, just as the artistic form of the dialogue avoids the fixity of the written word, and irony the danger of dogmatic seriousness. The achievement of the myth is that it renders intelligible the mysterious aspects of life, and it does so not only by evoking a vague sentiment. Our intuitive imagination is led along a clear and firm path of ancestral tradition; both the knowledge gained through the dialectical method and the moral obligations immediately felt lead to the myth, and the myth leads back to knowledge and obligation.[12]

Indeed, at the end of the myth Socrates reminds us that it is a likely story. The myth remains fundamentally ambiguous or uncertain. As such it is not something that we can remain neutral toward or passively accept. It compels commitment or participation, as does the dialogue form itself.

The same situation exists regarding Socrates' attitude toward death. In the *Phaedo* Socrates is allowed to participate in his own death. The context in which he goes through the process of dying is a familiar one—the dialogue setting. Socrates is allowed to die "at home," so to speak. Furthermore, decisions on his death are not made without his opinion. Right up to the end "the patient" (Socrates) is forced to defend his actions and is therefore acknowledged as important, as growing and contributing something even through the art of dying. Because Phaedo does not pity Socrates (which would really be to pity himself), he can learn from Socrates' dying. Xanthippe is put "on stage" only long enough to administer a dose of hysteria (or possibly self-pity). She cannot learn from his death, nor help him with the process of dying, so she is led away. (It must be said that her whole portrayal here remains quite questionable.) But in general Socrates is not deserted while dying; although there are occasional "relapses" into redefining his death by those present for their own purposes, nonetheless the sense of "being with" pervades the dialogue. And it does so on a level above that of pity. But as a final act of participation, Socrates' death is not something he can look at passively and objectively; rather it is something that he is involved with. It is, in short, mysterious, and fundamentally so.

Socrates then is wrongly seen as simply accepting death while others around him are angry (Crito) or hysterical (Xanthippe) about it. In other words, it is more accurate to say that Socrates' basic attitude toward death remains ironic rather than merely accepting. Death remains ambiguous for him. He believes in an afterlife, but has reflected on his belief long enough to realize that it entails the possibility of being wrong, and that this ambiguity is what is important about his belief state. Even concerning death he "knows that he doesn't know what he thought he knew" (*aporia*).[13] This is also the meaning of his statement in the *Apology:* "To be afraid of death is only another form of thinking that one is wise when one is not; it is to think that one knows what one does not know."[14]

In sum, our interpretation of the death scene reveals that Plato intentionally portrays Socrates' attitude toward death in an ironic way. An ironic situation is fundamentally ambiguous or indeterminate. It depends for its very being on "what might have been" or "what might yet be." At a second level, an open-textured situation, just because it is imprecise, compels a response or a commitment. It must be interpreted. Socrates' own death, as an ironic situation, cannot simply be acquiesced to. It must be appropriated, or dealt with. Furthermore, the appropriation presented by Plato in the portrait, precisely because it involves selectivity, also involves rejection. We return to this point below.

TOLSTOY'S IVAN ILYCH

On one level, Tolstoy's story of Ivan Ilych is a clear, realistic portrayal of the agonizing process of dying and the indifference a person's dying connotes to his so-called friends and, surprisingly, also to his wife.[15] Denial is a stance maintained by these people to the end, and Ivan himself goes through the stage of denial. However, Ivan arrives at the stage of confronting death—simply beholding it and not being able to do anything about it. He then enters into anger—particularly at the people around him who are in denial and who continually deceive him. He becomes depressed in two senses: First, in the sense of realizing that his past life may have been lived in vain. This makes no sense to him because he has lived so "properly" and "correctly." Second, Ivan becomes depressed in the sense that not only might his past life have been lived in vain, but he has no more time, no space of action, in short, no possibility of doing anything about it in the future. He finally reaches the stage of "acceptance." Ivan accomplishes this by *realizing* that he has lived in vain.[16] There is a sense here that the examined life is worth living, even if the examination is late in coming. Ivan's consummatory judgment that his life has been in vain gives meaning to his life and makes his life whole.

The assumption here seems to be that if one's life has meaning, even a last little bit as with Ivan, then death loses its sting. However, Ivan here knows that he hasn't lived the good life, but he doesn't know what the good life is. Said in another way, Ivan knows that what he's been attached to is worthless, so it's not the most difficult thing in the world to give it up. This is perhaps the beginning of an authentic existence, but it hardly seems strong enough to constitute the end. Realistically, one cognitive realization does not give one the courage to accept death objectively. As Hugh Fausset has noted, "When Ivan ceased to claim that his life had been good, he did not really comprehend in what a good life consists. He merely ceased to desire life for himself and so found death acceptable. . . . Tolstoy expressed in this story the identity between a mean, egotistic life and death, but . . . he invested a mere abandonment of the will to live with a moral value which it cannot possess."[17]

Ivan at this stage goes through a second act, or rather a second aspect of his first act of abandoning the will to live. He feels sorry for his son and his wife, and thinks he is making them wretched in continuing to live.[18] He replaces his egoic outlook not with an intersubjective experience, but rather with an altruistic abdication of self in the face of the other. Tolstoy would have us believe that this renunciation of self in favor of the other is sufficient to deny death's sting. Life here appears deceptively simple. One lives most authentically through self-effacement; one's goal should be to disappear in the midst of the other. But indeed Tolstoy's assertion rings false. Self-effacement is not synonymous with acceptance. It is, rather, its contrary. Lavrin seems quite correct in his thesis that "Tolstoy tried to conceal his fear by coquetting with death; by exalting it even into a semblance of joy."[19] There is, in short, irony in Tolstoy's portrait of death, but it is unintended. The irony exists in the fact that Tolstoy, in trying to advocate acceptance of death, failed to accomplish his task. One gets the impression that the artist in Tolstoy started portraying death realistically but that the moralist won out. In short, Tolstoy, in painting a picture of Ivan's accepting death, really painted a picture of deception or denial. Ruth Davies catches this point well: "It does not help that in his last moment of consciousness, as the disfigurements of life fall away from him, Ivan Ilyitch has an awareness of reconciliation and illumination as if cleansing waters have bathed his soul. Whether or not he intended to do so, Tolstoy created the impression that Ivan Ilyitch—Everyman—has to pay too much for that intimation of peace."[20]

This then is really an "absurd" situation. Tolstoy, in trying to portray death, fails to do so; and his portrait of Ivan as accepting death is really an indication of something Tolstoy either did not realize, or would not admit—that death could not be objectively accepted.

NIETZSCHE'S ZARATHUSTRA

Since Nietzsche set his whole philosophy over against that of "the rational Socrates," and since the latter, at least in Plato's portrait, viewed the study of philosophy as the "preparation for death,"[21] it is perhaps not inappropriate to look at the opposing portrait offered by Nietzsche. Just who is Zarathustra? Initially, he is presented as the herald of the overman or overperson. But as the text develops, it becomes more and more apparent that he is to take on the burden himself, rather than act as a beacon. Most important, as Kathleen Higgins has noted, Zarathustra, "although the harbinger of a new worldview, is presented as an ordinary human being. He has limitations, and often enough we see his limitations turning into foibles."[22] And again, "Zarathustra's glib formulations, pronounced to his disciples with increasing fluency, are only one aspect of Zarathustra's chronicle. Nietzsche also includes a number of scenes in which Zarathustra's composure and eloquence break down. The reports of Zarathustra's nightmare, visions, private emotional outbursts, etc., provide an ironic subtext that comments on Zarathustra's public presentations."[23]

It is this ironic subtext that is of most importance in looking at Zarathustra's approach toward death, which is not analyzable in a simple acceptance or denial "either/or" fashion. The message of Silenus, in *The Birth of Tragedy,* was that it would have been better not to have been born, and second, having been born, to die as quickly as possible.[24] The question posed by Nietzsche—wrongfully posed in an Apollonian fashion—was "Can one look into the abyss and laugh?" That is, can one note how fragile life is, sometimes how unsusceptible it is to rational analysis, and still "dance"—or write a tragedy?

Thus Spoke Zarathustra is a tragedy—or at least Nietzsche thought so. Zarathustra initially comes down from the mountain to teach people *not* the death of God, but the *consequences* of the death of God.[25] He is unsuccessful in addressing the people, managing to catch only one "dead soul," or corpse, whom he comforts just before death. The "Prologue" then, or preface, is a false start, going nowhere; it is "deadening," and Zarathustra has to begin anew, this time creating disciples rather than assuming the crowd's allegiance. Much of book one is devoted to this task. By its end, some disciples have indeed been created, and Zarathustra seems prepared to teach one last lesson, how to die, and equally important, *when* to die. "Many die too late, and a few die too early. The doctrine still sounds strange: 'Die at the right time!' "[26] And even this message is not for everyone, that is, not for the superfluous who have not lived at the right time. And just what is the "right time"? The answer is when one's death can serve as a "spur," prodding one's new-formed disciples to overcome one, to go further or pass one by. It is a freely accepted death, in the sense that willing it liberates the willer. "Unlike the Epicurean teaching on suicide, according to which life may be terminated when it is no longer pleasant, and unlike the Stoic teaching, which counsels suicide in the face of personal distress that cannot be mastered, Zarathustra's teaching requires that a free death be undertaken solely for its effect on an audience."[27] If "mankind" is to be overcome, if there is to be a bridge toward the future, then when Zarathustra has given his gift of "uneasiness," to live longer would be to become superfluous, to become a burden to the task at hand.

This then is the best way to die; there is, however, a runner-up: "Second to this [best way], . . . is to die fighting and to squander a great soul."[28] Rebellion here seems to triumph over mere acceptance. Worst of all are the avoiders. As Nietzsche says playfully: "Verily I do not want to be like the ropemakers: they drag out their threads and always walk backwards."[29] In other words, one must come to celebrate finitude.

Ironically enough, Zarathustra, having delivered this spur/ message to the chosen few, does *not* act as he spoke. Having "thrown his golden ball" to his disciples, he lingers awhile on the earth to see what will happen, and asks his disciples to forgive him for this. His desire here is personal and private, and as such it deprives his disciples of an important occasion. "His disciples would have done well to have thought hard about forgiving him, for they have become disciples of a master less dedicated to the cause that he himself invented than were those masters . . . whose teachings on life and death he aims to supplant—Socrates . . . and Jesus."[30] The possibility exists that this is not the right time, and furthermore, no bell ever goes off to indicate that a given moment *is* the right one. Indeed, the subsequent books of the text serve as evidence that Zarathustra has *not* given all that he can, that is, that there is more to be taught. Even the present failure to do as he preaches continues to teach; it discloses Zarathustra as human, as flawed, and hence as capable of being surpassed, whether by others or by himself.

Books two and three bear out this second interpretation, although in another sense (eternal recurrence) nothing changes; everything remains the same. Zarathustra realizes that he is not *only* the herald of the overman, but rather must himself freely undertake the task of becoming the overman. This process consists in realizing that will to truth depends upon will to power, but that ultimately the latter requires the affirmation of eternal return. By book three Zarathustra has realized that "in the end, one experiences only oneself."[31] This realization includes his confrontation with the dwarf or "spirit of gravity"; each tries to slay the other with alternative cyclical visions of time. The dwarf holds that time is circular and faces the future with a certain amount of contempt or loathing. Zarathustra intensifies the argument presented by the dwarf, asserting that everything will repeat itself *exactly,* and that he, Zarathustra, can say "yea" to this, that is, can say, "Was *that* life? Well then! Once more!"[32] Courage then is the weapon used by Zarathustra to club to death, first, dizziness before the abyss; second, pity; and third, even death itself by the affirmation of life as eternal recurrence. "It is clear from this hymn to courage that Zarathustra and the spirit of gravity are not polar opposites existing by virtue of one another in an endless oscillation of ascent and descent; rather, they are contraries or deadly enemies. Mastery for one is death for the other; as both speakers in the vision attest, 'I! or You!' To club the Dwarf to death is to club to death the whole rational, Socratic tradition."[33]

For many commentators, the natural culmination to the work takes place at the end of part three. Zarathustra has "overcome" the "choking knowledge" that accepting the doctrine of eternal recurrence entails accepting not only the "good," but also the "bad and the ugly," so to speak, and even the infirm or the "crippled." Zarathustra, convalescing and confronted by Life with his own mortality, has nonetheless not tried to alter her, has not chosen supposedly immortal wisdom over her. Rather naming Life "Eternity," he announces that she is the only woman with whom he wishes to have children. Zarathustra has realized that Will to Truth depends upon Will to Power, and that the latter requires him to joyfully affirm the doctrine of eternal recurrence. As the text itself says, "Thus *ends* Zarathustra's going-under."[34]

But the text does not end here. A fourth part was written, and circulated in secret, which for commentators like Lampert "violates the ending of Part III,"[35] but which Nietzsche himself termed the "Last Part."[36] One commentator who challenges the received view of the text properly ending with part three views the presentation of Zarathustra in part four as resembling in some respects the ass in Apuleius's satire *The Golden Ass*. Zarathustra is presented as a bit of a buffoon who is in danger, sometimes, of taking his own doctrine too seriously, and, consequently of *pitying* others. The richness of this interpretation cannot be dealt with in detail here, but one point is important to our theme, namely, the issue of acceptance versus denial of Life, and hence, of Death, since finitude accompanies her. In addition, *how* one accepts or denies, seriously or playfully, or both, now becomes of central importance. The heroic stance proffered in the earlier chapter "On Free Death" is here further undermined. Both Zarathustra and Lucius the ass function rather as "out-of-place heroes . . . [who] reveal a side of life that is not susceptible to direct observation."[37] Zarathustra is trying, still, to "love the earth," but realizing, and disclosing more and more that, ironically enough, taking life "seriously" means taking it as "play." While there is some validity to the assertion that "from the tragic point of view, the end of *Zarathustra* makes sense,"[38] there is even more validity in realizing that the text is outgrowing comedy and tragedy as *exclusive* alternatives, coming close, at times, to a "tragicomedy." We must remember that the subtitle of *Thus Spoke Zarathustra* is "A Book for All and None," that is, for everyone and no one. In returning to our major topic, the portrait of Zarathustra offered seems in the end to indirectly disclose that we can neither accept death and dying, nor deny them—or perhaps that we cannot avoid either. As Jacques Choron has noted, Nietzsche himself was ambivalent about the subject of death and dying:

> Eternal recurrence was for Nietzsche at once terrifying and sooth-ing. . . . There can be no doubt that . . . [his] attitude to death was ambivalent. At first death did appear to him to be a liberation from an unbearable existence. . . . On the other hand, death often appeared to him to be an enemy. There are utterances showing an attempt toward reconciliation with the necessity of dying: "One is certain to die, why should one not be gay? . . . Death belongs to the conditions of true progress . . . the act of dying is not so important after all." But then there is open resentment—"Hateful to the fighter is the sneering death"—and there is open revolt—"Let's break the tablets of the preachers of death!"[39]

CONCLUSION

The criticism might be raised that "portraits" of dying persons gleaned from literary or philosophical texts are too unrealistic. In response it may be pointed out that numerous contemporary bioethical articles on death and dying make at least passing references to Socrates or Ivan Ilych.[40] These references disclose a need we seem to have for role models in discussing the issue of death and dying. There are, admittedly, "real-life" alternatives, such as the portrait of Dax Cowart, which has become famous in the literature.[41] The case of Karen Anne Quinlan also comes to mind. While the latter two portraits can claim to be "real," they are not necessarily more "realistic." Indeed, because they have become matters of public record, they sometimes tend to be couched in overly legalistic terminology, thereby masking important dimensions of the human situation. On the other hand, Socrates and Ivan have stood the test of time, and in that sense have proven their reality as useful portrayals. They are clear instances of "thick description." However, sometimes their ability to endure through time has resulted in their been taken in too uncritical a fashion. We have argued that in both the case of Socrates and of Ivan there is more there than at first meets the eye, though the subtext may not have been intended by each author.

The case of Zarathustra may, at first glance, seem more out of place than the first two. After all, it remains somewhat debatable just how "human" Zarathustra is. But a recent article on assisted suicide by Margaret Battin clearly discloses how close a connection sometimes exists between literature and the real world. Battin contends that while the English language employs only one term for causing one's own death, *suicide,* German provides four: "Selbstmord," "Selbsttotung," "Suizid," and "Freitod."[42] She concentrates upon the first and last of these, arguing that *Selbstmord* "carries extremely negative connotations . . . including the implication of moral wrong."[43] It is, in this sense, analogous to the English term *suicide*, which also carries around negative conceptual baggage, due in large part to the influence of Christianity. The alternative German term, however, is positive in nature, and does not connote either pathological or moral wrongdoing. "*Selbstmord* is taken to involve a generally repugnant, tragic act, generally associated with despair, anger, or depression; *Freitod*, in contrast, is seen as expressing voluntary, idealistic choice."[44] Important for our purposes is Battin's contention that the etymological source of the word *Freitod* arises from Nietzsche's *Thus Spoke Zarathustra*, and specifically from section twenty-two, "On Free Death." To repeat, one must die at the right time. "The death to be avoided is the 'common, withered, patient death' of those who are 'like sour apples': their lot is to 'wait until the last day of autumn: and at the same time they become ripe, yellow, and shriveled.' The death that Zarathustra preaches is an active, extraordinary, heroic death, an earlier, self-willed death of which the ordinary man is hardly capable."[45] Achieving such a death is difficult but is viewed as both admirable and heroic. Today's Germans, then, make a distinction between "euthanasia," which they see as a political term associated with the Nazi tradition, and "assisted suicide," which they openly permit. They "see" the issue of assisted suicide differently than Americans, because the issue is framed in a different language. There simply is no term in English to correspond to *Freitod*. "Even in situations of terminal illness, the very concept of voluntary death resonates differently for the German speaker who conceives of it as *Freitod* than it does for the English speaker who conceives of it as *suicide*."[46] This is clearly a version of the Whorf-Sapir hypothesis,[47] and it raises anew some of the problems dealt with in Chapter 3, namely, to what extent can we see matters from the point of view of the other? And to what extent is the notion of personal autonomy socially constructed? "Language is crucial in shaping attitudes about end-of-life practices, and because of the very different lexical resources of English and German, it is clear that English speakers cannot straightforwardly understand the very different German conception of these matters."[48] Battin does not believe that translation across cultures is completely impossible. But the issue will be difficult, given the limitations of language, and perhaps necessarily incomplete. However, the attempt must be made, if we are to avoid "isolationist myopia about social issues," although our inability to distinguish in English between *Selbstmord* and *Freitod* may mean that "we English speakers cannot even fully understand our own assumptions and beliefs about these matters."[49]

There is an irony here, though it is unintended. Battin astutely reveals the origins of the German attitude toward "free death," as well as lending significant support to the Whorf-Sapir hypothesis. But she does not go on to deal with the character or portrait of Zarathustra beyond section twenty-two. Viewing Zarathustra more broadly, however, and including book four in the portrayal, creates a picture and an attitude toward death and dying much more complicated than the one disclosed in that single section. From this wider perspective, Zarathustra has some trouble with *either* complete acceptance *or* complete rebellion as alternatives.

In sum, the portraits of Socrates' and Ivan's deaths are often viewed as acceptance models. We have argued that this is at least overly simplistic. Though both characters seem to accept death, ultimately Socrates' position is more ironic, and more paradoxical. Ivan does accept death, but Tolstoy's portrayal leaves the reader with the sense of having been duped. Nietzsche's portrayal of Zarathustra is also intentionally ironic, seeking to overturn the entire rationalistic tradition in the West. Indeed, he lays the primary blame for rationalistic inquiry at the feet of Socrates, who did not comprehend and hence did not like what he saw in Greek tragedy, and therefore presumed to "correct existence."[50] With Socrates consciousness is centered and instinct marginalized; he therefore does not have "the natural fear of death," but rather approaches it with calmness; further, *"the dying Socrates* [as opposed to the tragic hero trying to look into the abyss and laugh when confronted with the message of Silenus] became the new ideal,"[51] in short, the new portrait. But this seeming "acceptance model," Nietzsche charges, is in reality only a dodge, a form of denial.

> What were we to say of the end (or worse, of the beginning) of all inquiry? Might it be that the "inquiring mind" was simply the human mind terrified by pessimism and trying to escape from it, a clever bulwark erected against the truth? Something craven and false, if one wanted to be moral about it? Or if one preferred to put it amorally, a dodge? Had this perhaps been your secret, great Socrates? Most secretive of ironists, had this been your deepest irony?[52]

In opposition, we have argued that the portrait of Socrates as found in Plato is more complicated than that allowed for by Nietzsche, and that the ironic stance is at least partly intentional rather than accidental as in Tolstoy. This puts Socrates closer to Zarathustra than to Ivan, and is in sympathy with Nietzsche's request for a "dancing Socrates." Nonetheless, Nietzsche's basic point remains untouched, that is, that complete acceptance seems to be an idealization, masking pieces of denial or rebellion. Going further, however, we have argued that portraits *as a genre* seem, in one sense of the term, to "idealize" their subject matter, that is, to concentrate on some aspects and leave others out. Given that portraits tend to reify or idealize their subject matter, can any portrait be proclaimed better than another? We would argue that intentional irony is better than unintended irony, and that intentional irony characterizes both Plato's and Nietzsche's positions. But why employ intentional irony? If portraits, as idealizations, do in a sense deceive, isn't intentional deception worse than unintentional deception? It has often been held that lying, or intentional deception, is far worse than error.[53] Further, one can lie and yet never speak an actual falsehood. Consider, for example, responding to a question with a particular glance, or gesture, or responding by changing the subject in some fashion, or even by uttering a truth that is not relevant to the situation. Most important, consider a response that is intentionally only a partial truth, such as the doctor's possible response to an unexpected question by a "friend" of a patient when the patient has a terminal disease and does not want it known. In such a situation the doctor might well simultaneously intend to deceive and to disclose. The situation may be that complex, that demanding. Analogously, Plato and Nietzsche are justified in intentionally deceiving if what they wish to disclose can be revealed only in an indirect manner. For Plato, this is clearly true. For example, the world of the Forms, the *eidos,* is not directly present to the reader. It is indirectly presented in the *Phaedo* as a "hypothesis." Plato advocates a metaphysical theory of participation where we are involved *with* the Forms rather than looking *at* them as spectators. Such a position cannot be simply "pointed out." It is only in and through the world of the visual, of true opinion, that one makes progress toward becoming aware of the Forms. Going further, Plato does not objectively prove the Forms through logic. As we have seen earlier in this chapter, even when he uses reason, he leaves the reader with a myth, that is, a likely story. In short, he uses language and reason to disclose, but also to point out the limitations of language and reason.

Nietzsche, too, wishes to disclose the situation indirectly, or, more strongly put, believes that only indirect revelation is possible. There are numerous indications of this in the text. First, there is Zarathustra's statement that "this is *my* way," and that "*the* way . . . does not exist,"[54] that is, all views are perspectival, *including* the author presently writing, namely, Nietzsche. This same point is made in the "transition" from *The Birth of Tragedy* to *Thus Spoke Zarathustra*. In the preface to *The Birth of Tragedy*, written some fourteen years after the text itself, Nietzsche admitted that he had made a false start, because "the problem of science cannot be discerned on the groundwork of science."[55] His labors had produced a dead text, and he called for a "dancing Socrates" who could learn to laugh. That is, he called for Zarathustra. But even here intentional irony and perspectivalism continue, as it becomes clearer that Zarathustra is not the herald of the *Ubermensch* but *is* himself trying to become the *Ubermensch* by "going under."

In short, personal portraits disclose the possibility of transcending the acceptance/denial dichotomy. But *how* this is shown is as important as *what* is revealed; the disclosure here is indirect, first-person rather than third-person, and, when successful, is a matter of style. In the following chapter we focus upon the issue of "the person."

[NINE]

Acceptance Versus Denial:
The Overall Implications

PAUL RAMSEY: THE BODILY SELF AND
THE DENIAL MODEL

Several times in the preceding chapters the issue of "acceptance versus denial" has come to the fore, but it has yet to receive the attention it deserves, for this seminal concept governs our entire investigation of the problematic. Does one exist most authentically accepting death as part of life? Or, does one live best if one tries to rebel or deny one's finite situation? Or, third, can this binary be either transcended or internalized? This chapter will focus upon these central questions.

The occasion for commencing our investigation is an insightful article by Paul Ramsey entitled "The Indignity of 'Death With Dignity.'" One of the first thinkers to stress the importance of *only* caring for the dying, that is, avoiding a good deal of seemingly necessary medical intervention, Ramsey has more recently begun to worry that too many people were not only agreeing with this position, but were generalizing it into an all-too-bland statement about death with dignity or "calisthenic dying."[1] In opposition, Ramsey argues that "there is nobility in caring for the dying, but not in dying itself."[2] We cannot hand dignity to the dying person like it was a billiard ball; rather the most we might be able to do is remove some obstacles and manage to get out of the way.

Ramsey's point is actually twofold: First, death itself is not

166

dignified, "whether accepted or raged against";[3] second, talk about death as dignified constitutes a further indignity or insult. To drive home his position he turns to and proceeds to refute a series of arguments offered by death-with-dignity advocates. First, we are told that "death is simply a part of life." But, for Ramsey, this is unpersuasive, for we are not told whether it is a good or bad part of life. Disease is also a part of life; that does not necessarily make it dignified, or acceptable. So too with the argument that death is part of the evolutionary process, and, as such, a necessity; "the man who is dying happens not to be in evolution."[4] The individual qua individual is dying as a whole.

A classic but much different argument for viewing death as dignified had its origins with Epicurus (341–270 B.C.), who argued that one should not fear death precisely because it was *not* part of life. More specifically, Epicurus argued that "good and evil imply sentience, and death is the privation of all sentience. . . . Whatsoever causes no annoyance when it is present, causes only groundless pain in the expectation. Death, therefore, the most awful of evils, is nothing to us, seeing that, when we are, death is not come, and, when death is come, we are not."[5] But it is precisely death viewed temporally, not spatially, as something we must live "up against," but which we cannot experience or conceptualize that is so disheartening.[6] This is to say nothing of the fact that Epicurus's argument does not deal at all with *dying*. Going further, this view of death as a limit and therefore as a "prod" to us to get our lives in order can as easily function as an invitation to "disorder," or despair.

The suggestion that only "untimely" death is unnatural, that there is "a time to die," fares no better. "We know better how to specify an untimely death than to define or describe a 'timely' one."[7] Opinions to the contrary run the risk of descending the "slippery slope" to the stage where one makes suggestions concerning the departure of old people. Statements that "death," like "birth," is (or can be) beautiful, are also found to be wanting in their attempt to attain "innocence by association." Language functions here not to reveal but rather to conceal. "Talk about death as a fact or a reality seasonally recurring in life with birth or planting, maturity and growth, may after all not be very rational. It smacks more of whistling before the darkness descends."[8] Thingifying or beautifying death then is the wrong solution. "Death means *finis*, not in itself *telos*."[9]

Ramsey is much more sympathetic to the approach of Pascal, whom he quotes as saying that "man is but a reed, the feeblest in nature, but he is a thinking reed. . . . Were the universe to crush him, man would still be nobler than that which kills him, for *he knows that he dies*, while the universe knows nothing of the advantage it has over him. Thus our whole dignity consists in thought."[10] Here we see, for Ramsey, the greatness of the human being fused with his or her misery in the experience of death. Death cannot be viewed then as completely acceptable. "To deny the indignity of death requires that the dignity of man be refused also."[11]

Writing as a Christian ethicist, that is, not neutral, Ramsey characterizes the Hebrew tradition as preoccupied with sin, with death playing only a subordinate role. By contrast, in Greek religion death was central, and sin, or disobedience, was subordinate. Christianity "inseparably fused" these two, namely death and sin, in Western culture's awareness of personal existence. The result, at least within this context, is that "death may be a good evil [in that it teaches us to number our days] or an evil evil [in that it's a threatening limit that begets evil], but it is perceived as an evil or experienced indignity in either case."[12]

If death is as undignified as Ramsey would have us believe, if a "newly dead" body arriving at a hospital emergency awakens feelings of awe and dread,[13] then why is it that we tend to dignify death, or to wholeheartedly accept an acceptance model? For Ramsey, there are two ways in which the dreadful picture of death is reduced or masked. One way is to view bodily life as unimportant. Ramsey accuses Plato of holding this view, in offering an idealized and dualistic picture of Socrates in the *Phaedo*.[14] The second way to repress the problem is to hold to a philosophy or view of human life that sees the uniqueness of the individual person as transient or interchangeable. Aristotle's philosophy is offered as an example. Here the form/matter distinction is primary, the individual secondary. Ramsey sees additional instances in Eastern philosophy, wherein "the individual has only transiency."[15]

These then are the main ways of working oneself into accepting the acceptance model by denying the fear of death.

> Whenever these two escapes are simultaneously rejected—i.e., if the "bodily life" is neither an ornament nor a drag but a part of man's very nature; and if the "personal life" of an individual in his unique life-span is accorded unrepeatable, noninterchangeable value—then it is that Death the Enemy again comes into view. A true humanism and the dread of death seem to be dependent variables. I suggest that it is better to have the indignity of death on our hands and in our outlooks than to "dignify" it in either of these two possible ways.[16]

In sum, Ramsey's article has raised three points of significant importance for the overall theme of this book. First, it has claimed that the "acceptance model" can be associated with several general philosophies, such as Platonism, Aristotelianism, and Eastern thought; we might add objective idealism (Hegel) and evolutionary naturalism (process philosophy), among others. Alternatively, one might turn to existentialism (at least some forms) and personalism, and, if Ramsey is correct, to Christianity (again certain forms only) for proponents of a "denial model." Various forms of denial may be articulated, from rebellion (Camus) to the Pascalian tragic awareness of the situation. (However, as we shall see below sometimes a specific philosopher—Plato, for example—is claimed by proponents of both the acceptance and the denial models.) Secondly, Ramsey has specifically highlighted the bodily and the uniqueness of the person, in a way similar to that emphasized by William James, John McDermott, and Hans Jonas in Chapters 5 and 7 and he has claimed that these features are or should be associated with the denial model. And third, he has again brought up the issue of language, and indicated that it can and does function in many ways, that is, not only to describe, but also to divert, and hopefully, also to direct (readers) beyond itself to the primary experience at hand. Omitted from the analysis is the issue of the social construction of the self.

We now turn to three advocates of the acceptance model: Robert Morison, Leon Kass, and H. Tristram Engelhardt, Jr.

MORISON: PROCESS AND
THE ACCEPTANCE MODEL

In "The Dignity of the Inevitable and Necessary," Robert Morison argues that it is unclear whether Ramsey is talking about how to die, or just raging against it, as Dylan Thomas did. Arguing from a "pagan" perspective, Morison wants to focus on dying (i.e., not death) with dignity, and he holds that "at a certain stage in the process of dying, it is basically *un*dignified to continue casting desperately about for this or that potion, philter, or device to prolong some minor sign of life, after all reasonable chance for the reappearance of its major attributes has disappeared."[17] Admitting that his reaction here is an instinctive one, Morison nonetheless holds that we should strive to identify this final stage in the "downward trajectory" of an individual, the latter being viewed as a series of interactions with the environment. "It is not breathing, urinating, and defecating that makes a human being important even when he can do these things by himself. How much greater is the indignity when all these things must be done for him, and he can do nothing else?

Not only have means been converted into ends; the very means themselves have become artificial."[18] Here Morison and Ramsey would seem to agree in arguing against various "forms" of dying with supposed dignity, but not about the possible indignity of death itself. Morison "find[s] something basically undignified in a failure to accept the inevitable logic or the empirically demonstrable structure of the natural world."[19] Ramsey utilized the work of Pascal to bolster his position on the unnaturalness of death. The Stoics constitute Morison's counterpart. Let us extend his position here a bit.

As opposed to the Epicureans who utilized a basic denial model, the Stoics tried to root the human being in nature, as part and parcel of the wider scheme of things. One strove to live "according to nature," and death belonged as much to the cosmic order of things as life did.[20] One tries then, to become "indifferent" to death, impervious to harassment (*apathia*), via a form of metaphysical pantheism. "All things are implicated with one another," Marcus Aurelius said in the *Meditations*, "and the bond is holy."[21] Death should not be viewed as unnatural, for it is "not contrary to the reason of our constitution."[22] Further, it is by the change of individual parts, that "the whole universe continues ever young and perfect."[23] One should therefore live one's life as if each day were one's last, since "it is possible that you may depart from life this very moment."[24] The emphasis here is upon death being natural, therefore acceptable, and on our constantly dwelling upon this. Morison sees similarities between his respect for the Stoics and Ramsey's respect for Pascal, but we would argue that this analogy is pushed too far. Pascal's reflections disclosed that death was at least partly unnatural, tragic, and in some sense unacceptable—at least in Ramsey's interpretation. The Stoic outlook is much more rational than Pascal's, for whom "the heart has its reasons which reason does not know."[25]

For Morison, social interdependence is a fact, and "every

human death is ultimately for the good of the group."[26] He suggests that we not adopt a Freudian view of civilization, and that indeed many individuals find "self-sacrifice" to be the greatest challenge. But mostly Morison is content to reaffirm his biological model. "To rage with Dylan Thomas and other rebellious Celts at the injustice of it all, is to rage at the very process which made one a human being in the first place. It is all these things that the pagan biologist has in mind when he says that death is part, parcel, and process of life and not some absurd event tacked on at the end out of divine spite or, worse still, as a punishment for sin."[27] In short, not much has changed since the Stoics—except we now enjoy a much more sophisticated evolutionary biology. The acceptance model is correct; the human self should be viewed as changing, rather than as a core substance. But ultimately the self should be seen as part of the overall picture.

KASS: ARISTOTLE AND
THE ACCEPTANCE MODEL

In "Averting One's Eyes, or Facing the Music?—on Dignity and Death," Leon Kass chooses to focus upon the first of Ramsey's theses, namely, that death is itself undignified (as opposed to Ramsey's second thesis that the language of "death with dignity" is itself somehow undignified). Like Ramsey, Kass believes that dignity is not some "thing" that is bestowed upon a person, or, for that matter, taken away from him or her. It is rather a question, for Kass, of a human being being allowed to *actualize* the *possibility* of accepting death. This is, for him, an inner disposition (note the Aristotelian language). But Kass *concludes* from all this that "death is, at the very least, neutral with respect to dignity; further, . . . human mortality may even be the necessary condition for the display of at least *some* aspects of a human being's dignity."[28] Both he and Ramsey agree that there are relatively undignified ways of dying. But Kass charges that Ramsey's view of "the indignity of death" rests upon a false personification and reification of death as "the enemy," "the dreadful visage," and so on. What Ramsey really seems to be talking about is "the indignity of human mortality." "Indeed, another way of stating Ramsey's claim is to say that there is no such thing as a timely death, as a death in season, because the 'contradiction' of our mortality means that there is never a right time to die. . . . [Also,] if mortality is an indignity, so are aging and senescence."[29] Kass believes that a good deal of confusion surrounds Ramsey's position, since he (Ramsey) floats back and forth between "a subjective perspective on a *particular* 'death' in its 'individuality,' . . . and . . . an objective perspective on human mortality itself."[30] In opposition, he argues that death itself should not be considered as an indignity; it might be a great evil, but it is better viewed as an "evil good" than as an "evil evil," or even a "good evil." In support of his position Kass offers the following: First, many people do lead full lives. For them death simply is not an indignity. This simply is not how people ordinarily speak about these deaths. Second, death is at least sometimes the occasion for heroism, for the display of human dignity. Third, "not having world enough and time" gives meaning and seriousness to human life.[31] Fourth, death is the condition of the possibility of renewed life and youth and hope. This is similar to Morison's position above. Fifth, death for Kass, "is natural and necessary and inextricably tied to life. To live is to be mortal; death is the necessary price for life."[32] Ramsey fails to see this because of his personification of the problematic. Like Morison, Kass asks, "Is there really dignity in attempting the impossible or in railing against the inevitable? Is there not more dignity in facing up to such things and in facing them nobly and bravely?"[33] Death for Kass is *not* like disease; it (death) is natural decline evolving from within the body, whereas the former is an attack on the body from an external agency. From an Aristotelian perspective, Ramsey "fails to give nature her due."[34] The issue, further, is not just that of Christianity versus secular humanism, or faith versus reason, for Kass can claim the support of thinkers like Aquinas for his position, although a complete rapprochement between the latter and the Pauline view of nature as debased may not be possible.

Finally, and most important, Kass realizes that the major issue between himself and Ramsey concerns generic human qualities versus specifically individuating ones. "Ultimately, though not in this paper, we shall have to ask whether the 'esteem' for the 'individual human being' is tied first and foremost to what is *individuated* or to what is human—that is, generic—about that *particular* human being."[35] Kass retreats slightly from his position at the end, admitting that if the whole human species were to become extinct the world would be robbed of its dignity, since "wo/man" (i.e., not *this* man or *this* woman) is the only being that can think, appreciate, and care for the whole. Pascal yes, but on a Platonic or Aristotelian scale, or better perhaps, Hegelian, as we shall see below.

For Kass, the whole is greater than the sum of its parts, and a biological approach is not only possible but desirable, as well as the realization that man or woman is a social animal, a member of the *polis*. This outlook, then, is rooted in Aristotle, and culminates by advocating acceptance of the acceptance model.

ENGELHARDT: HEGEL AND THE ACCEPTANCE MODEL

In "The Councils of Finitude" H. Tristram Engelhardt, Jr., argues that death is a "natural event in the course of human life,"[36] and that, as such, it should be accepted. He is somewhat surprised that this is not an obvious point and, in looking back into the Western cultural tradition, blames Plato, Aristotle, and the Christian tradition in general for having led us down the wrong path. Plato's dualism, particularly as found in the *Phaedo*, served to promote the thesis that the human being is immortal, and therefore that death could be *denied*. It is interesting to remember that earlier in this chapter Paul Ramsey had faulted Plato for advocating an *acceptance* position of death in the *Phaedo*, relying upon a view of the body as "indifferent."[37] Engelhardt also interprets Plato as "concluding" in the *Phaedo* that the "mind is as perduring as the ideas it knows."[38] In opposition to this, the view of Socrates presented above in Chapter 8 argued that Plato can be seen as offering either an acceptance or a denial model, depending upon the importance one wishes to allow for the ironic. In short, Engelhardt's Socrates, if allowed to stand by itself, may be a bit of a "straw person," especially if one begins to take into account the issue of style.

Engelhardt continues his historical analysis by presenting Aristotle and Aquinas as two thinkers who furthered the tradition of viewing the mind as independent of the body. This was only intensified by Christianity, which viewed "the body as corrupted due to human error, human sin."[39] All these positions confuse "distinguishability with separability," that is, they assume that if we make conceptual distinctions in discussing the human self, these distinctions must also possess an ontological status. Rather should the mind and body be viewed as "distinct inseparables," existing in a categorical relationship.

To oppose the Platonic-Christian outlook with its stress on dualism and infinity, Engelhardt draws on the Stoic tradition, as Morison did, viewing "death and disease . . . as natural to humans as life."[40] Here we should recall Ramsey's retort that "natural" does not necessarily mean "acceptable," either in the case of death or of disease. Charles Hartshorne's view that being finite in time is no more of an insult to human beings than only occupying a finite amount of space is aligned by Engelhardt with the Stoic tradition of naturalism. Further, an infinite life would be one without novelty, hence aesthetically displeasing.

Engelhardt is quite willing to admit that there are untimely deaths and also painful deaths, and that these should be struggled against; it is death *as such* that he argues needs to be accepted. Medicine often plays the role of mediator between the needs of an individual to avoid pain and live a full life, vis-à-vis the overall needs of the community. But "it is one thing to conceive the enemy of medicine to be death as such, and another to conceive the enemy to be an untimely or painful death."[41] In the twentieth century new philosophies have arisen that have accented the importance of the individual and marginalized the need for community. Camus's stance on the importance of individual rebellion, and especially Heidegger's view of how a person lives authentically, are singled out for criticism:

> For Heidegger, "freedom towards death" is effected only through release from "lostness in the they-self." In the individual's being-toward-death, the individual lives over against his death as an individual and ultimate limit which, in the end, separates him from others. Such notions define human existence in terms of an individual rebellion against [Camus] or anxiety over death, and suggest a covert desire for existence of non-finite proportions. Moreover, such anxiety is asocial if not antisocial. It fails to place death with regard to the general value of individual life and death for the community.[42]

For Engelhardt, the realization that not everyone's life can be extended indefinitely in and of itself constitutes an argument that human life must be reevaluated in less than absolute terms, and that the apparent tension between the goals of medicine and the individual on the one side, versus the needs of society on the other, needs a mediator. He offers Hegel, specifically Hegel's *Philosophy of Nature,* as espousing an ecological and contextual view of death. For Hegel, an individual, in his or her particularity, "only imperfectly and in a one-sided and partial fashion achieves the values of humanity."[43] The individual, in its particularity, is "not up to being universal," so to speak, and its life therefore is precarious, disease-laden, and ultimately, finite. "Death for Hegel is part and parcel of animal life; it is normal and natural and to be accepted as such."[44] The really important values are "trans-individual," that is, the community values of the spirit: state, art, religion, and philosophy. In what appears to be somewhat of a form of stereotyping, even old age and senility, with its lack of activity, are viewed as already mirroring death. In contrast to Heidegger, who "fails to appreciate the 'they,' "[45] Hegel offers a balance, suggesting that individuals can, and should, accept their individual deaths in the knowledge that their goals and values may be enduring in the community. Individual life then, while valuable, does not have absolute value, and the mere extension of life for the sake of extending it constitutes a "bad infinite." One needs rather to assess all technological extensions in terms of the overall needs of the community. Thus, "the issue of the quantity versus the quality of life has an essentially social dimension."[46] Engelhardt concludes by reiterating that, if death is "natural," as he and Hegel have argued, then it should not be viewed as the enemy of medicine—only untimely or painful death. In the final analysis, "death itself is even more natural to us than medicine."[47]

CONCLUSION

The three acceptance models outlined above have much in common. To begin with they all highlight the importance of death as "natural." But "natural" does not necessarily mean "self-evident," nor does it necessarily mean "acceptable." It may even be argued that "nature" is a social construct, as has been done to some extent above in Chapters 2 and 3. Second, the authors see nothing wrong with rebelling against an untimely death, but exactly what this term means is debatable, to say the least.

A third problem arises over the issue of the needs of an

individual versus the needs of *the* community. In this age of pluralism, it is important to recognize that there are multiple communities, that these may have different values, which may or may not be commensurate with each other. Josiah Royce may have been correct in stating that an individual should be loyal to a cause, and by further stressing that we should be loyal to that cause that furthers the principle of loyalty in the universe at large.[48] Engelhardt's version of this is to suggest that we "act always to ensure that the general achievement of cultural values by humans is not precluded by the investment of resources and energies in postponing death."[49] But it was also this same Josiah Royce who suggested the need for "wise provincialism," and in so doing at least hinted at the possibility that there may be several communities rather than one big one.[50]

The penchant for speaking in essentialist vocabulary surfaces in another way. All three authors argue as if "human finitude" requires acceptance—and they accuse Ramsey of rebelling against this. But the "this" here is more of a Platonic Form than anything else. Ramsey's point was, in a sense, to disclose such language as inadequate through his reference to the bodily and the individual self—and we would add, the importance of first-person over third-person accounts. He holds the position that the more one stresses the personal the more one will adopt a denial model of rebellion, for "selfish" reasons. To accuse him therefore of rejecting what he refuses to believe in somewhat misses the point—or perhaps suggests that there are "preferential" or "sentimental" elements operating on both sides.

In sum, the challenge presented by Ramsey is an important one, but it needs to be extended one step further. Chapter 8 began to challenge the sufficiency of overly descriptive accounts, by calling attention to the importance of portraits of dying persons. This attempt to let dying persons tell the story from their point of view is impossible to achieve completely—mainly because the very meaning of one's self is at least partly socially constructed through the use of language. Nonetheless, storytelling does serve as a reminder of the multiple functions of language. The present chapter focused upon the intermingling of the "personal" and the "unacceptable," regarding dying. It should be clear that the more one finds oneself in agreement with Ramsey's position, the more "unacceptable" one will find impartial, third-person accounts of dying to be. On the other hand, two of the portraits presented in Chapter 8 seemed to indicate at least some possibility of transcending the exclusivity of these alternatives (acceptance versus denial). In our Conclusion, we focus upon this "overcoming," as well as on the more dynamic use of language in dealing with dying persons, emphasizing the use of language as not merely *descriptive* but also *directive*.[51]

Conclusion

En Attendant la Mort

Previous chapters of this volume have disclosed two opposing stances toward death and dying, that of acceptance and that of denial or rebellion. These postures have emerged in both the historical and the biological contexts, though the specifics may differ in each situation. This issue was specifically tied to the personal or the individual by Ramsey. One consequence of this is that it brings us face to face with the issue of language, or, more specifically, with style. This is so because language is notorious for dealing well with universal characteristics of experience, but not very well with unique characteristics. After all, "unique" means, in a sense, "indescribable." And so what has emerged is not only the problematic itself of acceptance versus denial, but *how* it is to be presented, or "made present," if at all. The turn to portraits was an attempt to dramatize this issue, and to show its importance. As Nietzsche noted, "The problem of science cannot be discerned on the groundwork of science . . . [Rather must one] *view science through the eyes of the artist, and art through the eyes of life.*"[1] And again, a few lines later, "The existence of the world is *justified* only as an esthetic phenomenon."[2] In our century writers like Samuel Beckett are trying for the justification, but having some trouble achieving it.

WAITING FOR GODOT

In Samuel Beckett's *Waiting for Godot,*[3] we witness an attempt to resolve the acceptance-denial dilemma, and to do so utilizing a particular style or genre that forces us to reconfront the issue of language. The play consists of so much *inactivity* that it is difficult to describe. Two tramps, Vladimir and Estragon, seemingly spend their time waiting for the mysterious Mr. Godot. In the process of doing this, they encounter two other "persons," Pozzo and Lucky. Communication remains difficult throughout the play, with the characters talking *through* or *at* rather than *with* one another. Of course, the elusive Godot never arrives, and attention is gradually focused on the waiting, the attending. Godot has been interpreted in various ways, probably the most popular slant being that he is God. But Ramona Cormier and Janis L. Pallister, in a book entitled *Waiting for Death: The Philosophical Significance of Beckett's En* Attendant Godot, have provided an interesting alternative to the standard interpretation. For Beckett, the "source of man's troubles lies in his being born."[4] One spends or uses up one's life trying to "make up" for birth, and at the same time trying unsuccessfully to revolt against the situation. There is a certain "black humor" in it all. The more things change, the more they remain the same. Vladimir and Estragon continually say "let us go"—but they continually remain where they are. "They . . . are caught in a situation in which they cannot separate from one another, or give up waiting for Godot, or leave the place in which they find themselves. They appear to be condemned to an inertia that can only end with death. The play ends with Vladimir's suggestion that they depart, but both of the characters remain immobile. Stasis is their lot."[5]

The tramps say they would like the waiting to be over (death), but they are scared—afraid this might actually happen. The two invent games to pass the time. Language, for example, is often a game, a diversion, rather than a vehicle of communication. They talk of suicide several times during the play, but are never able to seriously consider it. Rather, the talk of suicide is *itself* a game, a diversion. "The important thing for them is not the content of the conversation but simply that there be conversation."[6] So long as they continue speaking, everything seems all right. It is silence that cannot be tolerated.

The characters have difficulty remembering or recollecting in the play, and yet in another sense, they don't want to remember that death is approaching. They themselves "recognize (and remember!) the defective nature of memory."[7] Their sense of who they are, where they have come from, where they are going, has broken down. They have lost their perspective. Indeed, they can't even stand up for much of the play. The biographical sedimentation of their lives has encased them in a "net" (Lucky's dance), which they try to accept and simultaneously try to reject. They have become conditioned or habituated to a significant degree in the play. Habit functions as the great "deadener" in the play, but again, they don't seem to be able simply to accept the habitual. They keep trying to rebel and yet continually fail to accomplish this. Indeed, they don't accomplish anything in the play. The result is sterile. (Note that there are no women in the play, and that Vladimir and Estragon are impotent.) As Cormier and Pallister put it, "There is 'nothing to be done' except to give . . . [oneself] the illusion, in one way or another, that . . . [one] is 'doing something.' "[8] But, of course, doing something would generate habit and hence perpetuate the boredom. On the surface at least, the play seems thoroughly pessimistic. "In conclusion, . . . the picture of man that emerges . . . is a nihilistic one. Man's use of reason, his senses, and his memory results in a skepticism about his identity as well as that of others, about time and about place, in short, about the cosmos. Since man has multiple identities, and no clear vision of self, he cannot position himself in time. Rather, he tends to adopt the temporal mode that best suits the immediate situation."[9]

But again, as was the case with Plato's Socrates and Nietzsche's Zarathustra, there is more here than appears at surface level. Here, too, there is an ironic quality present, and it is intended. "The need to express meaninglessness through meaningful form, and thus to give meaning, even though that meaning is meaninglessness, would constitute the greatest irony of all."[10] If language is used as a diversion by the characters in the play, at a meta-theoretical level we might well ask why Beckett himself writes. Is it to divert others (the audience) or primarily to distract himself? Or perhaps simply to disclose the chaotic nature of the human situation? "The ironist escapes the need to moralize. Instead, Beckett merely presents the human situation as he sees it. As a result of this, neither tragic nor comic catharsis is present in the play. It may be that Beckett condemns the human situation, but it cannot be said that he gives us either a remedy or a corrective."[11] Yet even here there is the additional irony that Beckett, in presenting such a pessimistic view of the human person, has already taken an implicit moral stand. "Ironically enough, it is through language itself that Beckett exhibits for us the limitations of language and it is through reason that he shows the limitations of reason, though we would have to admit that through an additional irony Beckett is only too well aware of this fact."[12]

Beckett, like Plato and Nietzsche, wishes or feels he has to reveal indirectly; hence he too intentionally deceives. The "really real" world for him is one in which we are immersed, "sedimented" so to speak, in a series of habits from which we continually try to escape. We can isolate the strands of *description, deception, denial, diversion,* and *direction* here in the way language is being used. True, on one level language is used to describe the tramps' situation, but as we have lately noted in linguistic philosophy, too great an emphasis upon the descriptive aspect of language can lead to a reductionist position, both linguistically and ontologically speaking. One can, for example, forget that words change their meaning from context to context, and hence require interpretation. Or, one can conflate the intentional aspect of "meaning" with the formal significance of that term.[13] In addition, as we have seen in Chapter 3, overemphasis upon description results in an inability to view matters from the point of view of the "other."

For Beckett, language can be used to describe reality, but its power is limited, and this is not a temporary problem. Since the description that language can accomplish is limited, by that very fact language denies, or leaves out, various aspects of reality. It concentrates on some features of a subject, while relegating others to a vague background or penumbra. In short, language, as selective, constitutes a form of denial.

Third, language is deceptive. It looks, on the face of it, like a black and white phenomenon, impartially there, like the type-oriented universe Marshall McLuhan refers to as the "Gutenberg galaxy."[14] While language does reveal, it also conceals, and if this twofold "amplification-reduction"[15] procedure is not seen, then language provides an overly simplistic picture of a complex state of affairs. That is, if language is not seen as simultaneously disclosing and concealing, what a given sentence overtly states is too often taken as all there is. The upshot is what William James termed "vicious intellectualism."[16]

Going further, language can be seen as diversionary. In Beckett, language is used to pass the time, to kill time, as we have seen. Language functions as a gloss or a screen. Instead of being employed as a wedge into the tissue of experience, language degenerates into rhetoric, and we interact with linguistic extensions of our own egos. Language here has the sole psychological purpose of merely sounding good, of making us feel good. There is a considerable amount of this in Beckett's play. Vladimir continually asks Estragon to "return the ball" in conversation, that is, to say something, anything. The two decide to abuse one another, and then to make up. There is also a "play within the play," as Vladimir and Estragon attend the performances of Pozzo and Lucky. Actually, there is even a "play within the play within the play," wherein the two tramps themselves "play" or mimic the characters of Pozzo and Lucky. And of course they talk of suicide, but only in a rhetorical fashion, as a new linguistic game.

Finally, language is directional; that is, it points beyond itself toward the existential, or more precisely in this case, the nihilistic situation at hand. The play itself constantly reminds the viewer/reader of the insufficiency of language, of its inability to communicate. As such, it is constantly reminding us that there is more "out there"—messy or not—than can at will be alluded to.

Interesting differences emerge if we compare and contrast the portrait of Socrates offered us by Plato, Nietzsche's Zarathustra, and that of the tramps provided by Beckett. Socrates appears to make progress while awaiting death, or "preparing for death," as he defined Philosophy. That is, he defends his position when it is challenged by those around him. He is able to make a contribution, even at his last moment. He uses language, and reason, to deny the crushing inevitability of death, but in a more ironic sense than Nietzsche allowed for. Also, language is not simply a diversionary tool for Socrates. Nietzsche's "dancing Socrates," Zarathustra, also makes progress in some sense of the term. But the progress is much less straightforward than it was with Socrates. This is so because the progress entails recognizing, and playfully embracing, the realization that the more things change, the more they will remain the same, affirming eternal recurrence. Beckett's tramps are also "attending death." But unlike Socrates, and to a lesser degree Zarathustra, they seem unable to make any progress at all. Socrates is able to make *some* progress through, for example, the argument from Recollection in the *Phaedo*,[17] even though that argument is incomplete, whereas the two tramps can only remember that they can't remember. Beckett presents the reader with a sedimentation situation so strong that the tramps seem unable to alleviate it. Indeed, the immersion in the rubble seems worse rather than better in the second act. While both Socrates and the tramps await death, Socrates seems able to rebel or deny some aspects of the situation, while the two tramps appear condemned to do the same thing in ever-changing ways. Here Beckett's nihilism emerges. Zarathustra appears to be located between Socrates and the tramps, on the one hand rejecting an overly logical approach to death, and on the other trying desperately to maintain the ability to laugh as one looks into the abyss—something Vladimir cannot do without experiencing physical pain in the play.

It is often overlooked that Socrates chooses his own form of death. That is, in a Sartrean sense,[18] he chooses to await the death that has been dictated by the Athenian jury, or perhaps more accurately, that he has forced from the jury by refusing to "cop a plea," or accept exile as an alternative proposal. He might be accused of acting in a "suicidal" manner here, but as we have seen with Nietzsche's concept of *Freitod,* much depends upon the connotations a particular word carries around with it. In any event we know that suicide was not an acceptable option for Socrates, who describes each of us here on earth as being at a "guard post"[19] that we cannot desert. While it might be granted that Socrates intended to place himself in an extremely dangerous situation, this was by no means his sole or his primary purpose. Socrates did not simply want to die. That is, he was not "awaiting" death *per se.* Rather he has, in a Sartrean sense, chosen a specific way to die. Socrates is rejecting death *itself* by selecting, and taking his chances on, how he will die. By contrast, the two tramps don't seem to be able to do this. They *do* await death *per se* and only occasionally try, unsuccessfully, to deny death *per se* by selecting a form of death, that is, perhaps not suicide so much as *Freitod.* In short, Socrates still has his freedom precisely because he has chosen a form of death to prepare for, whereas the two tramps seem impotent. Of course, in revealing or disclosing this, even in an indirect and intentionally deceitful fashion, Beckett has himself made it somewhat meaningful or comprehensible, and in that sense has taken an implicit stance against it, thus providing further justification for Sartre's position.

It will be noted that these matters were discussed previously, for example, in Chapter 6, dealing with euthanasia. What has

changed is the *style* of discussion. Attempts at impartial description have given way to portraits. The latter are admittedly selective, hence a form of denial. Furthermore, they are attempts to
disclose individuality *through* language, and in doing so only
partly and incompletely, they also disclose the limitations *and yet
the necessity* of language. Finally, they are attempts to take into
account the problem of the "other" initially raised in Chapters 2
and 3.

In sum, for Plato, Nietzsche, and Beckett, in a truly ironic
sense, one cannot simply wait for or prepare for death per se;
there are simply too many possibilities. On the other hand, one
cannot completely avoid the preparation for death. Attempts to
deny or rebel are at best only partly successful. Beckett shows us
the impossibility of awaiting death per se; Plato shows us the
same thing by demonstrating the necessity of selecting a specific
anticipated death. Nietzsche intensifies Plato's message by emphasizing dying at "the right time," by indicating that no bell
goes off to indicate exactly when that time is, and by disclosing
that such a death may not be available, even to heroes. Most
important, all three authors intentionally leave us with an ironic
feeling, because all three manage to disclose indirectly that attending or preparing for death is both necessary and impossible.

We have argued that no one discipline owns death; approaches to death and dying are inherently interdisciplinary—or
at least they should be. While many would agree to this proposition at first glance, the disciplines they have in mind are already
too closely aligned, for example, biology and chemistry, or law
and politics. A truly interdisciplinary approach to death must
strive to provide as "thick" a context as is possible, given any
author's particular limitations. But within those limitations care
should be taken to select diverse disciplines, to put together, for
example, biology and literature, mythology and economics. The
amount of material presented in the above chapters is sizable,
variegated, representative, and, perhaps most important, incon-

clusive. More specifically, a sustained analysis of various authors has disclosed two basic stances toward either death or dying or both, namely, acceptance versus denial or rebellion. (In this presentation, denial is viewed as a weak form of rebellion.) However, what also becomes clear is that neither of these alternatives exists in pure form; in other words, they are "transcended" by becoming internalized. This has become evident in two ways. First, through the realization that "stories" are more important than "stages," and that stories are idiosyncratic, that the lives of individual people, in real life or in selected literary instances, don't completely add up. This realization occurs only if the stories are unfolded utilizing "thick description" rather than the more truncated "case study" approach. Second, the insufficiency of stages is also disclosed by an anthropological or intercultural approach, which also argues that death and dying are not completely rational topics, though the unit of comparison changed here from the individual to the group.

There is an important line in Beckett's play which runs "Ce qui est terrible c'est d'avoir pensé" (What is terrible is to have thought).[20] It expresses in a more radical form the Socratic stance that "knowing that you don't know is the first step toward knowledge." It may now, however, also be seen as the last step—at least in terms of any complete answer. Attempts to deal with death and dying are both necessary and impossible, as noted above. Necessary in the sense that we cannot avoid death and its ramifications, pretend what we may. Impossible in that we cannot seem to solve the very many complex and multidimensional issues that it brings. This is conceptually traumatic, maybe even emotionally so. But perhaps the discomfort we feel tells us more about ourselves than we care to realize. The ironic is the real, the real is absurd. The absurd is, that one has to do this, and, that one can never accomplish the task of making death and dying meaningful.[21] However, once the "waiting" is undertaken, that is, once the investigation has begun, one "can't go home again." Having suspended or bracketed the everyday world of the habitual long enough to try consciously awaiting death and dying, the situation has now gained a momentum of its own. We are now "dis-eased" through thinking. The realization offered here, that is, that we can't wait for death, and that we can't rebel either, needs also to be taken in a self-reflexive manner. That is, is the attempt, offered here, admittedly doomed in advance to incompleteness, *itself* merely a diversion? Or, does it at least *indirectly* disclose something that cannot be neatly put into language, even though language itself is necessary in order to bring about the disclosure?

That question must be left to each reader to decide individually.

Chapter 1 contained a simple example of a dentist's probe. Hopefully its point (no pun intended) has by now become clear. The probe, *as* a probe, is not neutral. What we "see" or find is at least partly the result of what we probe for. Analogously, in death and dying, what we find is the result of what we probe for. The use of case studies in the context of death and dying is by no means null; indeed they have accomplished noteworthy results. But the death of a person must not be confused with a brief case study. Nor is the process of dying identical with a neutrally progressive series of abstract stages. Both case studies, and indeed in a more general sense language itself, are probes, that is, they simultaneously amplify and reduce dimensions of our experience. There is a temptation, both in the instance of case studies and in that of language itself, to take what is amplified or highlighted as constituting *all* there is. The pressure to do so is both intense and subtle. Nevertheless, it must be resisted. Only if we succeed in resisting can any meaningful sense of the person or of self-realization, fragile and socially constructed as it is, be preserved. Some methods of resistance have been outlined in this volume. They consist of

1. a recovery of the historicity of death, in both a Western and a non-Western context, and a realization that the term does not have one objective, transcendental meaning;
2. a realization that, in the biological context, uneasiness over lack of a contemporary, clear definition of death leads to a temptation to define the vagueness of the situation out of existence; and
3. a reaffirmation of the narrative dimension of dying, through portraits, of trying to allow each dying person to tell his or her own story, as opposed to categorizing all stories into stages.

These are only suggestions. They are beginnings, but even if successful, they are not sufficient. There is a final ironic sense in which all that is written here is *itself*—because it is language, only a probe, that is, "directional." As such, it has highlighted some aspects of the situation and marginalized others. The only difference is that the probing characteristic has been admitted and even highlighted from the beginning. It is also the case that what is highlighted in the present volume is somewhat different from what is generally emphasized, in that it focuses upon what probes do—just by virtue of being probes. Hopefully, the present probe has not been too painful, as opposed to the dentist's, and hopefully in the long run the "benefits" will outweigh the "cost." As Michael Ignatieff has noted in *The Needs of Strangers:* "We need words to keep us human. Being human is an accomplishment like playing an instrument. It takes practice. . . . Without a public language to help us find our own words, our needs will dry up in silence. . . . Without the light of language, we risk becoming strangers to our better selves."[22]

[NOTES]

PREFACE

1. See Paul Ramsey, "The Indignity of 'Death with Dignity,'" in *Death Inside Out*, edited by Peter Steinfels and Robert Veatch (New York: Harper and Row, 1975), pp. 95–96. In the present text, denial is construed as a weak form of rebellion and not as an alternative to it.

2. The thesis of "meaning invariance" has come under considerable criticism in twentieth-century philosophy. See, for example, Ludwig Wittgenstein, *Philosophical Investigations*, translated by G.E.M. Anscombe, 2d edition (New York: Macmillan, 1967), pp. 6–32; Friedrich Waismann, "Language Strata," in *Logic and Language, First and Second Series*, edited with introductions by Antony Flew (New York: Doubleday and Company, 1965), pp. 226–47; C. K. Ogden and I. A. Richards, *The Meaning of Meaning, A Study of the Influence of Language Upon Thought and of the Science of Symbolism* (New York: Harcourt, Brace and Company, 1923).

3. See Peter L. Berger and Thomas Luckman, *The Social Construction of Reality* (New York: Doubleday & Company, 1967), p. 3ff.; Benjamin Lee Whorf, *Language, Thought and Reality*, edited with an introduction by John B. Carroll (Cambridge: Massachusetts Institute of Technology Press, 1956).

CHAPTER ONE

1. As quoted in Roger B. Dworkin, "Death in Context," *Indiana Law Journal* 48 (Summer 1973), p. 623.

2. See the discussion of Hans Jonas's article "Against the Stream: Comments on the Definition and Redefinition of Death," in Chapter 5.

3. This case is taken and adapted from Robert Veatch, *Case Studies in Medical Ethics* (Cambridge: Harvard University Press, 1977), pp. 317–19, case 102.

4. See Robert Veatch, "Defining Death Anew: Technical and Ethical Problems," in *Ethical Issues in Death and Dying,* edited by Tom L. Beauchamp and Seymour Perlin (Englewood Cliffs, N.J.: Prentice-Hall, 1978), discussed in Chapter 5.

5. For the concept of "inventing the problematic," see John Dewey, "The Pattern of Inquiry," in *The Philosophy of John Dewey,* edited by John J. McDermott (Chicago: University of Chicago Press, 1981), p. 229.

6. This case is taken and adapted from Howard Brody, *Ethical Decisions in Medicine* (Boston: Little, Brown and Company, 1976), pp. 82–85.

7. Ibid., p. 83.

8. This case is taken and adapted from Veatch, *Case Studies in Medical Ethics,* pp. 319–25, case 103.

9. See Willard Gaylin, "Harvesting the Dead," *Harper's* 249 (September 23, 1974), pp. 23–46.

10. The account of this case is taken from William J. Gavin, "The Gardiner Case in Maine: Summary and Reflections," *American Philosophical Association Newsletter on Philosophy and Medicine* 88 (November 1988), pp. 44–46. Quotes from the actual case are from *In Re Joseph V. Gardiner,* Maine Supreme Judicial Court, argued September 18, 1987, decided December 3, 1987, Reporter of Decisions, decision no. 4574, Law Docket no. And-87-361.

11. See *In Re Storer,* New York Court of Appeals, 52 N.Y. 2d 363, 376–80, 20 N.E. 2d 64, 70–72, 438 N.Y.S. 2d 266 272–74, *cert. denied* 454 U.S. 858 (1981).

12. See *In the Matter of Karen Quinlan, An Alleged Incompetent,* 137 N.J. Supr. 227 (1975).

13. See *Superintendent of Belcher State School v. Joseph Saikewicz,* 370 N.E., 2nd 417 (Mass. 1977).

14. On this matter, see Richard W. Momeyer, *Confronting Death* (Bloomington: Indiana University Press, 1988), pp. 153–58, 169–70.

15. See *Cruzan v. Director, Missouri Dept. of Health,* United States Supreme Court, June 25, 1990.

16. See, in this respect, the excellent analysis of the case by George Annas, "Nancy Cruzan in China," *Hastings Center Report* 20 (September–October 1990), pp. 39–41.

17. Ronald Cranford, "A Hostage to Technology," *Hastings Center*

Report 20 (September–October 1990), p. 10. See also Gilbert Meilander, "*Terra es animata:* On Having a Life," *Hastings Center Report* 23 (July–August 1993), who notes: "When we are told that, within a month after the Supreme Court's *Cruzan* decision, 100,000 people sought information about living wills from the Society for the Right to Die, we can understand that this is not an issue for specialized academic disciplines alone" (pp. 29–30). Meilander goes on to note, however, that this legalistic way of approaching the issue is misleading and carries its own bias. "Such a procedural approach brings with it a certain vision of the person: to be a person is to be, or have the capacity to be, an autonomous chooser, to take control over one's personal history, determining its bounds and limits" (p. 30). In opposition, he argues for a more embodied view of the person, analogous to that of Paul Ramsey, though he fails to bring out Ramsey's connection between personal self and denial or rebellion (see Chapter 9). Nonetheless, Meilander's point about autonomy being "paradoxical" (p. 30), or in our terms, "socially constructed" or "relative," rings true.

18. See Derek Humphry, *Final Exit: The Practicalities of Self-Deliverance and Assisted Suicide for the Dying* (Eugene, Ore.: The Hemlock Society, 1991).

19. See Alastair MacIntyre, *After Virtue* (Notre Dame, Ind.: University of Notre Dame Press, 1981), chapters 9 and 12.

20. For the concept of "amplification-reduction" structure, see Don Ihde, *Technics and Praxis* (Dordrecht, Neth.: D. Reidel Publishing Company, 1979), p. 21.

21. Ibid., pp. 20–21.

22. For the concept of "thick description," see Dena Davis, "Rich Cases: The Ethics of Thick Description," *Hastings Center Report* 21 (July–August, 1991), pp. 12–17. See also Clifford Geertz, *The Interpretation of Cultures* (New York: Basic Books, 1973), and Chapter 3 of this volume. Robert Veatch makes a similar point when he argues for the need to distinguish four separate levels in any definition of death: the formal definition itself; the concept, that is, content, of death; the locus of death; and the criteria to be employed in determining death. See Chapter 5 of this volume.

23. See Alfred North Whitehead, *Science and the Modern World* (New York: Free Press, 1967), p. 51.

24. Dena Davis, "Rich Cases," p. 15. See also Robert Kleinman, *The Illness Narratives: Suffering, Healing, and the Human Condition* (New York: Basic Books, 1988), p. 28: "Clinical and behavioral science research . . . possess no category to describe suffering, no routine way of recording this most thickly human dimension of patients' and families' stories of experiencing illness. . . . The thinned-out image of patients and families that perforce must emerge from such research is scientifically replicable but ontologically invalid."

25. See John Dewey, "Context and Thought," in *Experience, Nature, and Freedom,* edited with an introduction by Richard J. Bernstein (Indianapolis: Bobbs-Merrill, 1960), pp. 88–110. In Dewey's opinion, "examination discloses three deepening levels or three expanding spheres of context. The narrowest and most superficial is that of the immediate scene. . . . The next deeper and wider one is that of the culture of the people in question. The widest and deepest is found in recourse to the need of general understanding of the workings of human nature" (pp. 108–9). While stressing the need for the third level, Dewey is himself aware of the danger contained in too universal an approach. The present work, proceeding from a Jamesian perspective, stresses this danger even more than Dewey did.

26. Robert Coles, *The Call of Stories: Teaching and the Moral Imagination* (Boston: Houghton Mifflin, 1989), pp. 13–14.

27. Ibid., p. 21.

28. Ibid., p. 29.

CHAPTER TWO

1. Ludwig Wittgenstein, *Philosophical Investigations* (New York: Macmillan, 1953), p. 47e.

2. John J. McDermott, "The American Angle of Vision," *Cross Currents* 15 (Winter 1965), p. 70.

3. Geoffrey Gorer, "The Pornography of Death," in *Death: Current Perspectives,* edited by Edwin S. Sheneidman (Palo Alto: Mayfield Publishing Company, 1976), p. 74.

4. Ibid., p. 76.

5. Peter Steinfels, Introduction to *Death Inside Out,* edited by Peter Steinfels and Robert M. Veatch (New York: Harper & Row, 1975), p. 1.

6. Philippe Ariès, *Western Attitudes Toward Death: From the Middle Ages to the Present* (Baltimore: Johns Hopkins University Press, 1974); *The Hour of Our Death* (New York: Knopf, dist. Random House, 1981); "Death Inside Out," in *Death Inside Out*, 1975.

7. As quoted in Ariès, *Western Attitudes Toward Death*, p. 3.

8. Ibid., p. 56.

9. Ariès, "Death Inside Out," p. 12.

10. Ariès, *Western Attitudes Toward Death*, pp. 88–89.

11. Ibid., p. 106.

12. Ariès, "Death Inside Out," p. 24.

13. Ariès, *Western Attitudes Toward Death*, p. 100.

14. Ibid., p. 103.

15. Ariès, "Death Inside Out," p. 21.

16. Ariès, *Western Attitudes Toward Death*, p. 100.

17. Ariès, "Death Inside Out," p. 24. In "Pursuing a Peaceful Death," Daniel Callahan agrees that "we have come to feel only now the loss of what the late French historian Philippe Ariès called a 'tame death'" (*Hastings Center Report* 23 [July–August 1993], p. 33). However, he argues that we can "have both the advantages of the older tame death and, with the help of technology, many improvements in contemporary death" (p. 36). But in order to do so, we must reject "technological brinkmanship." In other words, for Callahan, "we should begin backward. Death should be seen as the necessary and inevitable end point of medical care" (p. 33). Unfortunately, it is currently viewed as "what happens when medicine fails" (p. 34).

18. Ivan Illich, "The Political Uses of Natural Death," in *Death Inside Out*, p. 25.

19. Ibid., p. 28.

20. Ibid., p. 35.

21. Ibid., p. 36.

22. Ibid., pp. 40–41. Robert Veatch, however, argues that Illich's position can be viewed in a different way. While agreeing that "the concept of natural death is at least dreadfully ambiguous and dangerous and possibly elitist," he nonetheless maintains that "it is clear that making complex biomedical technologies necessary for a natural death was a blatant contradiction that could not survive long. Nor could the radical egalitarianism of the proletarian form of natural death. It is

natural that someone would seize upon the ambiguities in the term *natural*, that the death-with-dignity movement would recognize that the artifacts of biomedical technology need not be called natural. Those who no longer need worry about life's necessities—food, shelter, and especially medical care—now seem to have discovered the right to die the new natural death.

"If that is the case, then Illich's clever analysis may be open to reinterpretation. He sees the proletariat enslaved by a medical elite and demanding what as 'health consumers' they have been taught is the natural death of the intensive care unit. But it could also be that the elite is outflanking the masses, preparing the ground for a new stage in the combat—a stage where a basically healthy group can undermine the newly won right to life-extending interventions. The new natural death is the gnosis, accepted willingly by the enlightened and enforced upon the masses" (*Death, Dying and the Biological Revolution: Our Last Quest for Responsibility*, revised edition [New Haven: Yale University Press, 1989], pp. 225–26). The issue of death with dignity is taken up in Chapter 9.

23. Ibid., p. 38.

24. Eric J. Cassell, "Dying in a Technological Society," in *Death Inside Out*, p. 44.

25. Ibid., p. 45.

26. Ibid., p. 47.

27. See Chapter 4 of this volume.

28. Cassell, "Dying in a Technological Society," in *Death Inside Out*, p. 47.

29. Ibid., p. 45.

30. Ibid., pp. 45–46.

31. Ibid., p. 46.

32. Ibid., p. 48.

33. See Chapter 8 and Conclusion of this volume.

34. Joseph Campbell, *Myths to Live By* (New York: Viking Press, 1972), p. 22.

35. See Paul Tillich, *Dynamics of Faith* (New York: Harper Torchbooks, Harper & Row, 1958), p. 50: "A myth which is understood as a myth, but not removed or replaced, can be called a 'broken myth.'" In the cases alluded to above, however, we are not necessarily arguing that

all the elements of the ritual mythology in cultural attitudes toward death be preserved.

CHAPTER THREE

1. Ruth Benedict, *The Chrysanthemum and the Sword: Patterns of Japanese Culture* (New York: Meridian Books, New American Library, 1974), p. 2.

2. Ibid., p. 223.

3. As quoted in Esyun Hamaguchi, "A Contextual Model of the Japanese: Toward a Methodological Innovation in Japan Studies," *The Journal of Japanese Studies* 11 (Summer 1985), p. 292. Original reference: Keiichi Sakuta *Kachi no shakaigaku (Sociology of Value)* (Tokyo: Iwanami Shoten, 1972), p. 295.

4. Hamaguchi, "A Contextual Model," pp. 292–93.

5. Rihito Kimura, "Fiduciary Relationships and the Medical Profession: A Japanese Point of View," in *Ethics, Trust, and the Professions: Philosophical and Cultural Aspects,* edited by Edmund Pellegrino, Robert Veatch, and John Langan (Washington: Georgetown University Press, 1991), p. 235. See also Arthur Kleinman, *The Illness Narratives: Suffering, Healing, and the Human Condition* (New York: Basic Books, 1988): "For members of Western societies, the body is a discrete entity, a thing, an 'it,' machinelike and objective, separate from thought and emotion. For members of many non-Western societies, the body is an open system linking social relations to the self, a vital balance between interrelated elements in a holistic cosmos. . . . We do not discover our bodies and inner worlds *de novo*" (pp. 11–13). Kleinman's primary non-Western example of the social construction of self and illness is China. See Kleinman, chapter 6, "Neurasthenia: Weakness and Exhaustion in the United States and China."

6. Ibid., pp. 235–36.

7. In a similar fashion, Alasdair MacIntyre notes that "comparisons of American moral culture with Japanese, in terms of a contrast between the greater individualism of the former and the greater solidarity of the latter . . . may be . . . fundamentally mistaken . . . just because and insofar as they presuppose . . . a culturally neutral conception of the distinction between *the social* and *the individual*. . . . We have to ask not

how do Japanese differ from Americans in respect of the social and individual aspects or components of morality, but rather how does a Japanese view of the difference between Americans and Japanese differ from an American view of that same difference." ("Individual and Social Morality in Japan and the United States: Rival Conceptions of the Self," *Philosophy East and West* 40 [October 1990], pp. 489–90).

8. See Conclusion to this chapter.

9. Tetsuo Najita, "On Culture and Technology in Postmodern Japan," in *Postmodernism and Japan,* edited by Maseo Miyoshi and H. D. Hartootunian (Durham, N.C.: Duke University Press, 1989), p. 14.

10. Ibid., p. 14. Original reference: Takeo Doi, *Amae no kozo (The Anatomy of Dependence,* trans. John Bester (New York: Kodansha International, distributed by Harper & Row, 1973).

11. Bradd Shore, "An Introduction to the Work of Clifford Geertz," *Soundings* 71 (Spring 1988), p. 16.

12. Clifford Geertz, "From the Native's Point of View: On the Nature of Anthropological Understanding," in *Interpretive Social Science, A Reader,* edited by Paul Rabinow and William M. Sullivan (Berkeley: University of California Press, 1979), p. 229.

13. Ibid., pp. 227–28.

14. Clifford Geertz, "Deep Play: Notes on the Balinese Cockfight," in *The Interpretation of Cultures: Selected Essays* (New York: Basic Books, 1973), p. 453.

15. Ibid., p. 452.

16. Ibid.

17. Shore, "Clifford Geertz," p. 24.

18. Ibid.

19. Emiko Ohnuki-Tierney, *The Monkey as Mirror: Symbolic Transformations in Japanese History and Ritual* (Princeton, N.J.: Princeton University Press, 1987), p. 3.

20. Emiko Ohnuki-Tierney, *Illness and Culture in Contemporary Japan, An Anthropological View* (Cambridge: Cambridge University Press, 1984), p. 1.

21. Ibid., p. 1.

22. Ibid., p. 50.

23. Ibid.

24. See ibid., p. 7. Analogously, Howard Brody notes that "a member

of another society may have symptoms that, on an individual basis, Western physicians might unanimously and unambiguously label as constituting a serious disease. But if the members of that society do not regard that individual as being diseased and continue to respond to that person precisely the same as they do to healthy members of their society, then, insofar as those people are concerned, *no sickness exists"* (*Stories of Sickness* [New Haven, Conn.: Yale University Press, 1987], pp. 34–35). Arthur Kleinman, in *The Illness Narratives,* also distinguishes "illness" from "disease": "By invoking the term illness, I mean to conjure up the innately human experience of symptoms and suffering. Illness refers to how the sick person and the members of the family or wider social network perceive, live with, and respond to symptoms and disability. . . . Disease, however, is what the practitioner creates in the recasting of illness in terms of theories of disorder. . . . The practitioner reconfigures the patient's and family's illness problems as narrow technical issues, disease problems. . . . Illness [in contrast] is polysemic or multivocal; illness experiences and events usually radiate (or conceal) more than one meaning" (pp. 3–8).

25. Ohnuki-Tierney, *Ilness and Culture,* p. 31. Emphasis mine.

26. Ibid., p. 44.

27. Ibid., p. 46.

28. Ibid., p. 48.

29. Ibid., p. 60.

30. Ibid., p. 68.

31. Ibid., p. 69.

32. Ibid., pp. 69–70.

33. Ibid., p. 70.

34. Ibid., pp. 73–74.

35. Ibid., p. 213. See also Ohnuki-Tierney, "Brain Death and Organ Transplantation," *Current Anthropology* 35 (June 1994), pp. 233–54. This insightful article was published too recently to be included in the present analysis.

36. This comparison should not be taken as an indication that Kimura would necessarily agree with Ohnuki-Tierney's position as it is described here.

37. Ohnuki-Tierney, *Illness and Culture in Contemporary Japan,* p. 216.

38. Ibid.

39. See William James, "The Sentiment of Rationality," in *The Writings of William James,* edited with an introduction by John J. McDermott (New York: Modern Library, Random House, 1967), pp. 317–45.

40. See Ichiro Kato and Ilkufuni Nimi, "New Health Care and Laws," in *Medical Science and Health Care in the Coming Century, A Report from Japan,* edited by W. Mori and S. Homma (Amsterdam: Elsevier Science Publishers, 1987), p. 43.

41. Rihito Kimura, "Ethics Committees For 'High Tech' Innovations in Japan," in *Journal of Medicine and Philosophy* 14 (August 1989), p. 460.

42. See Eric Feldman, "Medical Ethics the Japanese Way," *Hastings Center Report* 15 (October 1985), p. 23. According to the *Japan Times,* what was only the fourth liver transplant operation was completed on October 23, 1993. The newspaper noted that "transplants from brain-dead donors have been in legal limbo since 1968" ("Fourth Liver Transplant Operation Begins," October 23, 1993). How the actual event unfolded discloses the mixed attitudes toward death still prevalent in Japan. "Doctors initially planned to extract the liver of a 53-year-old man in Osaka after he was diagnosed Thursday as brain dead in a hospital and his family agreed to donate his internal organs. . . . But they gave up the idea because the head of Osaka Prefecture's health department urged 'prudence' in removing organs at the brain-dead stage [and waited until] the man's heart stopped functioning early Friday" (*Japan Times,* October 23, 1993). It is quite clear here that "Japanese law does not accept brain death as death" ("Kyushu Doctors Complete Liver Transplant," *Japan Times,* October 24, 1993).

43. Rihito Kimura, "Japan's Dilemma with the Definition of Death," *Kennedy Institute of Ethics Journal* 1 (June 1991), p. 127.

44. Rihito Kimura, "Anencephalic Organ Donation: A Japanese Case," *Journal of Medicine and Philosophy* 14 (February 1989), p. 100.

45. See Omine Akira, "Right and Wrong in the Brain-Death Debate," *Japan Echo* 17 (Spring 1991), p. 69.

46. Ibid., p. 70.

47. Ibid.

48. Rihito Kimura, "Bioethics as a Prescription for Civic Action: The Japanese Interpretation," *Journal of Medicine and Philosophy* 12 (August 1987), p. 271.

49. Ibid.

50. Rihito Kimura, "Japan's Dilemma with the Definition of Death," *Kennedy Institute of Ethics Journal* 1 (June 1991), p. 127. Indeed, Kimura notes elswhere that this same concept of "En," or "sense of relatedness of all life, along with various Buddhist strictures about the integrity of the human body, helps to explain why Japan is one of the few medically advanced nations that has not a definitive clinical standard of brain death" ("Anencephalic Organ Donation: A Japanese Case," p. 101).

51. Emiko Namihira, "Prolonging Death," *Mainichi Shimbun*, June 15, 1988. Source: *Translation Service Center*, 1988: Social and Educational Affairs.

52. Ibid.

53. Umehara Takeshi, "A Buddhist Approach to Organ Transplants," *Japan Echo* 16, no. 4 (1989), pp. 80–81.

54. Ibid., p. 80.

55. Ibid., pp. 79–81.

56. Tomoaki Tsuchida, "Bioethics and Japanese Attitudes to Life and Death," *Bulletin of the Nanzan Institute for Religion and Culture* 10 (Summer 1986), pp. 23–24.

57. Kimura, "Fiduciary Relationships and the Medical Profession: A Japanese Point of View," p. 236.

58. Ibid.

59. Koichi Bai, Yasuko Shirai, and Michiko Ishii, "In Japan, Consensus Has Limits," *Hastings Center Report* 17 (June 1987), p. 18.

60. It should be noted, however, that Kimura sometimes argues in a more Kantian fashion. For example: "Clearly, persons ought to be fully respected, for it is they who make moral choices in this age of secular pluralism. Further, the dignity and rights of persons should not be disregarded simply because of cultural differences" ("Ethics Committees for 'High Tech' Innovations in Japan," *Journal of Medicine and Philosophy,* 14 [August 1989], p. 458).

61. See E. R. Dodds, *The Greeks and the Irrational* (Berkeley: University of California Press, 1951), p. 179. Original source: Gilbert Murray, *Greek Studies,* p. 66.

62. Ichiro Kato "Brain Death and the Myth of Social Consensus," *Japan Echo* 15 (Summer 1988), p. 53. See also Robert Veatch on "pluralism," pp. 101ff.

63. Kato, "Brain Death," p. 54.

64. Ibid., pp. 54–55.

65. For example, wouldn't higher brain failure, with its affinity to a view of the person as a soul/matter complex, really maintain a closer tie with the past? See Chapter 5 of this volume.

66. See Chapters 5 and 6.

67. Soichi Yagisawa, "User-Friendly Funerals," *Yomiuri Shimbun*, March 23, 1989. Source: *Translation Service Center*, 1989: Social and Educational Affairs.

68. Ibid.

69. As quoted in Mizuho Ishikawa, "The Japanese Way of Death," *Sankei Shimbun*, February 23, 1986. Source: *Translation Service Center*, 1986: Lifestyles. See also William R. LaFleur, *Liquid Life, Abortion and Buddhism in Japan* (Princeton, N.J.: Princeton University Press, 1992), who notes that "in fact, the whole of the ancestral cult in Japan insists that dying, at least in cultural and social terms, must be a prolonged, protracted, and many-staged passing. The Buddhist memorial services are held, at least when according to tradition, on an exact schedule. The sequence of rites consists in the funeral day, seventh day, forty-ninth day, hundredth day, first year, third year, seventh year, thirteenth year, seventeenth year, twenty-third year, and thirty-third year. . . . Thought to be progressively integrated into the world of the gods and Buddhas, the dead person is less and less dangerous to those who inhabit the world of living humans. Not only is he or she forgotten but the living also feel safe in forgetting. . . . A kind of ontological thinning takes place" (pp. 32–33).

70. Marx Wartofsky, "Beyond a Whole-Brain Definition of Death: Reconsidering the Metaphysics of Death," in *Death: Beyond Whole-Brain Criteria*, edited by Richard M. Zaner (Dordrecht, Neth.: Kluwer Academic Publishers, 1988), p. 219.

71. Ibid., p. 221.

72. Ibid., p. 222.

73. See, in this regard, Charles Scott, "The Many Times of Death," in *Death: Beyond Whole-Brain Criteria*, who notes that "the *Report* is an exceptionally fine example of a society-forming document that ignores the social identity of its subject matter, dying and dead people" (p. 229). The issue of medicine and science is taken up in Chapter 4 of this volume.

74. Wartofsky, "Beyond a Whole-Brain Definition of Death," p. 224.

75. Ibid., p. 224.

76. Ibid., p. 226.

77. Marx Wartofsky, "Organs, Organisms and Disease: Human Ontology and Medical Practice," in *Evaluation and Explanation in the Biomedical Sciences,* edited by H. Tristram Engelhardt, Jr., and Stuart F.
Spicker (Dordrecht, Neth.: D. Reidel Publishing Company, 1975), p. 67.
See end of Chapter 3 of this volume.

78. Wartofsky, "Organs, Organisms and Disease," p. 73.

79. Ibid., p. 74.

80. Ibid., p. 76.

81. Wartofsky, "Beyond a Whole-Brain Definition of Death," p. 220.

82. Charles Scott, "The Many Times of Death," p. 231.

83. Ibid., p. 230.

84. Wartofsky, "Organs, Organisms and Disease," p. 77.

85. John Lachs, "The Element of Choice in Criteria of Death," in
Death: Beyond Whole-Brain Criteria, p. 237.

86. Ibid., p. 238.

87. Ibid., p. 244.

88. Ibid., p. 248.

89. Ibid., p. 250.

CHAPTER FOUR

1. Ronald Munson, "Why Medicine Cannot Be a Science," *The
Journal of Medicine and Philosophy* 6 (May 1981), p. 183.

2. Daniel Callahan, *The Troubled Dream of Life, Living with Mortality*
(New York: Simon & Schuster, 1993), p. 61.

3. Ibid., p. 32.

4. John Dewey, "The Pattern of Inquiry," in *Pragmatism, The Classic
Writings,* edited by H. S. Thayer (Indianapolis: Hackett Publishing Company, 1982), p. 323.

5. Ibid.

6. Peter Steinfels, "Introduction," *Death Inside Out,* edited by Peter
Steinfels and Robert M. Veatch (New York: Harper & Row, 1975), p. 5.
For the distinction between a "problem" and a "mystery," see Gabriel
Marcel, *Being and Having: An Existentialist Diary* (New York: Harper and
Row, 1965), pp. 100–121.

7. Callahan, *Troubled Dream*, p. 32.

8. See P. W. Bridgman, *The Logic of Modern Physics* (New York: Macmillan, 1927).

9. See Rudolf Carnap, "Testability and Meaning," *Philosophy of Science* 3 (1936), pp. 419–71; and "Testability and Meaning," *Philosophy of Science* 4 (1937), pp. 1–40.

10. Thomas Kuhn, *The Copernician Revolution: Planetary Astronomy in the Development of Western Thought* (New York: Vintage Books, Random House, 1959).

11. Thomas Kuhn, *The Structure of Scientific Revolutions*, 2d edition, enlarged (Chicago: University of Chicago Press, 1970).

12. Kuhn, *Copernician Revolution*, p. ix.

13. Ibid., p. 94.

14. Ibid., p. 132.

15. Ibid., p. 38.

16. Ibid., p. 76. W. H. Newton-Smith criticizes Kuhn for "over-reacting to the discovery that there is no algorithm [for theory choice], for he seems to fail to appreciate that even if there is no rationally grounded algorithm to guide our decisions there may none the less be rational considerations which it is relevant to appeal to in justifying our decisions" (*The Rationality of Science* [London: Routledge & Kegan Paul, 1981], p. 116).

17. See Margaret Masterman, "The Nature of a Paradigm," in *Criticism and the Growth of Knowledge*, edited by Imre Lakatos and Alan Musgrave (Cambridge: Cambridge University Press, 1970), pp. 59–89.

18. See Kuhn, *The Structure of Scientific Revolutions*, p. 10. Israel Scheffler takes specific issue with Kuhn's restriction of rationality to taking place only within a specific paradigm: "To assume . . . that deliberation and interpretation are *restricted* to normal science is to beg the very point at issue"; and again, Kuhn's argument "fails to make the critical distinction between those standards or criteria which are internal to a paradigm, and those by which the paradigm is itself judged" (*Science and Subjectivity* [Indianapolis: Bobbs-Merrill Company, 1967], pp. 80, 84).

19. See Kuhn, *The Structure of Scientific Revolutions*, pp. 182–87.

20. Ibid., p. 187.

21. Alan E. Musgrave, "Kuhn's Second Thoughts," in *Paradigms and*

Revolutions, edited by Gary Gutting (Notre Dame, Ind.: University of Notre Dame Press, 1980), p. 51. See also Newton-Smith, *The Rationality of Science,* where he states: "In response to criticism Kuhn has so modified and altered or re-interpreted the position advanced in the first edition of *The Structure of Scientific Revolutions* that it is no longer clear whether a rationalist is committed to denying anything that Kuhn asserts" (p. 103). Israel Scheffler's analysis of Kuhn, which takes place before the "Postscript" was written, alleges that, even there, Kuhn "seems to reinstate the very distinction between discovery and justification with which we started. For despite his strong emphasis on the conversion experience and the gestalt switch, he suggests several considerations relative to the critical evaluation of theories as actual elements of scientific functioning: the predictive criterion . . . , the existence of anomaly and crisis, the preservation of previously acquired problem-solving abilities, and the promise 'to resolve some outstanding and generally recognized problem that can be met in no other way'" (*Science and Subjectivity,* p. 89).

22. Herrman L. Blumgart, M.D., "Medicine: The Art and the Science," in *Hippocrates Revisited,* edited by Roger J. Bulger, M.D. (New York: Medcom Press, 1973), p. 34.

23. Ibid., p. 33.

24. Ibid., p. 38.

25. Richard M. Magraw, M.D., "Science and Humanism: Medicine and Existential Anguish," in *Hippocrates Revisited,* p. 48. In *The Illness Narratives: Suffering, Healing and the Human Condition* (New York: Basic Books, 1988), Arthur Kleinman argues for an "alternative therapeutic approach [which] originates in the reconceptualization of medical care as (1) empathic witnessing of the existential experience of suffering and (2) practical coping with the major psychosocial crises that constitute the menacing chronicity of that experience" (p. 10). For Kleinman, "empathic witnessing is a moral act, not a technical procedure" (p. 154).

26. Magraw, "Science and Humanism," p. 49.

27. Kleinman, *Illness Narratives,* p. 17.

28. H. Tristram Engelhardt, Jr., "Explanatory Models in Medicine: Facts, Theories, and Values," *Texas Reports on Biology and Medicine* 32 (Spring 1974), p. 225.

29. Ibid., p. 226.

30. Ibid., p. 232. See also Paul Ramsey, who writes, of one particular individual, in *The Patient as Person:* "The patient is not exhaustively characterized by one disease, two separate diseases, or the interconnected diseases from which he may be suffering, both incurable, one involving prolonged dying. . . . A proper description of the human acts of caring for mortal man terminates in that man. He is the unity of the diseases he suffers when one his quietus makes. Doctors do not treat diseases, though often they conquer them. They treat patients, and here finally all fail" (New Haven, Conn.: Yale University Press, 1970), p. 130. See also Howard Brody, *Stories of Sickness* (New Haven, Conn.: Yale University Press, 1987): "When, for example, someone suffers gastritis with mucosal hemorrhages, the effect can be noted upon the stomach, upon the cells of the gastric mucosa, upon the molecules being secreted by those cells, upon the person herself, and perhaps upon the person's family and coworkers who must respond to the sufferer's altered functional status. The gastris itself might have its origins partly within a medication being taken for some other malady and partly within the stress that person is experiencing because of recent intepersonal pressures. . . . Causes and effects make up complex, interacting networks. Something becomes *the* cause when we *choose* to isolate or manipulate it for certain practical purposes" (pp. 39–40).

31. Martin Pernick, "Back from the Grave: Recurring Controversies over Defining and Diagnosing Death in History," in *Death Beyond Whole Brain Criteria,* edited by Richard M. Zaner (Dordrecht, Neth.: Kluwer Academic Publishers, 1988), p. 17.

32. Ibid., p. 20.

33. Michael Crichton, *The Great Train Robbery* (New York: Knopf: dis. by Random House, 1975), p. 193.

34. See Chapter 2 of this volume.

35. See *Ethical Issues in Death and Dying,* edited by Tom L. Beauchamp and Seymour Perlin (Englewood Cliffs, N.J.: Prentice-Hall, 1978), p. 3.

CHAPTER FIVE

1. As quoted in "A Definition of Irreversible Coma," Report of the Ad Hoc Committee of the Harvard Medical School to Examine the Definition of Death, in *Ethical Issues in Death and Dying,* edited by Tom L.

Beauchamp and Seymour Perlin (Englewood Cliffs, N.J.: Prentice-Hall, 1978), p. 14.

2. See ibid., p. 11.

3. Ibid.

4. Ibid.

5. Peter Black, "Definitions of Brain Death," in *Ethical Issues in Death and Dying,* ed. Beauchamp and Perlin, pp. 9–10.

6. Ibid.

7. Ibid., p. 13.

8. See the Tucker case in Chapter 1, and the reference to Willard Gaylin, "Harvesting the Dead," *Harpers* 249 (September 23, 1974), pp. 23–46.

9. Robert M. Veatch, *Death, Dying, and the Biological Revolution* (New Haven, Conn., Yale University Press, 1976).

10. Robert Veatch, "Defining Death Anew: Technical and Ethical Problems," in *Ethical Issues in Death and Dying,* p. 21.

11. See Chapter 4 of this volume.

12. Though as we shall see in the section on public policy in this chapter, Veatch has increasing problems with the concept of "person."

13. Robert Schwager, "Life, Death, and the Irreversibly Comatose," in *Ethical Issues in Death and Dying,* p. 44.

14. Ibid., p. 43.

15. Ibid., p. 44.

16. Hans Jonas, "Against the Stream: Comments on the Definition and Redefinition of Death," in *Ethical Issues in Death and Dying,* pp. 51–52.

17. Ibid., p. 52.

18. Ibid., p. 53. See also William James, *The Principles of Psychology* (New York: Dover Publications, 1950), vol. 1, p. 254, where James says: "It is, in short, the re-instatement of the vague to its proper place in our mental life which I am so anxious to press on the attention." See also the present writer's *William James and the Reinstatement of the Vague* (Philadelphia: Temple University Press, 1992).

19. Jonas, "Against the Stream," p. 57.

20. Ibid., p. 55.

21. Willard Gaylin, "Harvesting the Dead," *Harpers* 249 (September 23, 1974), pp. 23–46.

22. Jonas, "Against the Stream," p. 56.

23. Ibid., pp. 57–58.

24. As quoted in "A Definition of Irreversible Coma," Report of the Ad Hoc Committee of the Harvard Medical School to Examine the Definition of Death, in *Ethical Issues in Death and Dying*, p. 14.

25. Ibid., p. 15.

26. Ibid.

27. As quoted in the President's Commission for the Study of Ethical Problems in Medicine and Biomedical and Behavioral Research, *Defining Death* (Washington, D.C.: U.S. Government Printing Office, 1981), p. 62.

28. David Lamb, *Death, Brain Death, and Ethics* (Albany: State University of New York Press, 1985), p. 20.

29. A similar issue will arise in Chapter 6 of this volume concerning the use of anencephalics for organ transplants.

30. Alexander M. Capron and Leon R. Kass, "A Statutory Definition of the Standards for Determining Human Death: An Appraisal and a Proposal," in *Ethical Issues in Death and Dying*, p. 63.

31. Ibid., p. 69.

32. Ibid., pp. 69–70.

33. David Lamb, *Death, Brain Death, and Ethics*, p. 22.

34. President's Commission, *Defining Death*, p. 2.

35. James L. Bernat, Charles M. Culver, and Bernard Gert, "Defining Death in Theory and Practice," *Hastings Center Report* 12 (February 1982), p. 5.

36. See Lamb, *Death, Brain Death, and Ethics*, p. 24.

37. See ibid., p. 25.

38. President's Commission, *Defining Death*, p. 59.

39. Bernat, Culver, and Gert, "Defining Death," p. 8.

40. President's Commission, *Defining Death*, pp. 58–59.

41. Lamb, *Death, Brain Death, and Ethics*, p. 25. See also Robert M. Veatch, "The Impending Collapse of the Whole-Brain Definition of Death," *Hastings Center Report* 23 (July–August 1993): "It is very doubtful . . . that the move to a whole-brain-oriented concept of death is any less of a fundamental change in concept than movement to a higher-brain-oriented one" (p. 19).

42. Bernat, Culver, and Gert, "Defining Death," p. 8.

43. For the concepts of "manifest image" versus "scientific image," see Wilfred Sellars, "Philosophy and the Scientific Image of Man," in *Science, Perception and Reality* (London: Routledge & Kegan Paul, 1963), pp. 1–40.

44. Robert M. Veatch, "Defining Death Anew: Policy Options," in *Ethical Issues in Death and Dying*, pp. 81–83. More recently, Veatch has added to this: "I did not say at the time, but should have, that the choices would have to be restricted to those that avoid violating the rights of others and avoid creating insurmountable social problems for the rest of society" ("The Impending Collapse of the Whole-Brain Definition of Death," *Hastings Center Report* 23 [July–August 1993], p. 22). This addendum does place significant limitations upon autonomy as a sufficient principle.

45. In "Whole-Brain, Neocortical, and Higher Brain Related Concepts," Veatch states that "I have never in my own discussions of the concept of death made my formulation dependent on the concept of the person" (*Death: Beyond Whole-Brain Criteria*, edited by Richard M. Zaner [Dordrecht, Neth.: Kluwer Academic Publishers, 1988], p. 174). See also "The Impending Collapse of the Whole-Brain Definition of Death," p. 20.

46. See President's Commission, *Defining Death*, pp. 38–39.

47. Robert Veatch, "Whole-Brain, Neocortical, and Higher Brain Related Concepts," in *Death: Beyond Whole-Brain Criteria*, pp. 180–81.

48. Ibid., p. 181.

49. Ibid., p. 182.

50. See Richard M. Zaner, "Brains and Persons: A Critique of Veatch's View," in *Death: Beyond Whole-Brain Criteria*, p. 189.

51. President's Commission, *Defining Death*, p. 39.

52. See William James, *Pragmatism* (New York: Longmans, Green, and Co., 1908), p. 240: "The whole notion of *the* truth is an abstraction from the fact of truths in the plural, a mere useful summarizing phrase like *the* Latin Language or *the* Law."

53. Richard M. Zaner, "Brains and Persons: A Critique of Veatch's View," in *Death: Beyond Whole-Brain Criteria*, p. 196.

54. See ibid., p. 193. See also Robert Neville's suggestion that "people become responsible in special contexts and in small increments because the social situation first allows them the opportunity to exercise

responsibility, and then *demands* it of them" ("On the National Commission: A Puritan Critique of Consensus Ethics," *Hastings Center Report* 9 (April 1979), p. 26.

55. Patricia D. White, "Should the Law Define Death?—A Genuine Question," in *Death: Beyond Whole-Brain Criteria,* pp. 104—6.

56. Roger Dworkin, "Death in Context," *Indiana Law Journal* 48 (Summer 1973), p. 633. See also Robert M. Veatch, "The Impending Collapse of the Whole-Brain Definition of Death," where he states: "It is increasingly apparent . . . that . . . [the] consensus [on whole-brain death] is coming apart" (p. 18).

CHAPTER SIX

1. Robert C. Cefalo and H. Tristram Engelhardt, Jr., "The Use of Fetal and Anencephalic Tissue for Transplantation," *Journal of Medicine and Philosophy* 14 (February 1989), p. 28.

2. Cefalo and Engelhardt say that "50 percent are born alive" (ibid., p. 28), whereas James W. Walters and Stephen Ashwal contend that "between 25 and 45 percent are live births" ("Organ Prolongation in Anencephalic Infants: Ethical & Medical Issues," *Hastings Center Report* 18 [October—November 1988], p. 19).

3. Walters and Ashwal, "Organ Prolongation," p. 19.

4. Richard M. Zaner, "Anencephalics as Organ Donors," *Journal of Medicine and Philosophy* 14 (February 1989), p. 61.

5. Walters and Ashwal, "Organ Prolongation," p. 20. However, this is contested by J. C. Willke and Dave Andrusko, who hold organ transplants from anencephalics to be "a procedure with a track record of very few successes" ("Personhood Redux," *Hastings Center Report* 18 [October—November 1988], p. 33).

6. Alexander Capron, "Anencephalic Donors: Separate the Dead from the Living," *Hastings Center Report* 17 (February 1987), p. 6.

7. Ibid., p. 7.

8. Ibid. p. 8.

9. Zaner, "Anencephalics as Organ Donors," p. 69.

10. Ibid., p. 68. See also Engelhardt, "Medicine and the Concept of Person," in *Ethical Issues in Death and Dying,* edited by Tom L. Beau-

champ and Seymour Perlin (Englewood Cliffs, N.J.: Prentice-Hall, 1978), pp. 271–84.

11. Zaner points out that this point has already been made in the courts in the Federal Republic of Germany ("Anencephalics as Organ Donors," p. 69).

12. Ibid., p. 74.

13. Ibid., p. 70.

14. Mary B. Mahowald, Jerry Silver, and Robert A. Ratcheson, "The Ethical Options in Transplanting Fetal Tissue," *Hastings Center Report* 17 (February 1987), p. 15.

15. Michael Harrison, "The Anencephalic Newborn as Organ Donor: Commentary," *Hastings Center Report* 16 (April 1986), p. 21.

16. Ibid.

17. Norman Fost, "Organs from Anencephalic Infants: An Idea Whose Time Has Not Yet Come," *Hastings Center Report* 18 (October–November 1988), p. 8.

18. Mahowald, Silver, and Ratcheson, "Ethical Options," p. 13. See also Zaner, "Anencephalics as Organ Donors," p. 68.

19. See Fost, "Organs from Anencephalic Infants," p. 8.

20. Ibid., p. 7.

21. See Engelhardt, "Medicine and the Concept of Person," in *Ethical Issues in Death and Dying,* p. 272.

22. Ibid., p. 273.

23. See Michael Tooley, "A Defense of Abortion and Infanticide," in *The Problem of Abortion,* edited by Joel Feinberg (Belmont, Calif.: Wadsworth Publishing Company, 1973), pp. 51–92.

24. Engelhardt, "Medicine and the Concept of Person," p. 277.

25. Ibid.

26. Ibid., p. 278.

27. Ibid., p. 280.

28. Engelhardt, "Ethical Issues in Aiding the Death of Young Children," in *Killing and Letting Die,* edited by Bonnie Steinbock (Englewood Cliffs, N.J.: Prentice-Hall, 1980), p. 85.

29. Ibid., p. 86.

30. Engelhardt, "Medicine and the Concept of Person," in *Ethical Issues in Death and Dying,* pp. 278–79.

31. David Smith, "On Letting Some Babies Die," in *Death Inside Out,* edited by Peter Steinfels and Robert M. Veatch (New York: Harper and Row, 1975), p. 129.

32. The film *Who Should Survive?* was produced by the Joseph P. Kennedy, Jr., Foundation. It is available from Film Service, 999 Asylum Avenue, Hartford, CT 06105.

33. See "The Baby Jane Doe Case," in Gregory E. Pence, *Classic Cases in Medical Ethics* (New York: McGraw-Hill, 1990), p. 138.

34. Smith, "On Letting Some Babies Die," p. 138.

35. Pence, *Classic Cases,* p. 141.

36. Ibid., p. 142.

37. See *Federal Registrar* 49, no. 238 (December 10, 1984), p. 48161.

38. Ibid.

39. Thomas H. Murray, "The Final, Anticlimactic Rule on Baby Doe," *Hastings Center Report* 15 (June 1985), p. 7.

40. Ibid., p. 8.

41. See Pence, *Classic Cases,* pp. 140–41.

42. Murray, "The Final, Anticlimactic Rule," p. 8.

43. John D. Arras, "Toward an Ethic of Ambiguity," *Hastings Center Report* 14 (April 1984), p. 26.

44. Ibid., p. 28.

45. Ibid., p. 30.

46. Ibid., p. 31.

47. Ibid., p. 32.

48. Ibid., pp. 32–33.

49. Ibid., p. 33.

50. See "Imperiled Newborns," edited by Arthur Caplan and Cynthia B. Cohen, *Hastings Center Report* 17 (December 1987), p. 11.

51. Ibid., p. 11.

52. Ibid., p. 13.

53. James Rachels, "Active and Passive Euthanasia," in *Ethical Issues in Death and Dying,* p. 242.

54. Ibid., p. 243.

55. Ibid., p. 244.

56. Ibid.

57. It is perhaps appropriate to remember here that the killing of newborns was also not always looked at negatively. Both Plato and

Aristotle advocated the killing of defective newborns in the *Republic* and the *Politics,* respectively. "For most of two millennia, Bedouin tribes of Arabia, the Chinese, and much of India practiced female infanticide. [In Christianity, while it was illegal to kill children after A.D. 300], it was not illegal to abandon them in rural fields to die of exposure. The exposure of defective babies was a very common practice during the first four centuries A.D. and such 'letting die' was not considered infanticide (or active killing). . . . In the eighteenth century, Europe was overrun by exploding populations, resulting in exposure and infanticide functioning as birth control. Overpopulation revived institutionalized abandonment in France, Germany, and England. . . . In France in 1833, over a hundred thousand babies were abandoned." (Pence, *Classic Cases,* pp. 136–37). Here again, the social context needs to be taken into account, but not necessarily as a justification of all forms of infanticide mentioned, such as, for example, gender-based ones.

58. See "Imperiled Newborns," edited by Caplan and Cohen, p. 22.

59. See ibid., p. 23.

60. Tom Beauchamp, "A Reply to Rachels on Active and Passive Euthanasia," in *Ethical Issues in Death and Dying,* p. 251.

61. Ibid., p. 253.

62. Ibid., p. 256.

63. See "Imperiled Newborns," edited by Caplan and Cohen, p. 24. In *Death, Dying and the Biological Revolution: Our Last Quest for Responsibility,* Robert Veatch develops an argument for the distinction between killing and letting die based upon deontological principles: "Letting die is not a wrong at all unless it is a violation of beneficence or promise keeping, while killing is always a violation of the duty to avoid killing. . . . While active killing is always a violation of the prima facie principle to avoid killing another human being, letting die, when the decision maker is outside the nexus of responsibility, is nothing more than fulfilling the prima facie principle of respecting autonomy" (revised edition [New Haven, Conn.: Yale University Press, 1989], pp. 72–73). Veatch's position assumes that the killing of human beings is a wrong we have a duty to avoid.

64. See John Dewey, "The Pattern of Inquiry," in *The Philosophy of John Dewey,* edited by John J. McDermott (Chicago: University of Chicago Press, 1981), p. 229, and Chapters 1 and 4 of this volume.

65. Maurice A. M. de Wachter, "Euthanasia in the Netherlands," *Hastings Center Report* 22 (March–April 1992), p. 23.

66. Ibid.

67. Dan W. Brock, "Voluntary Active Euthanasia," *Hastings Center Report* 22 (March–April 1992), p. 11.

68. Daniel Callahan, "When Self-Determination Runs Amok," *Hastings Center Report* 22 (March–April 1992), p. 52. See also "Pursuing a Peaceful Death," where Callahan says: "The most obvious way the dying self can be deformed is by allowing the fear of death, or the fear of what dying may do to our ideal self, itself to corrupt the self. . . . One way to resist the force of this fear is to be willing to accept some loss of control. . . . It is at least as likely that we could create the possibility of a peaceful death for a majority of people by changing our medical attitudes and expectations as by the more violent course of euthanasia and assisted suicide, and with far less loss of other values in the process" (*Hastings Center Report* 23 [July–August 1993], pp. 35–36).

69. Ibid., p. 52.

70. Maurice A. M. de Wachter, "Euthanasia in the Netherlands," p. 29.

71. Robert Veatch has noted that "if in this confusing time we cannot agree on a definition of death, we have hardly begun to ask what it means to be dying" (*Death, Dying and the Biological Revolution: Our Last Quest for Responsibility,* revised edition [New Haven, Conn.: Yale University Press, 1989], p. 3).

CHAPTER SEVEN

1. See Alfred North Whitehead, *Science and the Modern World* (New York: Free Press, 1967), p. 51, and Chapter 1 of this volume.

2. Robert S. Morison, "Death: Process or Event?" in *Death Inside Out,* edited by Peter Steinfels and Robert M. Veatch (New York: Harper and Row, 1975), p. 64.

3. Ibid., pp. 65–66.

4. Ibid., p. 68.

5. Ibid. p. 70.

6. See William James, *The Principles of Psychology* (New York: Dover Publications, 1950), vol. 1, pp. 224–90; *Essays in Radical Empiricism,* in

Essays in Radical Empiricism & A Pluralistic Universe (Gloucester: Peter Smith, 1967), pp. 39–91.

7. Leon Kass, "Death as an Event," in *Death Inside Out,* p. 72.

8. Ibid., p. 73.

9. David Lamb, *Death, Brain Death and Ethics* (Albany: State University of New York Press, 1985), p. 71.

10. Ibid., p. 79.

11. Ibid., p. 76.

12. Kass, "Death as an Event," p. 76.

13. Ibid., p. 78.

14. Ibid.

15. Ibid., p. 76n.

16. On this issue, see Barbara MacKinnon, "Death: Process or Event?" in *Biomedical Ethics and the Law,* edited by James M. Humber and Robert F. Almeder (New York: Plenum Press, 1976), pp. 527–28.

17. See ibid., pp. 528–30.

18. Morison, "Death," p. 67.

19. As Barbara MacKinnon has noted, "The alternatives of regarding death as an event that occurs more or less instantaneously (or as a definite occurrence) and regarding it as a more vaguely defined process occurring over an extended period of time are not the only ones. Death could be an *event* which is a definite happening causing a dramatic change and yet take some time" ("Death: Process or Event?" in *Biomedical Ethics,* pp. 530–31).

20. See Jean-Paul Sartre, *Being and Nothingness: An Essay on Phenomenological Ontology,* translated and with an Introduction by Hazel E. Barnes (New York: Washington Square Press, 1966), pp. 26–55.

21. See Chapter 5.

22. Hans Jonas, "Against the Stream: Comments on the Definition and Redefinition of Death," in *Ethical Issues in Death and Dying,* edited by Tom L. Beauchamp and Seymour Perlin (Englewood Cliffs, N.J.: Prentice-Hall, 1978), pp. 57–58.

23. William James, *Psychology: Briefer Course* (New York: Henry Holt and Co., 1892), p. 165.

24. William James, *Essays in Radical Empiricism,* p. 34.

25. Ibid., p. 35.

26. Ibid., p. 146.

27. John J. McDermott, "Feeling as Insight: The Affective Dimension in Social Diagnosis," in *Hippocrates Revisited,* edited by Roger J. Bulger, M.D. (New York: Medcom Press, 1973), p. 168. See also Arthur Kleinman, *The Illness Narratives: Suffering, Healing, and the Human Condition:* "Health professionals, when they stop to think about it (and in the exigency of the clinical day most do not), recognize that how they listen to . . . [patients'] accounts constrains the telling and the hearing. . . . Moreover, the priorities of the practitioner lead to selective attention to the patient's account, so that some aspects are carefully listened for and heard (sometimes when they are not spoken), while other things that are said—and even repeated—are literally not heard. The physician's training also encourages the dangerous fallacy of over-literal interpretation of accounts best understood metaphorically" ([New York: Basic Books, 1988], p. 52).

28. McDermott, "Feeling as Insight," p. 170.

29. Ibid., p. 171.

30. Ibid., p. 172.

31. William James, *Essays in Radical Empiricism,* p. 170n.

32. McDermott, "Feeling as Insight," p. 175.

33. William James, *Pragmatism* (New York: Longmans, Green and Co., 1908), p. 295. See also, in this connection, John J. McDermott, "Why Bother: Is Life Worth Living?" *Journal of Philosophy* 88 (November 1991), pp. 677–83.

34. Elisabeth Kübler-Ross, *On Death and Dying* (New York: Macmillan, 1970), p. 8.

35. Ibid., p. 35.

36. Ibid., p. 77.

37. Ibid., p. 99.

38. Ibid., p. 122.

39. Ibid., p. 123.

40. Ibid., p. 123.

41. Ibid., p. 9.

42. Elisabeth Kübler-Ross, *Questions and Answers on Death and Dying* (New York: Collier Books, Macmillan Publishing Co. 1974), p. 37.

43. Ibid., p. 36.

44. Ibid., p. 34.

45. See Roy Branson, "Is Acceptance a Denial of Death? Another Look at Kübler-Ross," *The Christian Century,* May 7, 1975, p. 464.

46. Ibid., p. 467.

47. James Carpenter, "Accepting Death: A Critique of Kübler-Ross," *Hastings Center Report* 9 (October 1979), p. 42.

48. Elisabeth Kübler-Ross, *To Live Until We Say Good-Bye* (Englewood Cliffs, N.J.: Prentice-Hall, 1978).

49. Carpenter, "Accepting Death," p. 43.

50. Ibid., p. 43.

51. Ron Rosenbaum, "Turn On, Tune In, Drop Dead," *Harpers* 265 (July 1982), p. 33.

52. Ibid., p. 33.

53. Ibid., p. 40.

54. Ibid., p. 36.

55. Ibid., p. 42.

56. Larry Churchill, "The Human Experience of Dying: The Moral Primacy of Stories over Stages," *Soundings* 62 (Spring 1979), p. 27.

57. Ibid., p. 29. For an analysis of the concept of "story," see Howard Brody, *Stories of Sickness* (New Haven, Conn.: Yale University Press, 1987), pp. 13–19.

58. Churchill, "The Human Experience of Dying," p. 30. See also Arthur Kleinman, *Illness Narratives*, "Patients order their experience of illness—what it means to them and to significant others—as personal narratives. The illness narrative is a story the patient tells, and significant others retell, to give coherence to the distinctive events and long-term course of suffering. . . . The personal narrative does not merely reflect illness experience, but rather it contributes to the experience of symptoms and suffering" (p. 49).

59. Ibid., p. 30.

60. Ibid., p. 31. Analogously, Arthur Kleinman opposes "mechanical models of the stages of dying." For Kleinman, "there is no single, timeless pathway toward death that is most serviceable for the dying person. An individual's course of death, like that of life, may take dozens of different turns, circle back to the start, or enter a state previously unknown. The practitioner cannot know in advance where the patient is headed or what is best" (*The Illness Narratives: Suffering, Healing, and the Human Condition*, p. 154).

61. Ibid., p. 32.

62. William James, *A Pluralistic Universe*, in *Essays in Radical Empiricism & A Pluralistic Universe* (Gloucester: Peter Smith, 1967), p. 330.

63. See Chapter 1 of this volume.

64. Larry Churchill, "The Human Experience of Dying," p. 32.

65. Ibid., p. 33.

66. Ibid.

67. William Carlos Williams, *Paterson* (New York: New Directions, 1946–58), p. 3. Reprinted by permission of New Directions Pub. Corp.

CHAPTER EIGHT

1. Plato, *Phaedo*, in *The Collected Dialogues of Plato*, edited by Edith Hamilton and Huntington Cairns (New York: Pantheon Books, Random House, 1961), 64a (p. 46).

2. Plato, *Crito*, in *The Collected Dialogues*, 44c (p. 29).

3. See Plato, *Phaedo*, 116e (p. 96).

4. See Plato, *Republic*, in *The Collected Dialogues*, 434d–441c (pp. 676–83).

5. Plato, *Symposium* in *The Collected Dialogues*, 216d (p. 568).

6. Plato, *Apology* in *The Collected Dialogues*, 42a (p. 26).

7. See Plato, *Phaedo*, 118a (p. 98).

8. See Plato, *Crito*, 47a (p. 31).

9. Robert C. S. Downs, *Going Gently* (Indianapolis: Bobbs-Merrill Company, 1973), p. 76.

10. Gregory Vlastos, "The Paradox of Socrates," in *The Philosophy of Socrates*, edited by Gregory Vlastos (New York: Doubleday Anchor, 1971), pp. 16–17.

11. See J. E. Raven, *Plato's Thought in the Making* (Cambridge: Cambridge University Press, 1965), p. 103.

12. Paul Friedlander, *Plato: An Introduction* (New York: Harper Torchbooks, Harper and Row, 1964), p. 210.

13. *Aporia:* embarrassment; perplexity; doubt; need; difficulty; impassableness (*Handy Dictionary of the Greek and English Languages*, edited by Karl Feyerabend [New York: David McKay Company, 1919], p. 55).

14. Plato, *Apology*, 29a (p. 15).

15. See Leo Tolstoy, *The Death of Ivan Illych and Other Stories* (New York: New American Library, 1960), pp. 96–97, for the reaction of his friends; pp. 100–101, 123, for his wife's reaction.

16. See ibid., p. 152.

17. Hugh Fausset, *Tolstoy: The Inner Drama* (New York: Russell and Russell, 1968), p. 255.

18. See Tolstoy, *Ivan Ilych*, p. 155.

19. Janko Lavrin, *Tolstoy: A Psycho-Critical Study* (London: W. Collins Sons & Co., Ltd., 1924), pp. 110–11. However, we must once again note that the particular notion of "self" being discussed is at least partly socially constructed.

20. Ruth Davies, *The Great Books of Russia* (Norman: University of Oklahoma Press, 1968), p. 295.

21. Plato, *Phaedo*, 64a (p. 46).

22. Kathleen M. Higgins, "Reading *Zarathustra*," in *Reading Nietzsche*, edited by Robert C. Solomon and Kathleen M. Higgins (New York: Oxford University Press, 1988), p. 134.

23. Ibid., p. 147.

24. See Friedrich Nietzsche, *The Birth of Tragedy*, in *The Philosophy of Nietzsche* (New York: Modern Library, Random House, 1927), pp. 961–62.

25. See Laurence Lampert, *Nietzsche's Teaching* (New Haven, Conn.: Yale University Press, 1986), p. 17.

26. Friedrich Nietzsche, *Thus Spoke Zarathustra*, in *The Portable Nietzsche*, edited and translated by Walter Kaufmann (New York: Penguin Books, 1959), p. 183.

27. Lampert, *Nietzsche's Teaching*, p. 71.

28. Nietzsche, *Thus Spoke Zarathustra*, p. 184.

29. Ibid., p. 184.

30. Lampert, *Nietzsche's Teaching*, p. 72.

31. Nietzsche, *Thus Spoke Zarathustra*, p. 264.

32. Ibid., p. 269.

33. Lampert, *Nietzsche's Teaching*, p. 164.

34. Nietzsche, *Thus Spoke Zarathustra*, p. 333.

35. Lampert, *Nietzsche's Teaching*, p. 287.

36. Nietzsche, *Thus Spoke Zarathustra*, p. 343.

37. Kathleen Marie Higgins, *Nietzsche's* Zarathustra (Philadelphia: Temple University Press, 1987), p. 224.

38. Ibid., p. 235.

39. Jacques Choron, *Death and Western Thought* (New York: Collier Books, 1963), p. 204.

40. See, for example, William May, "The Metaphysical Plight of the Family," and H. Tristram Engelhardt, Jr., "The Counsels of Finitude," both in *Death Inside Out* edited by Peter Steinfels and Robert M. Veatch (New York: Harper & Row, 1975).

41. See *Dax's Case, Essays in Medical Ethics and Human Meaning,* edited by Lonnie D. Kliever (Dallas: Southern Methodist University Press, 1989).

42. See Margaret Battin, "Assisted Suicide: Can We Learn from Germany?" *Hastings Center Report* 22 (March–April 1992), p. 47.

43. Ibid.

44. Ibid.

45. Ibid., p. 48.

46. Ibid.

47. The Whorf-Sapir hypothesis holds that the specific language people speak conditions their view of reality. See, for example, Benjamin Lee Whorf, *Language, Thought, and Reality,* edited by J. R. Carroll (Cambridge: Massachusetts Institute of Technology Press, 1956).

48. Battin, "Assisted Suicide," p. 48.

49. Ibid., p. 50.

50. See Nietzsche, *The Birth of Tragedy,* p. 1019.

51. Ibid., p. 1021.

52. Friedrich Nietzsche, *The Birth of Tragedy and The Genealogy of Morals,* translated by Francis Golffing (New York: Doubleday Anchor Books, 1956), pp. 4–5.

53. See, for example, Sissela Bok, *Lying: Moral Choice in Public and Private Life* (New York: Pantheon Books, 1978).

54. Nietzsche, *Thus Spoke Zarathustra,* in *The Portable Nietzsche,* p. 307.

55. Friedrich Nietzsche, "An Attempt at Self-Crticism," in *The Philosophy of Nietzsche,* p. 936.

CHAPTER NINE

1. Paul Ramsey, "Death's Pedagogy," *Commonweal,* September 20, 1974, p. 502, as quoted in Peter Steinfels, Introduction to *Death Inside Out,* edited by Peter Steinfels and Robert M. Veatch (New York: Harper & Row, 1975), p. 3.

2. Paul Ramsey, "The Indignity of 'Death With Dignity,'" in *Death Inside Out*, p. 82. Robert Veatch also "remain[s] uncomfortable with the thought that the death of a person can really be called something of 'dignity.'" Of the two scenarios, "death is dignified" versus "death is evil," Veatch believes that "a case can be made that the second view—that death is combatible and ought to be combatted—is the more human course." This argument for the "ideal of immortality" ultimately holds that "overcoming death—my own and my fellow man's—is the final step in overcoming evil and building human community" (*Death, Dying and the Biological Revolution: Our Last Quest for Responsibility*, revised edition [New Haven, Conn.: Yale University Press, 1989], pp. 224–37). Veatch, however, does not emphasize the uniquely personal in the way that Ramsey does.

3. Ramsey, "The Indignity of 'Death with Dignity,'" p. 82.

4. Ibid., p. 83.

5. Epicurus, "Letter to Menoeceus," *Greek and Roman Philosophy After Aristotle*, edited by Jason Saunders (New York: The Free Press, 1966), p. 50.

6. See Ramsey, "The Indignity of 'Death With Dignity,'" p. 83.

7. Ibid., p. 84.

8. Ibid., p. 86.

9. Ibid., p. 87.

10. As quoted in ibid., pp. 89–90. See also, in this regard, the approach of William James to dying, in Chapter 7 of this volume.

11. Ibid., p. 90.

12. Ibid., p. 92.

13. See also, in this respect, the Japanese attitude toward the newly dead, as presented in Chapter 3.

14. We would tend to disagree with Ramsey's example here, as our portrait or Socrates in the preceding chapter makes evident, but we do not disagree with his overall point.

15. Ramsey, "The Indignity of 'Death With Dignity,'" p. 95.

16. Ibid., pp. 95–96.

17. Robert Morison, "The Dignity of the Inevitable and Necessary," in *Death Inside Out*, p. 97.

18. Ibid., p. 98. For Morison's description of the individual as a series of interactions, see Chapter 7 of this volume.

19. Ibid., p. 99.

20. See Jacques Choron, *Death and Western Thought* (New York: Collier Books, Macmillan Publishing Co., 1963), pp. 64–77.

21. Marcus Aurelius, *Meditations*, in *Essential Works of Stoicism*, edited with an introduction by Mosas Hadas (New York: Bantam Books, 1961), p. 152.

22. Ibid., p. 124.

23. Ibid., p. 202.

24. Ibid., p. 113.

25. Blaise Pascal, *Thoughts*, translated by W. F. Trotter, *The Harvard Classics*, edited by Charles W. Eliot (New York: P. F. Collier & Son, 1938), vol. 48, p. 98.

26. Morison, "The Indignity," p. 99.

27. Ibid., p. 100.

28. Leon Kass, "Averting One's Eyes, or Facing the Music?—On Dignity and Death," in *Death Inside Out*, p. 103.

29. Ibid., p. 104.

30. Ibid.

31. Kass does admit to having some discomfort with this view (p. 108).

32. Kass, "Averting One's Eyes," p. 109.

33. Ibid., p. 109.

34. Ibid., p. 110.

35. Ibid., p. 110.

36. H. Tristram Engelhardt, Jr., "The Councils of Finitude," in *Death Inside Out*, p. 115.

37. See Ramsey, "The Indignity of 'Death With Dignity,'" p. 94.

38. Engelhardt, "The Councils of Finitude," p. 116. As we have seen in Chapter 8, some commentators disagree with this interpretation. See J. D. Raven, *Plato's Thought in the Making* (Cambridge: Cambridge University Press, 1965), p. 103.

39. Engelhardt, "The Councils of Finitude," p. 117.

40. Ibid.

41. Ibid., p. 118.

42. Ibid., p. 119.

43. Ibid., p. 121.

44. Ibid.

45. Ibid., p. 122.

46. Ibid., p. 123.

47. Ibid., p. 125.

48. See Josiah Royce, "Loyalty to Loyalty," in *The Basic Writings of Josiah Royce,* edited with an introduction by John J. McDermott (Chicago: University of Chicago Press, 1969), vol. 2, pp. 894–913.

49. Engelhardt, "The Councils of Finitude," p. 125.

50. See Josiah Royce, "Race Questions and Prejudices," in *The Basic Writings of Josiah Royce,* vol. 2, pp. 1067–88, and Chapter 3 of this volume.

51. For an analysis of these terms, see the present writer's *William James and the Reinstatement of the Vague* (Philadelphia: Temple University Press, 1992), pp. 72–75, 189–93.

CONCLUSION

1. Friedrich Nietzsche, "An Attempt at Self-Criticism," in *The Philosophy of Nietzsche* (New York: Modern Library, Random House, 1954), pp. 936–37. See Chapter 8 of this volume.

2. Ibid., p. 940.

3. Samuel Beckett, *Waiting for Godot* (New York: Grove Press, 1954).

4. Ramona Cormier and Janis L. Pallister, *Waiting For Death: The Philosophical Significance of Beckett's* En Attendant Godot (Tuscaloosa: University of Alabama Press, 1979), p. 1.

5. Ibid., p. 15.

6. Ibid., p. 44.

7. Ibid., p. 24.

8. Ibid., p. 2.

9. Ibid., p. 51.

10. Ibid., p. 105.

11. Ibid., p. 108.

12. Ibid., p. 113.

13. See, among others, Frederick Waismann, "Language Strata," in *Logic and Language,* first and second series, edited by Anthony Flew (New York: Anchor Books, Doubleday and Co., 1965), pp. 226–47; Ludwig Wittgenstein, *Philosophical Investigations* (New York: Macmillan, 1953), pp. 6–32.

14. See Marshall McLuhan, *The Gutenberg Galaxy* (New York: Signet Books, New American Library, 1969), pp. 19–313.

15. See Don Ihde, *Technics and Praxis* (Dordrecht, Neth.: D. Reidel Publishing Company, 1979), p. 21, and Chapter 1 of this volume.

16. See William James, *A Pluralistic Universe*, where he defines vicious intellectualism as "the treating of a name as excluding from the fact named what the name's definition fails positively to include" (in *Essays in Radical Empiricism & A Pluralistic Universe* [Gloucester: Peter Smith, 1967], p. 60).

17. See Plato, *Phaedo*, in *The Collected Dialogues of Plato*, edited by Edith Hamilton and Huntington Cairns (New York: Pantheon Books, Random House, 1961), 72e–78b (pp. 55–61).

18. Jean-Paul Sartre, *Being and Nothingness, An Essay on Phenomenological Ontology*, translated and with an Introduction by Hazel E. Barnes (New York: Washington Square Press, 1966), pp. 650–81.

19. Plato, *Phaedo*, 62b (p. 45).

20. Beckett, *Waiting for Godot*, p. 41.

21. One is reminded here of the line toward the end of Franz Kafka's novel *The Trial*, where the priest says to Joseph K.: "It is not necessary to accept everything as true, one must only accept it as necessary" ([New York: Schocken Books, 1968], p. 220).

22. Michael Ignatieff, *The Needs of Strangers* (New York: Viking Penguin, 1985), pp. 141–42. Recently Daniel Callahan has stated that his own definition of a "peaceful death . . . blends personal, medical, and social strands" (*Hastings Center Report* 23 [July–August 1993], p. 36). The present text has been divided into three parts, each dealing with one of these aspects. However, one of these parts, namely, the one dealing with the personal, has, through Paul Ramsey's observation, placed limitations upon the acceptability of a peaceful death, and, further, raised questions concerning both the importance of style and the possibility of communication.

[INDEX]